TONY
and the IRA

THE 'ON THE RUNS' SCANDAL

AUSTEN MORGAN

THE BELFAST PRESS

Published by The Belfast Press Limited

22 The Quadrant
Richmond
Surrey
TW9 1BP

First published 2016

Austen Morgan © 2016
The moral right of the author has been asserted.

Typeset in Adobe Garamond Pro 10.5

ISBN 978-0-9539287-7-4 (Paperback)

ISBN 978-0-9539287-8-1 (Kindle)

The cover illustration is of Tony Blair (with his Downing Street chief of
staff Jonathan Powell) meeting Gerry Adams and Martin McGuinness
in his office at the house of commons on 13 June 2007. Photograph
by Stefan Rousseau © PA Archive/Press Association Images.

To the victims of
republican and loyalist terrorism
and unlawful state killings
(especially those denied OTR prosecutions)

CONTENTS

PREFACE

On Tuesday, 25 February 2014, a story – of considerable constitutional significance – broke in London. Sitting in the high court, Mr Justice Sweeney lifted reporting restrictions on his judgment of the previous Friday. On 21 February 2014, he had ruled (in the Old Bailey), that it would be an abuse of process to prosecute an Irish national called John Downey, aged 62 years. This was in spite of the defendant having been charged with murdering four soldiers in the Hyde Park bombing in 1982. Following that unreportable judicial ruling, the crown prosecution service – consulting the attorney general, Dominic Grieve QC – decided quickly on the Monday not to seek leave to appeal.

Relatives of the soldiers, who had been following the case, were dignified but devastated, at John Downey being set free without having to face a criminal trial in front of a jury. (Even if he had been tried, convicted and sentenced for murder, he would have been released most likely within two years.) Their further loss was much greater, in human terms, that February 2014 morning, than John Downey's personal and political courtroom gain.

Mr Justice Sweeney was no friend of terrorists, having been (when a barrister) first senior treasury counsel at the Old Bailey.[1] It was not disputed that John Downey was an Irish republican: born in Co. Clare in 1952, he had been convicted in the Republic of Ireland in 1974 of being a member of the Irish Republican Army ('IRA'); by the 2000s, and living in Co. Donegal, he was a member of Sinn Féin – a supporter of its president, Gerry Adams', so-called peace strategy, he denied, and denies, all involvement in the Hyde Park car bombing. John Downey seemingly is to have the last word on his criminal liability.

On 20 July 1982 at 10.40 – nearly 32 years previously – Irish republicans had killed: Anthony Daly (23 years) and Simon Tipper (19); Jeffrey Young (19) and Roy Bright (36) died shortly afterwards

---

[1] As a junior barrister, he had helped prosecute the Brighton bombing case, following the unsuccessful attempt to kill Margaret Thatcher in October 1984.

of their injuries. They were members of a sixteen-strong, household cavalry troop on its way to change the guard at Horse Guards Parade in Whitehall. (Media images of seven dead military horses in Hyde Park, put down because of their injuries, have become iconic over the decades.) Thirty-one people were injured, some seriously. Later that same day, this time in London's Regent's Park, Irish republicans killed seven military bandsmen during a lunchtime public concert. Most likely, given the need to coordinate, the same paramilitary unit was responsible, though individuals may have been involved in one or other atrocity. Hyde Park and Regent's Park – with eleven dead ceremonial soldiers that day in the capital – was one of the worst terrorist attacks upon the army in Great Britain, during the thirty years of the Northern Ireland ('NI') troubles.

When John Downey was arrested at Gatwick airport at 08.00 on 19 May 2013, *en route* to a family holiday in Greece, he had been sent (but was not carrying) an official letter – signed by a senior civil servant, Mark Sweeney, dated 20 July 2007. Mark Sweeney was not related to the judge.[2] But the date of the letter – irony of ironies – was the twenty-fifth anniversary of the Hyde Park bombing! The letter stated erroneously that, though a warrant for his arrest had been issued in London on 29 May 1983, John Downey was not wanted by any police force in the United Kingdom ('UK').[3]

Despite the mistake by Mark Sweeney in Whitehall, the decision was made to prosecute John Downey on four counts of murder and one of intending to cause an explosion. The letter was not considered an obstacle to prosecution. However, the defence argued in advance that it would be an abuse of process to proceed, that the letter granted John Downey in effect immunity from prosecution. This was in spite of the fact that he had not been entitled to the letter; he knew he was wanted in London. Legal argument ensued for several days. Mr Justice Sweeney eventually threw out the prosecution case in a carefully drafted

---

[2] The family name Sweeney, while of Scottish origin, is closely associated with Ireland.

[3] A copy of the covering letter to Gerry Kelly, and a copy of the letter to John Downey, is placed at pp. 119 to 121 below.

57-page judgment, which permitted John Downey to return to Co. Donegal a free person: 'Clearly [the judge concluded] ... the public interest in ensuring that those who are accused of serious crime should be tried is a very strong one (with the plight of the victims and their families firmly in mind). However, in the very particular circumstances of this case it seems to me that it is very significantly outweighed in the balancing exercise by the overlapping public interests in ensuring that executive misconduct does not undermine public confidence in the criminal justice system and bring it into disrepute, and the public interest in holding officials of the state to promises they have made in full understanding of what is involved in the bargain.'[4]

This judgment of 21 February 2014 revealed definitively for the first time (when published four days later), hundreds of pages of official documents having been made public through disclosure to the court: four secret written agreements between Tony Blair and Gerry Adams in 1999–2006; which dealt with so-called 'on the runs' (a topic not included in the Belfast agreement of 10 April 1998); this led to what was called in Whitehall an 'administrative scheme', involving the police and the public prosecutor in NI; it was run by the political director of the Northern Ireland Office ('NIO') in London (a senior civil servant); the first so-called comfort letters had been issued in June 2000, from number 10 (by the prime minister's chief of staff, Jonathan Powell), and the last in December 2012 (though the administrative scheme was not abandoned finally until after the Downey judgment); altogether, some 228 presumed members of the IRA (but not dissident republicans much less loyalists) applied for what they believed to be immunity (before and after the failed legislative amnesty of 2005–6); over the years, under Tony Blair, Gordon Brown and even David Cameron, at least 187 men and women, having been told by senior officials that they were not wanted for any terrorist crimes, were permitted to live freely in NI or any other part of the UK. They, or rather Sinn Féin, were holding official letters (similar to John Downey's), which the republicans be-lieved guaranteed they were safe for life from prosecution for alleged

---

[4] Para 175. There is a fuller extract from the judgment in the appendix, pp. 206-11.

IRA activities. Neither Sinn Féin nor any government has published a list of those 187 men and women, most of whom now live in NI.

From the beginning of the 'on the runs' scandal, ministers, officials and others who had been involved repeated a number of reassuring myths about the administrative scheme, including:

- *one*, the administrative scheme was lawful;
- *two*, the administrative scheme had not been secret;
- *three*, ministers were not involved in the administrative scheme;
- *four*, the comfort letters were only statements of facts;
- *five*, the 'on the runs' were not granted immunity;
- *six*, there was no amnesty for IRA crimes (committed before 10 April 1998);
- *seven*, the administrative scheme was necessary to implement the 1998 Belfast, and 2007 St Andrews, agreement;
- *eight*, the judgment of Mr Justice Sweeney was particular to a unique set of facts;
- *nine*, the Police Service of Northern Ireland ('PSNI') – in particular the Operation Rapid team – was responsible for John Downey escaping prosecution; and
- *ten*, no ministers nor officials in Belfast or London did anything wrong.

The word myth does not imply intellectual dishonesty, even if some of these arguments were mobilized in desperation. It refers to beliefs, which were articulated by many of those involved. Like most myths, each contains a grain of truth. This book, however, reveals a much more complicated picture of public administration (in which there are no scapegoats), but one where there was incontrovertibly serious political involvement in the criminal justice system.[5]

I consider in chapter 12 the following official reports, produced in 2014-15 in response to the shocking John Downey judgment:

- *first*, that of Dame Heather Hallett, published on 17 July 2014, which has been of considerable use;

---

[5] I return to the ten official myths in chapter 13.

- *second*, that of the Police Ombudsman for Northern Ireland, published on 20 October 2014, which contains little original information; and
- *third*, that of the Northern Ireland Affairs Committee ('NIAC') of the house of commons, published on 24 March 2015 (after a year's inquiry), on which I have relied heavily.

Each report, in its way, contributes to our understanding of the OTR issue. But, I believe, there is nothing to beat the documents disclosed in the John Downey trial: republicans preferred oral communication and the body language which accompanies it; but servants of the state, who no doubt whispered as well, wrote down a great deal that they must have believed would remain secret for a very long time, if not forever.

I am the author of a number of books on British and Irish, nineteenth- and twentieth-century history. I became a barrister in the mid-1990s in London, and also later in Belfast. This book is based upon the official papers made public in the Downey case, and given wider circulation by NIAC during its lengthy parliamentary inquiry in 2014–15. I refer to the Downey case papers, and identify each document relied upon. This book is an account of an important area of public policy. But for Mr Justice Sweeney, the Downey case papers would not have been made public in 2014. Even after twenty or more years, they might never have been released as public records by the national archives in London, because they deal with individual terrorist suspects. This is a unique opportunity to consider a secret part of government. I write as a historian with the benefit of legal experience. This book is written to reveal – pretty much for the first time – an important aspect of the relationship between Tony Blair, as prime minister, and the IRA, a terrorist organization reluctant to give up its arms. It is a political drama: there is a cast of characters, some larger than life and others mere organization men and women in the state bureaucracy. I characterize the story of the OTRs as a scandal, because the key players risked breaching – and Tony Blair did breach – the principle that, when it comes to criminal justice, all persons should be treated equally.

ABBREVIATIONS

DUP	Democratic Unionist Party
IG	Irish Government list of OTRs (undated)
IRA	Irish Republican Army
NI	Northern Ireland
NIAC	Northern Ireland Affairs Committee (of the House of Commons)
NIO	Northern Ireland Office
NIOB	Northern Ireland (Offences) Bill
PONI	Police Ombudsman for Northern Ireland
OTRs	On The Runs
PL	Prison List of OTRs (11 February 2001)
PPSNI	Public Prosecution Service for Northern Ireland
PSNI	Police Service of Northern Ireland
RPM	Royal Prerogative of Mercy
RUC	Royal Ulster Constabulary
SDLP	Social Democratic and Labour Party
SF1	Sinn Féin One list of OTRs (19 May 2000)
SF2	Sinn Féin Two list of OTRs (30 March 2001)
SF3	Sinn Féin Three list of OTRs (19 May 2008)
UK	United Kingdom of Great Britain and Northern Ireland
US	United States (of America)

NOTE ON TERMINOLOGY

The term on the runs is unknown to the criminal justice system in the UK, the terms fugitive suspect, fugitive defendant or fugitive offender being used; one becomes a fugitive from criminal justice by fleeing England and Wales, and/or NI, after committing a crime in one or other jurisdiction.[6]

On the runs comes from the language of Irish republicanism; it is highly ideological, and self-glorifying, and does not readily permit of constitutional analysis, as will be seen; it is irrelevant, for example, that John Downey was not on the run from NI, because he lived in the Republic of Ireland: he was a fugitive from justice in England and Wales until 25 February 2014.

At the beginning of the administrative scheme in 2000, the NIO – at the behest of the attorney general – tried to counter this thinking by referring to Irish 'terrorists on the run'. In time, ministers and officials acceded to negotiating pressure from Sinn Féin, and adopted the term on the runs, quickly abbreviated to OTRs.

I use the term on the runs or OTRs, because it now clearly refers to the 228 presumed members of the IRA who sought effective immunity from criminal prosecution, in the years 2000 to 2014, either through a comfort letter (such as John Downey's) and/or, in a minority of cases, the granting of the royal prerogative of mercy.

---

[6] There is no consideration of Scotland in this book, because the issue has not arisen.

CHAPTER ONE

Key Players in the OTR Scandal

The OTR story runs from 1999 until 2014, a significant period of 15 years. The high point was 2007, the year Tony Blair resigned as prime minister. The principals in the OTR scandal were: the new labour leader; and Gerry Adams, the Irish republican president. But a number of other individuals, in Westminster and Whitehall, was crucial to the administrative scheme. Not everyone within government in those years knew about the IRA letters. The issue never went to the cabinet. On the contrary, the existence of comfort letters was limited to a very small number of key players in a number of institutions, in London and Belfast. The secretary of state for NI was not completely in control of what some officials were doing, because of the role of number 10 during the three Blair governments.

Here, I list those key players within the UK state, relying upon an accompanying table.[7] It may be considered a road map to the following narrative. Most of those names were publicly identifiable to informed observers. Lesser figures, in a number of institutions, are mentioned in the detail in subsequent chapters. When it comes to the John Downey mistake, the latter come to the fore; I name names, high and low, exonerating those, I believe, who have been blamed unfairly, redistributing responsibility to where it belongs properly. The ultimate responsibility for OTRs, however, rests with Tony Blair and Gerry Adams; and, between the head of government, and the IRA leader who continues to deny ever having been a member of a terrorist organization, it is the former who needs to be held to account constitutionally (the latter still being at risk of criminal sanction[8]). All of the individuals mentioned

---

7 P. 2 below.

8 Though no longer apparently for the murder of Jean McConville in 1972, a widowed mother of ten from Belfast who was abducted and killed by the IRA: *Guardian,* 29 September 2015. A total of four men and four women, including

KEY PLAYERS
May 1997 to July 2016

	Tony Blair (05.97–06.07)					Gordon Brown (06.07–05.10)	David Cameron (05.10–07.16)	
Prime Minister	Tony Blair (05.97–06.07)					Gordon Brown (06.07–05.10)	David Cameron (05.10–07.16)	
No. 10 Officials	Jonathan Powell John Sawers							
Secretary of State	Mo Mowlam* (05.97–10.99)	Peter Mandelson (10.99–01.01)	John Reid (01.01–10.02)	Paul Murphy (10.02–05.05)	Peter Hain (05.05–06.07)	Shaun Woodward (06.07–05.10)	Owen Paterson (05.10–09.12)	Theresa Villiers (09.12–07.16)
NIO Permanent Secretary	Sir Joseph Pilling (1997–2005)				Sir Jonathan Phillips (2005–10)		Hilary Jackson (2010–11)	Sir Jonathan Stephens (2014–)
Other Officials	Sir Quentin Thomas Sir Bill Jeffrey William Fittall Mark Sweeney							
Attorney General	John Morris QC (05.97–07.99)	Lord Williams QC* (07.99–06.01)	Lord Goldsmith QC (06.01–06.07)			Baroness Scotland (06.07–05.10)	Dominic Grieve QC (05.10–07.14)	Jeremy Wright QC (07.14–)
AGO Officials	Kevin McGinty							
Police Chief Constable	Sir Ronnie Flanagan (1996–2002)			Sir Hugh Orde (05.02–09.09)		Sir Matt Baggot (09.09–06.14)	George Hamilton (06.14–)	
Director of Public Prosecutions	Sir Alasdair Fraser QC* (04.89–09.10)					Barra McGrory (11.11–)		

* Deceased

below, will be encountered in the detailed narrative in following chapters. They are introduced here.

Prime Ministers

First, heads of government. It remains a quirk of the UK state that the prime minister, perceived to be the chief executive officer of UK plc, has limited formal powers and responsibilities. He/she is not head of a department; number 10 is an office at the centre, and the cabinet office is separate. Each holder of the premiership has, therefore, fashioned it in his or her style of management; their premierships have been exercises in administrative leadership by elected politicians. Margaret Thatcher made a lasting impact in the 1980s; and Tony Blair, with continuities and variations, similarly left his managerial mark on the machinery of government in the 2000s.

Three prime ministers (as the table shows) have been involved in the OTR issue: Tony Blair (May 1997 to June 2007); Gordon Brown (June 2007 to May 2010); and David Cameron (May 2010 – July 2016).

Tony Blair was something of an iconoclast, when it came to governing; paradoxically, he applied a critical view of officialdom (identified with Tony Benn), in order to advance progressive politics (modernization). His administrative radicalism is recounted in his unusual memoirs, *A Journey* (London 2010),[9] showing how theory guided practice in his case. He believed himself to have a charismatic personality, and some officials were dazzled by Blairism for a time. His style, however, was criticized – as sofa government – by his first (of four) cabinet secretaries, each of whom found him challenging to handle as head of government.[10] He was to be accused of cronyism by non-cronies, during and after his time in Downing Street.

Gerry Adams, was arrested in March/April 2014, but only Ivor Bell – a former chief of staff of the IRA – was charged with involvement in her death.

[9] Introduction, pp. xv–xvii & chapter 9 (forces of conservatism), pp. 254–86.

[10] Lord Butler, *Review of Intelligence on Weapons of Mass Destruction*, HC 898, 14 July 2004, paras 606–11. The term sofa government does not appear in the report! It does, in Tony Blair, *A Journey*, pp. 16–19.

Tony Blair's legacy – based upon the 2003 Iraq war (to 2011), and the Afghanistan war (2001–14) – obscures how his ten years at number 10 were lived. It must be remembered that he had a continuing electoral mandate: 418 parliamentary seats in 1997 (and 43.2 per cent of the popular vote); 412 seats in 2001 (and 40.7 per cent); and 355 seats in 2005 (and 35.2 per cent) – and the latter after the Iraq war, for which, on 18 March 2003, 412 MPs (many labour) had voted for with only 149 against.[11] His cabinet secretaries could not overlook this political power, and the official checks and balances of Whitehall did not work as before in all areas. Sir John Chilcot, who pronounced belatedly on Blair and Iraq (but not Afghanistan[12]) in July 2016, narrowly escapes inclusion in the above table as a mandarin (in the NIO), by virtue of his retirement from the civil service in late 1997, though his fingerprints remain on the formulation of the NI peace process.

The Report of the Iraq Inquiry[13] (the Chilcot report) – the revenge of the mandarinate? – destroyed Tony Blair's historical reputation (between the EU referendum and Theresa May entering number 10), with an intellectual sniper shot propelled by the following principal findings about his conduct of UK policy: one, secret support in December 2001 – an '[extremely] clever strategy' – for regime change in Iraq;[14] two, an assumption – following the Crawford, Texas meeting with president Bush on 5–6 April 2002 – that there could be UK military participation in a US-led war;[15] three, the deliberately ambiguous security council resolution 1441 of 8 November 2002 (to rid Saddam Hussein finally of weapons of mass destruction), following US cooperation with the UK in the united nations;[16] four, perhaps the most extraordinary finding regarding Tony Blair's articulated *casus belli*, that UK officials never

---

[11] House of Commons, *Hansard,* vol. 401, cols. 907–11.

[12] Or his other wars: Iraq (1998), Kosovo (1999) and Sierra Leone (2000).

[13] *Report of a committee of privy councillors*, HC 264, in 12 volumes plus executive summary, 6 July 2016.

[14] Chilcot report, vol. 1, section 3.1, para 420.

[15] Chilcot report, vol. 1, section 3.2, para 755.

[16] Chilcot report, vol. 2, section 3.5, paras 1116–7.

considered whether, following the first gulf war of 1990–1, Iraq might have got rid of all its chemical, nuclear and biological weapons (it had done so, as post-war inspectors concluded in 2004);[17] five, belated legal advice from the attorney general, Lord Goldsmith QC, on 7 March 2003, that a (domestic or international?) court might well conclude that a second security council resolution was needed for military action;[18] six, Lord Goldsmith (under pressure from the armed forces and the treasury solicitor) plumping by 15 March 2003 for a legal war without a second resolution (relying on security council resolutions 678 and 687 regarding Kuwait in 1990–1!), on the basis solely of a number 10 official confirming that there was 'hard evidence' that Saddam was in material breach of resolution 1441;[19] and seven, a cabinet decision of 17 March 2003 to go to war (followed by the attorney general's written parliamentary answer that this would be lawful).[20]

The war began on 20 March 2003 and concluded, with Saddam overthrown (and hiding in a hole), on 1 May 2003. The rest – including a sectarian Iraq – is still history.

Sir John Chilcot and his privy council colleagues, none of whom is a lawyer, did not conclude that Tony Blair led the UK into an unlawful war: 'the Inquiry [he said in his televised statement on 6 July 2016] has not expressed a view on whether military action was legal. That could, of course, only be resolved by a properly constituted and internationally recognised Court.' One detects here the advice of Dame Rosalyn Higgins, a former UK president of the international court of justice in The Hague, who advised the inquiry on international law. The reference to this court may well be significant, however unlikely a case may be (the best bet would be an advisory opinion requested by the united nations[21]). It adds to Sir John's second conclusion regarding legality:

---

[17]   Chilcot report, vol. 4, section 4.3, para 671.
[18]   Chilcot report, vol. 5, section 5, para 920–6.
[19]   Chilcot report, vol. 5, section 5, paras 930–6.
[20]   Chilcot report, vol. 5, section 5, paras 945–57.
[21]   Charter of the united nations, art 96(1): security council or general assembly may request an advisory opinion.

'We have, however, concluded that the circumstances in which it was decided that there was a legal basis for UK military action were far from satisfactory.'[22] Far from satisfactory is important official understatement; Tony Blair, following Chilcot on 6 July 2016, is no longer a past premier who may be remembered fondly in his senior years. He may continue to fly the skies as an international businessman, and general prophet, but he is no longer a member of the UK establishment.

Northern Ireland is not Iraq (however much Tony Blair clings to this reputational comfort blanket). But this case study of OTR policy shows many of the same traits as the Chilcot report has revealed. Lord Goldsmith QC also played a legal role, and, in the case of Northern Ireland, I exonerate him – just. After Chilcot, and 6 July 2016, it will be impossible to consider Tony Blair's time in number 10, outside the framework now established by the Iraq inquiry.

There were few Whitehall checks and balances regarding NI, particularly after the 1998 Belfast agreement – which remains Tony Blair's substantial contribution to UK statecraft.[23] The OTR issue, however, threatens that surviving reputation, his ignoring of legal advice on NI being clearly distinguishable from the position on Iraq (where he obtained legal cover).[24]

Gordon Brown (June 2007 to May 2010) occupied the premiership when a great number of OTR letters was issued. But he seemed to leave NI to crystallize in his predecessor's historical legacy. The key decisions preceded his premiership. This conclusion, of course, could be a function of the Downey case papers petering out in July 2007, and it is difficult to exonerate later ministers and officials on the basis simply of no disclosure to Mr Justice Sweeney. Gordon Brown – uniquely among modern premiers – has chosen not to publish his memoirs

---

[22] Statement, p. 4.

[23] Anthony Seldon, *Blair,* London 2005, pp. 349–63 and *Blair Unbound*, London 2008, p. 541.

[24] Anthony Seldon, in an article drafted in advance of Tony Blair's evidence to NIAC on 13 January 2015, reprised his assessment of the premiership: *Daily Telegraph,* 13 January 2015.

(yet?), though he is the author of a string of books, including some with an autobiographical approach to politics.[25] If he had been interested in NI, we might have heard from him after he lost the 2010 election, including on the Blairite question of the OTRs.

David Cameron (May 2010 – July 2016) did try and withdraw from the NI question after his acceptance of the Bloody Sunday report.[26] However, the coalition government continued unhappily with the administrative scheme until after the John Downey judgment. Again, the lack of disclosed documents should not lead one to report simply that nothing happened.

Number 10

Under Tony Blair, a key role was played by Jonathan Powell. He was the prime minister's chief of staff, 1997–2007. Though a former diplomat, he came into government as a special advisor. The cabinet secretary was not comfortable with his (and Alistair Campbell's) exercise of power, and there had to be a statutory instrument to permit them to instruct civil servants.

Tony Blair made NI, following the 1998 Belfast agreement, a personal priority. Jonathan Powell became his 'chief negotiator'. Prime ministerial power was mediated by a person, who played a role in his own right and not just as a temporary civil servant. OTRs became one of the issues.

After leaving government with his patron, Jonathan Powell wrote (invoking Yeats) *Great Hatred, Little Room: making peace in Northern Ireland*, London 2008. He discussed OTRs with assurance, to little public comment following publication.[27] (This was followed by: *The New Machiavelli: how to wield power in the modern world* (London, 2010),

---

[25] Including: *Beyond the Crash* (London, 2010); *My Scotland, Our Britain* (London, 2014).

[26] Lord Saville, *Report of the Bloody Sunday Inquiry,* 10 vols., HC29, 15 June 2010; HC, *Hansard,* vol. 511, cols. 739–42, 15 June 2010; Anthony Seldon & Peter Snowdon, *Cameron at 10: the inside story, 2010–2015*, London 2015, pp. 47–54.

[27] Pp. 162, 179–80, 181, 185, 241, 271 and 274.

where he compared himself, in the preface, to Voltaire's *Candide* – 'an innocent unable to stop asking gauche questions and blurting out the truth' – rather than the Florentine administrator!). Some of the NI material from *Great Hatred, Little Room* reappeared in his third book, after some years of trying to generalize his peace-process experience through his non-governmental organization, Inter Mediate: *Talking to Terrorists: how to end armed conflicts,* London 2014. OTRs as a topic was drowned in the celebrated Blair/IRA peace process. The title of this more academic book, challenges conventional public policy in liberal democracies. But the fundamental flaw in his diplomatic iconoclasm is surely: why must statespeople talk to all terrorists who have some political support, when it is precisely such recognition which gives the latter traction as radical actors (as was the case of NI, with the republicans eclipsing the constitutional nationalists)? There is a little-articulated theory that, given the poor state of the IRA by the early 1990s, John Major's early negotiations with the Irish government, was mistaken – because unnecessary – statecraft.[28] Talking to Tamil terrorists in Sri Lanka led, after a more extensive peace process in 2002–9 (in which there was NI involvement), to total Sinhalese military victory.

Mention should also be made of John Sawers, Tony Blair's private secretary for foreign affairs (January 1999 to mid-2001), when the administrative scheme was established. Reportedly an intelligence officer, he had a successful career in the foreign office (before and after number 10), until, in November 2009, he became chief ('C') of the secret intelligence service. He retired from public service in November 2014. He was evidently more than a regular foreign office private secretary in number 10.

Secretaries of State

There have been eight NI secretaries of state, from May 1997 to July 2016. All have been involved in the OTR issue, but to varying

---

[28] Private information; Michael Gove, *The price of peace: an analysis of British policy in Northern Ireland,* London (centre for policy studies) 2000, pp. 12–13; James Dingley, *The IRA*, Santa Barbara, California 2012, pp. 103–4, 122 & 206.

extents. The NIO, created in 1972, ran NI until May 2007: since then, there has been devolution, with a reduced role for this Whitehall department (which survives still separate from the Wales and Scottish offices).

The eight secretaries of state are:

Mo Mowlam (May 1997 to October 1999);
Peter Mandelson (October 1999 to January 2001);
John Reid (January 2001 to October 2002);
Paul Murphy (October 2002 to May 2005);
Peter Hain (May 2005 to June 2007);
Shaun Woodward (June 2007 to May 2010);
Owen Paterson (May 2010 to September 2012);
Theresa Villiers (September 2012 to July 2016).

The first five of these eight were appointed by Tony Blair. Mo Mowlam was the first (of two) women. Gordon Brown had one secretary of state (Shaun Woodward, a former conservative). This was during devolution. David Cameron had two NI secretaries, the last occupant of the post – Theresa Villiers – being the longest serving since 1997.

Mo Mowlam was responsible, single handedly, for prisoner releases being included in the Belfast agreement. For that, we rely upon Tony Blair, who agreed release after one (but maybe two) years, personally with Gerry Adams.[29] The secretary of state, who was described by her head of government, as 'a little removed from the negotiations',[30] also single handedly conceded OTRs to republicans and seemingly loyalists (who would never benefit). Mo Mowlam made a distinct contribution to statecraft, which may now be assessed with the benefit of a little hindsight. Officials had prepared for neither prisoner releases nor OTRs, and implementation of the Belfast agreement was to be beset by these problems. The elision of prisoner releases and OTRs was, of course, characteristic of republican thinking. One did not naturally follow the other, since OTRs had not been included in the Belfast agreement.

Tony Blair had to move his NI secretary, in October 1999, because

---

[29] Tony Blair, *A Journey*, London 2010, pp. 172–3 & 179.
[30] P. 171.

of her lack of empathy for unionists. Mo Mowlam left parliament at the 2001 general election, and was to die in August 2005. In 2002, she published her memoirs: *Momentum: the struggle for peace, politics and the people*, London. The book was mainly about her less than three years as NI secretary of state. It mentions prisoner releases.[31] It does not mention on the runs. Nor does it mention Rita O'Hare, a leading Belfast republican living in Dublin (chapter 3).

Two other secretaries of state have also published their memoirs: Peter Mandelson, *The Third Man: life at the heart of new labour*, London 2010; and Peter Hain, *Outside In*, London 2012. They differed from each other. Peter Mandelson helped create new labour (placing himself alongside Tony Blair and Gordon Brown as the third man), and, as part of his sensitivity for electoral politics, was respectful generally of police officers and soldiers. NI warrants much of one chapter of his memoirs.[32] While he says nothing about OTRs, he subsequently – after the John Downey case – showed himself to have a serious constitutional understanding of the question. (The title of my chapter 2 includes a term he used about the exercise of state power.) Peter Hain, in contrast, entered parliament as a liberal-turned-labour supporter: his South African background was important; as was Irish nationalism in its republican form. He worked closely with Tony Blair, when a junior foreign office minister, to put Gibraltar under joint UK/Spanish sovereignty, unsuccessfully.[33] Peter Hain too has a chapter on NI in his memoirs. But he does not mention OTRs. He was voluble at the time of the John Downey case, and indeed figured in Mr Justice Sweeney's reasoning. The documents from the case show that the Downey letter leaving NI is attributable to him, as the secretary of state on his last full day in office (27 June 2007).

Neither John Reid, less an autodidact, and more a welfare state, intellectual, and Paul Murphy, a Welsh catholic with considerable patience, has produced memoirs. They, of course, were in post during the

---

[31] Pp. 220, 221, 227–8, 242–3, 249–50 & 269–70.

[32] Pp. 287–315.

[33] Tony Blair does not mention Gibraltar in his memoirs; *Outside In*, pp. 274–85.

totality of the second Blair government. This was a low point in the history of OTRs, but, as will be seen, the issue simmered, occasionally flaring up.

Civil Servants

The administrative scheme, as it developed, was the work of civil servants. They, of course, were acting on the instructions of ministers. They are entitled – in their own estimations – to hide from contemporary history; the civil service has been described as the invisible part of the constitution.[34] But, in the case of OTRs, official advice included going much further than the Belfast agreement, in which the people of NI – in the 1998 referendum – had set the democratic limits. Moreover, the officials concerned were exceptional as regards the positions they occupied in Whitehall. I do not seek to out officials, simply because they exist. But the story of the OTRs can only be told, if one does appreciate the individual, and significant, contributions of a handful of senior officials in designated posts.

It is an interesting question as to whether officials could, or would, have run the administrative scheme without input from Tony Blair and Jonathan Powell. They did not originate the idea of prisoner releases, and it took the head of government to fall for elision with OTRs, before they advised on the extension of the prisoner-release policy to fugitive suspects.

It has been claimed in the wake of Downey (somewhat unconvincingly) that telling suspected terrorists they were not wanted, was a normal public function applying generally to all who come into contact with the law. The various incidents of this cited – such as solicitors inquiring of the police as to whether their clients are going to be prosecuted for motoring offences – hardly amounts to a justification for the policy on OTRs as it was played out over many years.

The NIO had five official heads, called permanent secretaries (though two were lesser directors general) during the administrative

---

[34] Some, however, have come out on the NI peace process: Graham Spencer, ed., *The British and Peace in Northern Ireland,* Cambridge 2015.

scheme. Permanent secretaries know everything about their departments. In the case of the NIO, its official heads knew a great deal, if not everything, about NI. The five official heads were:

Sir Joseph Pilling (1997–2005);
Sir Jonathan Phillips (2005–10);
Hilary Jackson (a woman who was not made a dame) (2010–11);
Sir Julian King (2011–14);
Sir Jonathan Stephens (2014–).

Sir Joseph Pilling was especially involved in what the NIO came to call simply, the peace process.[35] Sir Jonathan Phillips was there at the time of the Downey letter.[36] Sir Julian King helped establish the Hallett review. And Sir Jonathan Stephens returned to the NIO, in time to help deal with the fallout from the Downey case.

While the official heads of the NIO knew about the administrative scheme, because of its significance for the IRA, it was located in one part of the department: in what became the political affairs directorate. This was headed by a political director and an associate political director. This directorate was located in: the rights and international relations division, which was based in London rather than Belfast. The division, as the name suggests, turned out to the world from Whitehall. The directorate looked, not exclusively to NI's elected representatives, but to its paramilitaries, and especially the IRA. Most officials in the NIO busied themselves with their particular jobs, oblivious to some of the dealings of the political affairs directorate. 'The way the NIO worked', a former official (distancing himself) told NIAC, 'information was extremely compartmentalised and held on a need to know basis, so I had no involvement in the scheme.'[37]

The following occupants of those two latter offices (political director and associate political director) were decisively involved in the OTR issue:

---

[35] Spencer, *The British*, pp. 201–28.
[36] Spencer, *The British*, pp. 277–301.
[37] Nick Perry, NIAC, *Report*, Q1001, 9 June 2014.

Political director:

> Sir Quentin Thomas (1991–8) after retiring,[38]
> Sir Bill Jeffrey (1998–2002),[39]
> Sir Jonathan Phillips (2002–5);

Associate political director:

> Sir Jonathan Stephens (1991–2000);
> William Fittall (2000–2),[40]
> David Cooke (2002–4).[41]

Sir Bill Jeffrey, giving evidence to NIAC, explained the uniqueness of the position of political director in the civil service: 'it is a civil service post but it reports – or reported in those days, anyway – to the Secretary of State through the Permanent Secretary. It is the main source of official advice for Ministers on the political process.'[42]

One other official deserves listing, in this introduction to key players: Mark Sweeney, head of the rights and international relations division, from early 2004 until late 2007. After devolution in May 2007, OTRs was to be dealt with at an even higher level of a more strategic Whitehall department.

Attorneys General

The key office holders in this narrative were the successive attorneys general for England and Wales (most of whom were also the attorney general for NI). There were six:

> John Morris QC (May 1997 – July 1999);
> Lord Williams of Mostyn QC (July 1999 – June 2001);
> Lord Goldsmith QC (June 2001 – June 2007);
> Baroness Scotland QC (June 2007 – May 2010);

---

[38] Spencer, *The British,* pp. 101–19.
[39] Spencer, *The British,* pp. 229–51.
[40] Spencer, *The British*, pp. 252–76.
[41] Spencer, *The British*, pp. 147–76.
[42] NIAC, *Report,* Q3315, 19 November 2014.

Dominic Grieve QC (May 2010 – July 2014);
Jeremy Wright QC (July 2014–).

John Morris QC had a brief initial involvement, but he was gone by July 1999.[43] A key OTR role was played by Lord Williams QC. Lord Goldsmith QC was long-serving, during the administrative scheme. Baroness Scotland QC was Gordon Brown's attorney general. Dominic Grieve QC had some involvement, under David Cameron. He was also the first advocate general for NI (from May 2010), being followed by Jeremy Wright QC in both positions.

Lords Williams and Goldsmith – both successful barristers before they went into government – played major roles in the OTR story. It is interesting that the attorneys general, between 1999 and 2010, were members of the upper house. Lords Williams and Goldsmith are the sources of the legal advice which went to number 10. Both criticized the administrative scheme. Of the two, Lord Williams showed greater courage, and independence of mind, in advising the prime minister.

Police

The police in NI was the first important institution, entrusted with the administrative scheme. As noted, the RUC became the PSNI in November 2001. There have been four chief constables:

Sir Ronnie Flanagan, 1996 – 2002;
Sir Hugh Orde, May 2002 – September 2009;
Sir Matt Baggott, September 2009 – June 2014;
George Hamilton, June 2014 –.

The last chief constable of the RUC, and first of the PSNI, was Sir Ronnie Flanagan. The second chief constable dealing with OTRs was Sir Hugh Orde, who served for over seven years. During his time, Sinn Féin came out in support of the police (in January 2007). He was followed by Matt Baggott, who served less than his five years. The current chief constable is George Hamilton, an Ulsterman.

---

[43] Lord Morris, *Fifty Years in Politics and the Law*, Cardiff 2011. On Russia Today, the television station, and after Chilcot, he articulated an extremely critical view of Tony Blair: *Belfast Telegraph,* 9 July 2016.

The three former were all involved in the administrative scheme, to the extent that OTRs were being dealt with by a varying number of police officers and staff. Sir Ronnie Flanagan has been out of NI – in England and Wales and further afield – for well over a decade. Sir Hugh Orde was the police chief most involved with OTRs: he was responsible most notably for Operation Rapid, during which the John Downey mistake occurred. Matt Baggott (knighted after retirement) dealt with the immediate outworking of the criminal case.

Director of Public Prosecutions

The second most important institution, or rather office holder, was the director of public prosecutions in NI.

This post was occupied by one individual, for a considerable period: Sir Alasdair Fraser QC (a Scot who grew up in NI), from April 1989 to September 2010. However, Sir Alasdair fell ill in the 2000s, and there were a number of acting directors in his later years. He was involved in the first half of 2006, but he was gone by the time of Operation Rapid.

The first director of public prosecutions, appointed in November 2011, by the attorney general for NI (after devolution), is Barra McGrory QC, Sir Alasdair Fraser's successor. However, Barra McGrory had a preceding role, as Sinn Féin's solicitor, in the OTR story, from 2006 through 2010.

Two Groups of Key Players

It is helpful to indicate in this introduction who, on the basis of all the evidence to be considered, deserves an accolade for doing his/her job properly. First place goes undoubtedly to the late Sir Alasdair Fraser QC. There would have been no John Downey catastrophe, if he had remained in effective charge of the administrative scheme. Second place goes to the late Lord Williams of Mostyn QC, Tony Blair's attorney general until the 2001 general election. He stopped a great deal for a period of time. Third place (some way behind) goes to his successor, Lord Goldsmith QC, despite two NI reservations (the unsuccessful 2002 attempt to change the question asked and Operation Rapid towards the end of this time). Two of these three nominees are deceased, and dead heroes are often not scrutinized sufficiently. They attempted to maintain the rule of law at relevant points: up to 2001, in the case of Lord Williams; up to 2006, in the case of Sir Alasdair Fraser; and up to 2007 (with reservations), in the case of Lord Goldsmith.

That they did not succeed completely is due to a second group of key players. The first key player is Tony Blair. The second is Jonathan Powell, with Sir Bill Jeffrey tying in the period 1998–2002. The third key player is Peter Hain, and the fourth (hitherto unrecognized) should be Sir Hugh Orde. All (except Sir Bill Jeffrey) were in post until 27 June 2007, when the prime minister resigned. No doubt, they would all claim a part of the UK victory – peace in NI – which has seen far fewer victims there than there might have been the position. They may be dubbed the peace processors, who believed it was expedient, and indeed essential, to make private concessions to the IRA. The date of 27 June 2007 (when Tony Blair left Downing Street) has an additional significance: it is the day the NI decision was made which led to the John Downey letter of 20 July 2007. Nearly seven years' later, the OTR administrative scheme was to be immolated in the court of Mr Justice Sweeney. We now know that the rule of law in NI had been interrupted significantly by the peace process.

What was it about Tony Blair's relationship with Gerry Adams, which led to the OTR scandal? At heart, the latter believed that the former could, in the words of Peter Mandelson, simply wave a magic wand as prime minister to give the republicans what they wanted.

CHAPTER TWO

Tony Blair and Gerry Adams: Waving a Magic Wand

Without Tony Blair, assisted by Jonathan Powell, and Gerry Adams, in tandem with Martin McGuinness, the administrative scheme of 2000–14 would not have existed.

A press photograph of the four (now on the cover of this book), in the prime minister's Westminster room, on 13 June 2007, two weeks before he resigned, reveals a great deal about the conduct of NI policy during his three governments.[44] One can read the body language of these four men. Blair looks irritated, while maintaining control. Powell is equally good mannered, but seems sheepish. Adams is open, relaxed and expansive (though he has not taken his shoes off this time). And McGuinness, with a comparable paramilitary reputation, leans forward as the good cop playing the UK prime minister.

The Two Interlocutors

The two leaders – Tony Blair (born 1953) and Gerry Adams (born 1948) – may be contrasted. Tony Blair, with Irish roots through his mother, was an English/Scottish public-school boy, and London barrister. He was to adopt the catholic religion of his Merseyside wife, Cherie Booth QC. Gerry Adams, not acknowledging possible English or Scottish roots, was a catholic grammar-school boy turned teenage Belfast barman. The former was, of course, the UK prime minister, having been elected a labour MP in 1983 and a modernizing party leader in 1994. The latter is believed to have joined the IRA in 1966, and the army council in 1977, though he persists in asserting he has been only a member of a democratic political party, Sinn Féin, whose president he has been for thirty-three years. One had the status of holding the highest office, under the sovereign, the other – in republican constitutional

---

44   Stefan Rousseau, PA Archive/Press Association Images.

thinking, the president of Ireland (sic) – had been forged in a west Belfast subculture of failed republicanism, unfamiliar to even the student Tony Blair in Oxford, with his guitar and interest in Anglicanism.

As men, and as negotiators (because Adams was not deferential to the UK prime minister), Gerry Adams was senior to Tony Blair. The year Adams joined the IRA, Blair went to Fettes college in Edinburgh as a boarder. When Adams first negotiated with 'the British' in 1972, Blair was on a pre-university gap year in London trying to get into the music business. The year Adams became a member of the army council, Blair was on the first rung of the legal ladder.

If Tony Blair was disadvantaged against Gerry Adams, the UK government was also disarmed in the face of the republicans. Blair headed three governments, in 1997 to 2007, but there were endless turnovers of ministers and officials, as political fortunes and civil service careers interrupted political continuity. On the other side, there was extraordinary continuity. Adams and McGuinness were in charge throughout the Blair years. Gerry Kelly, who was the same age as Blair (but had been convicted of the Old Bailey bombing in 1973), also ran the republican side of the administration scheme, between 2000 and 2014, from Sinn Féin's Connolly House in Belfast. The IRA was, and continued to be, a family of a particular sort. But, a point seemingly not spotted by the prime minister, its leaders were aging grandfathers, with complicated feelings for their adult children and their progeny.

Jonathan Powell recalls that Senator George Mitchell described Adams and McGuinness, after the Belfast agreement, as 'natural-born chisellers': 'It was true [Powell comments] that the Republicans were addicted to over-negotiating.'[45] The UK government, it may be argued, did not evidently benefit from that perceived addiction: on the contrary, as with the OTR *imbroglio*, it became the victim of the other's over-negotiation.

In his memoirs, looking back in 2010, Tony Blair wrote of the republican leaders with excruciating honesty: 'They were an extraordinary

---

[45] Powell, *Great Hatred*, p. 162. Sherard Cowper-Coles, in *Ever the Diplomat: confessions of a foreign office mandarin*, London 2012, p. 112, makes the same point.

couple. Over time I came to like both greatly, probably more than I should have, if truth be told.'[46] Either he did not know, or he had forgotten (or forgiven), that the IRA's code name for him was 'the naïve idiot'.[47] That is what the IRA leadership told its base, about the continuing Ireland versus Britain struggle, where Gerry Adams and Martin McGuinness were reported to be making considerable headway in secret negotiations with the historic enemy. The superior attitude of the republican leaders may be indicative of its opposite, but there is nothing in the other side's negotiating strategy – Tony Blair was no Lloyd George (and the UK was no longer the British empire) – which suggests the two republicans were out-smarted by the two Oxford graduates[48] successfully occupying number 10.

Shortly after the Downey case, David Trimble provided an insight, in the house of lords, into the Blair/Powell relationship with Adams/McGuinness: 'I was particularly attracted to [Lord Alderdice's] analogy of teenagers, although he should perhaps go a little further and bear in mind that some teenagers have delinquent tendencies and it is slightly better to view the matter in that way. We all know that it is absolutely essential that teenagers with delinquent tendencies have clear boundaries. In that situation, nothing is worse than letting people think that the boundaries can be blurred and that they can get away with things. Unfortunately, that has been done again and again over the past 15 years with regard to the republican movement.'[49]

The Bicycle Theory

Tony Blair brought a particular insight to his NI policy, if not to his statecraft generally. The Belfast agreement was not a historic compromise, to be simply implemented. The UK government had to keep momentum going. The republicans had to be fed concessions on demand. Thus, the idea of a continuing peace process. The analogy

---

[46] Tony Blair, *A Journey,* London 2010, p. 196.
[47] *Daily Telegraph,* 6 October 2002.
[48] Law for Blair, history for Powell.
[49] HL, *Hansard,* vol. 752, col. 1242, 4 March 2014.

was a bicycle being pedalled to prevent it falling over. In his memoirs, Tony Blair wrote: 'A peace process never stands still – it goes forward or back.'[50]

David Trimble and Mark Durkan told NIAC separately that, even though Sinn Féin had not voted for the Belfast agreement, there was no risk of the IRA going back to war.[51] These are important political opinions, from both sides of the divide in NI. David Trimble had had to manoeuvre into negotiations with Sinn Féin after 1998. Mark Durkan saw the republicans undermine his social democratic and labour party. The NI referendum in May 1998 had been crucial: the catholic community indicated its overwhelming approval of the Belfast agreement (almost regardless of what it meant). The republicans took serious note, and exercised collective discipline. '… Gerry Adams had told Tim Dalton [a leading Irish official] that the IRA would not go back to violence because their own community would not allow them to do so.'[52] This was a strategic weakness for the republicans, which the UK failed to use tactically. Tony Blair never came to see them as just ethnic nationalists for whom democracy was a constraint.

Jonathan Powell, in contrast, told NIAC that there was a risk of return to violence: 'there are reasons for thinking that right through to really quite late in this process. Again, people like to write history backwards and say it was all solved after 9/11. It is just not true. At any stage you could have tipped this back into war if you had taken a misstep.'[53]

If that is true, then he and the prime minister were negotiating

---

[50] *Journey*, p. 198. Jonathan Powell, a regular London cyclist, suggests he imparted this wisdom to Tony Blair: '… that is what makes me believe so strongly in my bicycle theory. You have to keep the process moving forward, however slowly. Never let it fall over.' (*Great Hatred*, p. 322)

The originator of the bicycle theory, applied to managing the labour party, was, in fact, Harold Wilson. It is interesting that neither the prime minister nor his chief of staff knew this!

[51] NIAC, *Report*, Q827, 13 May 2014; Q867, 4 June 2014.

[52] Powell, *Great Hatred*, p. 265.

[53] NIAC, *Report*, Q2540, 8 September 2014.

under a perceived threat of republican violence. If they deny that they were (as they must), then David Trimble and Mark Durkan have a better understanding of the NI republicans. The threat, of course, which was there, may have been largely hollow, given the successful diversion of Adams and McGuinness into political negotiations.

Late in the NIAC inquiry, Tony Blair told MPs of his inner motive regarding OTRs: 'Well, I did believe there was a chance of it [the peace process] collapsing … Look, there were points in time when the thing was more fragile than at other points … The three dates that stand out in my mind are: 1998, when this issue first arose; 2002, when the whole issue to do with decommissioning was very live; and late 2006, when the question was whether you could get [Stormont] up and running or not.'[54]

The year 1998 refers to prisoner releases. The year 2002 could be correct. Tony Blair referred especially to December 2006, when he countenanced 'that this thing [the peace process] was going to go down',[55] on several occasions during his evidence.

Such a counter-factual prime ministerial statement deserves close study. Unfortunately, some share in the prime ministerial panic, and do not properly consider the evidence. It is true that the IRA had broken its first ceasefire in February 1996, but it was then still out in the cold. The Northern Bank robbery in December 2004 (the biggest then in UK history), was a terrorist tactic. Jonathan Powell continued to travel to Belfast, and Adams and McGuinness were invited to Chequers in January 2005. Is Tony Blair really asking observers to accept that, having decommissioned its weapons in September 2005, the IRA was going to return to war in December 2006? That was after nine years' participation in the Blair circle, during which the republicans acquired a status of *primus inter pares* among the NI parties. Tony Blair, described by his biographer as 'essentially a courteous man',[56] knew in December 2006 his time in number 10 was limited to a matter of months (his

---

[54] NIAC, *Report,* Q3736, 13 January 2015.

[55] NIAC, *Report,* Q3708, 13 January 2015.

[56] Anthony Seldon, *Daily Telegraph,* 13 January 2015.

legacy was beckoning): Gerry Adams and Martin McGuinness had a timescale of decades, and a negotiating prize of the IRA escaping criminal punishment. Tony Blair and Jonathan Powell were not the hard men in that relationship. The prime minister was nervous in December 2006, not about what the security service may have been telling him about the IRA, but about his ability to stay in number 10 and sign off on the NI problem before Gordon Brown unseated him.

Sinn Féin

Sinn Féin, though republicans and others seek to suggest the contrary, had not 'signed up' to the Belfast agreement, in April 1998. Nevertheless, it came to rely increasingly upon it. The principal concession was the early release of prisoners, which came to have the end point of 28 July 2000. But Sinn Féin was thinking outside that box. There was the Rita O'Hare problem, and seemingly a number of other named republicans (including Owen Carron) who wanted to come in from the cold. There were also the escaped prisoners, and those facing extradition from the Republic of Ireland and other states. Gradually, the republicans formulated a demand that all non-prisoners – whom they came to call the on the runs – should essentially be let off; they were not all necessarily outside NI. Adams and McGuinness did not mind how it would be done. They did not need lessons in the UK constitution. They were talking to the head of government, in various grand locations. This was around the mythical conference table of Irish nationalism, where everything would be resolved. Peter Mandelson characterized them as wanting the prime minister to wave a magic wand (an image he used repeatedly), to give them what they wanted.[57]

Irish republicans had always had an exaggerated view of UK power: Gerry Adams and Martin McGuinness approached Tony Blair, demanding that he give them what they wanted by executive action from number 10. Gradually, he persuaded them that the executive action – under the name of public interest – would have to come from

---

[57] NIAC, *Report*, Q2936, 4 November 2014.

the attorney general, Lord Williams of Mostyn QC, a person known more to English lawyers than NI politicians. The prime minister was constitutionally incorrect: there was little or no such flexibility in the relevant public interest concept, as he would be advised more than once.

The formulation of the OTR policy had a secret official contemporary historian: on 3 September 2002, William Fittall, the associate political director in the NIO, wrote a handover document for his successor, David Cooke. He called it: 'OTRs – a brief history of crime'. He retired from the civil service, and became an official in the church of England.

William Fittall – who was not involved until after July 2000 – wrote in his handover: 'This is pre-eminently an area where two worldviews have collided. For the Provisionals, peace means not only the release of the "prisoners of war" from British custody, but also the removal of any continued sanctions or threats of prosecution against other "combatants" ... Ever since 1998, the Provisionals have been chiselling away [that word again!], exploiting their leverage over decommissioning to advance their objectives. Repeated private commitments were eventually turned into public commitments during 2001 and we now have a reasonably well worked-up legislative scheme for discharging them ... Meanwhile the grinding – and only partially avowed – private process of checking Sinn Fein names within present law continues.'[58] William Fittall was correct about the republican concept of peace, but he failed to appreciate that, given the UK was not linking prisoner releases to decommissioning under the Belfast agreement, the republicans were able to trade the continuing promise of decommissioning for the practical down payment of OTR gains.

The handover document contained a reference to the public OTR policy, which emerged on 8 March 2001, but also to the secret administrative scheme, which was 'only partially avowed' in the words of the retiring associate political director in September 2002. That was after the John Reid written parliamentary answers earlier in the summer, which have been relied upon to prove the administrative scheme was admitted at the time (see chapter 4).

---

[58]   Paras 2 & 3.

Much later, in a published interview with an academic (Graham Spencer), William Fittall alluded to the Adams/Blair relationship: 'They loved dealing with Number 10, partly because of the status and going to the top .... They were ruthlessly focused throughout and the advantage they had with Number 10, as opposed to the NIO..., was that the prime minister and Jonathan [Powell], because they had so many other things to attend to, were inclined to cut to the chase ... The point of having a governmental system is making sure that you have discipline and coherence and you do not give things away. The process had its own self-correcting mechanisms and, since the British Government's role was essentially facilitative [as between unionists and nationalists], there was not a serious risk that we were going to go off on a frolic, with one side and give them all they wanted because that would have been a ridiculous thing to do. But it did mean that sometimes on the details in the negotiations, the republicans would remorselessly keep chiselling away and would get more than perhaps they should. It is my own belief, as with the OTR's issue, that dealing with the past was unfinished business. On this Number 10 was absolutely right. But some of the promises given in those negotiations were given without the full dimensions of the issue being properly scoped out. That was pragmatism based on having to get some movement.'[59] It is also serious civil service criticism of the prime minister.

Sean O'Callaghan, a former associate of Adams and McGuinness, has recently commented upon their relationship with number 10: 'Blair and some of his advisers, though I exclude Peter Mandelson, seemed to have little sense of the dangers in negotiating with a so-called po-litical party whose leadership was still involved with an active terrorist organisation (the Provision IRA), and their immersion in group-think peacemaking meant they were soon in danger of speaking the same language as Adams and McGuinness.'[60] Irish peace process is the main example, where the republicans imposed their rhetoric eventually on

---

[59] *The British and Peace in Northern Ireland*, Cambridge 2015, p. 275.

[60] *James Connolly: my search for the man, the myth and his legacy*, London 2015, pp. 256–7.

established politicians.[61] OTRs is a good instance of intellectual laziness, where a republican category was adopted by the state, confusing the criminal justice practitioners who had to implement policy.

The Irish Government

The Irish government – introducing an important external actor – had taken the side of the IRA on the OTR issue from late 1999, while working with the democratically accountable government of the UK to implement the Belfast agreement. It was to act as a member of the Irish nationalist family, while being a neighbouring liberal-democratic state, with important obligations towards the UK in international law.

On 17 December 1999 (shortly after devolution to NI), the first meeting of the British-Irish intergovernmental conference took place in Downing Street. Though the communiqué does not mention it, the Irish taoiseach, Bertie Ahern, suggested to Tony Blair, that the early release scheme for prisoners, in the UK and the Republic of Ireland, should be developed to become two amnesties. He elaborated in a letter of 23 December 1999. The Irish premier wanted an agreement regarding Rita O'Hare, and some others, by that Christmas! One can only assume that the letter had been in draft for a number of days if not weeks.

Blair/Adams

Between November 1999 and May 2000, Tony Blair entered into a private agreement with Gerry Adams regarding OTRs. This was not simply a political agreement. The head of government made administrative promises to the leader of a NI party (who was also an abstaining Westminster MP). These promises were implemented, through seemingly sofa government – with Jonathan Powell omnipresent – rather than cabinet government, by ministers and officials. While some on the UK side tried to downplay the private agreement, Gerry Adams was

---

[61] Gerry Adams was the author of inter alia: *A Pathway to Peace* (1988); *An Irish Voice: the quest for peace* (1997); *Free Ireland: towards a lasting peace* (1995); *Hope and History: making peace in Ireland* (2003).

firm – and unsubtle – in holding Tony Blair's feet to the fire.

The pertinent documents proving the private agreement (really two separate ones) may be listed:

(1) Tony Blair to Gerry Adams, 5 November 1999;
(2) Tony Blair to Gerry Adams, 6 November 1999;
(3) John Sawers to NIO (Nick Perry), 20 December 1999;
(4) Bertie Ahern to Tony Blair, 23 December 1999;
(5) Gerry Adams to Tony Blair, 8 March 2000;
(6) John Sawers to NIO (Nick Perry), 13 March 2000;
(7) Jonathan Stephens, note, 3 May 2000;
(8) Sinn Féin text, 4 May 2000;
(9) Tony Blair to Gerry Adams, 5 May 2000.

The overall effect of the nine documents cannot be conjured away.[62] The main points follow, regarding the first agreement of 5/6 November 1999 and the second of 5 May 2000.

Tony Blair and Gerry Adams had met secretly, on 4 November 1999. The following day, the prime minister made a cryptic written promise: 'You raised certain matters with me last night. I understand the importance of them to you and I am prepared to do what I can.' One of the matters was extradition. Another was OTRs. In a second letter, on 6 November 1999, the prime minister promised that the attorney general would have reviewed extradition by Christmas or the early new year. Extradition, at this stage, was one of the entry points to OTR policy (see chapter 3). That was the first written agreement.

On 8 March 2000 – following the first suspension of Stormont – Gerry Adams wrote reproaching the prime minister: 'I ... have to say that I, at a personal as well as political level, feel your failure to honour these commitments is deeply damaging.' He recalled (correctly or incorrectly) that the attorney general was also reviewing OTRs, by Christmas or the early new year.[63] Gerry Adams did not often put things

---

[62] They are available in: Downey case papers, tab 8, pp. 5–7, 8–9, 12, 12A–12B, 13–14, 15, 23–35, 36 & 37–38.

[63] John Sawers, sending this to Nick Perry, on 13 March 2000, referred to Tony

in writing. But he had learned to accuse the young, and inexperienced, prime minister of dishonourable conduct without blushing.

On 2 May 2000, at the Irish embassy in London, UK officials continued talks with Irish officials and Sinn Fein.[64] The following day, Jonathan Stephens recorded: 'On OTRs, the British side undertook to operate the Irish procedure of clarifying the position of named individuals and reviewing cases where appropriate but with no guarantees of the outcome: Sinn Fein want an undertaking that the general principle of not pursuing OTRs will be recognised by July. [] Sinn Fein warn that they still do not have a package they are prepared to put to the IRA: even if they go to the IRA, they are not sure they will get an answer by Thursday and warn that the language may not be exactly what the Government want.'

Jonathan Stephens' note of 3 May 2000 indicates that there was a precedent in Dublin for an OTR policy: 'the Irish procedure of clarifying the position of named individuals and reviewing cases where appropriate but with no guarantees of the outcome'. The Irish practice (without a name) was to be imported by the UK, and established later in 2000 in NI and separately in England and Wales.[65]

Two days after the Irish embassy gathering, Sinn Féin handed Jonathan Powell and Bill Jeffrey a draft text of a public OTR policy. Sinn Féin rarely put things in writing. The UK government was to state: 'We will deal, on an individual basis, with an initial batch of OTRs. Further to this and when the last prisoners are released … [28 July 2000] … the Attorney General will outline his belief, in this new political context and the on-going process of conflict resolution, that the public interest would no longer be served by pursuing prosecution in cases relating to offences which pre-date The Good Friday Agreement

---

Blair's 'commitments' of November 1999.

[64] The participants were: Jonathan Powell, Bill Jeffrey and Jonathan Stephens (UK government); Paddy Teahon, Dermot Gallagher, Tim Dalton and Ted Barrington (Irish government); and Gerry Adams, Martin McGuinness, Bairbre de Brún, Aidan McAteer, Richard Macaulay and Leo Green (Sinn Féin).

[65] *Sunday Telegraph*, 17 & 24 May 2015; *Irish Independent*, 25 May 2015.

as anyone convicted on this basis would have qualified for release under the terms of the Agreement.'

They had taken the point about public interest, probably inaccurately communicated by Tony Blair initially, and the decisive role of the attorney general, whom they seemed to think would bend to the prime minister's will.

Also on Thursday, 4 May 2000, Tony Blair and Bertie Ahern travelled separately to Belfast, for political talks at Hillsborough. The following day, the prime minister wrote to Gerry Adams from Downing Street: 'You have raised a number of issues about prisoners and people in whom the police and the prosecuting authorities still have an interest.'

This letter of 5 May 2000 contains a clear OTR promise, with again an optimistic deadline: 'I can confirm that, if you can provide details of a number of cases involving people "on the run" we will arrange for them to be considered by the Attorney General, consulting the Director of Public Prosecutions and the police as appropriate, with a view to giving you a response within a month if at all possible.' This was the second written agreement.

It was the birth of the administrative scheme, the parents being improbably Tony Blair and Gerry Adams, in the context of an emerging public OTR policy. A number of points requires to be made about the conception. First, on 5 November 1999, the prime minister indicated that the attorney general would review the public interest in extradition cases. (This was legally incorrect: it was the responsibility of the NI secretary of state.) Second, the letter of 6 November 1999, set a timetable of Christmas/new year. Third, the prime minister only then sought legal advice from the NIO. Fourth, the rare letter from Gerry Adams, on 8 March 2000, treated the Christmas/new year deadline as applying to all OTRs. Fifth, the Sinn Féin text of 4 May 2000, made clear they wanted the attorney general to announce on 31 July 2000 that all prosecutions would be abandoned. And sixth, the Blair letter of 5 May 2000 – containing a promise about an unknown number of cases – repeated his earlier mistake of a deadline: 'within a month if at all possible'.[66]

---

[66] For evidence of a possible official reaction, see Bill Jeffrey, memo to [redacted]

Such promises were to become characteristically Blairite over the years. The prime minister, in negotiations, or simply political debate, would articulate a wish, for the benefit of his audience to believe, but then seek to protect himself by qualifying, and effectively denying, it. People believed him, and continued to do so when it was in their interest. But his credibility, starting from the high of his political success in May 1997, would, through repetition of the tactic, slide down a curve of growing disenchantment during his time in office.

There is another letter – from Gerry Kelly (also an occasional correspondent) on 10 July 2000 to Peter Mandelson (then the NI secretary of state) – which repeats Gerry Adams' complaint of dishonour of 8 March 2000. Again, the republicans referred to the one 'month' promise of 5 May 2000: 'whilst it is acknowledged that there are legal and other obstacles to be overcome[,] the situation is totally unsatisfactory and causing difficulties for Sinn Fein and the process.'[67] The next paragraph of the letter is redacted, in the version disclosed in the Downey case. However, an unredacted version is available from John Downey's lawyers; it reveals Gerry Kelly's familiarity with the IRA: '... the unresolved nature of all of these matters in the wake of the IRA delivering on its commitments sends entirely the wrong signal to those republican activists who have been positive in their support for the peace process...'.[68] The letter was signed on his behalf by Siobhán O'Hanlon, a former IRA prisoner who avoided being shot by the SAS in Gibraltar in 1988;[69] she was to die of natural causes in 2006.

Illegality or What?

The prime minister did nothing illegal, in the sense of breaching the criminal law. Nor was he completely naïve: Tony Blair must have known that Gerry Adams was pushing him. However, he tried to charm terrorists into becoming politicians.

---

12 May 2000. (Downey case papers, tab 8, pp. 40–1)

[67] Downey case papers, tab 8, pp. 91–2.

[68] Defence skeleton argument, 3 January 2014, para 87.

[69] BBC, 9 October 2009.

His conduct is constitutionally questionable. He was not implementing the Belfast agreement, which was his duty. Having failed to link prisoner releases to a timetable for decommissioning, he made promises (on 6 November 1999 and 5 May 2000) which could not be kept. He should have known that as a lawyer (and the husband of a part-time judge), if not as a statesman in the making. There is no evidence that he feared the IRA returning to war in 1999–2000. So why was the prime minister giving the republicans more? The answer can only be the bicycle theory; as an inexperienced, and insecure, ruler, he feared falling off his new machine. He and Jonathan Powell were no negotiating match for Gerry Adams and Martin McGuinness, educated in a different national university of life.[70]

Ministerial policy may be subject to judicial review, and possible findings of unlawful decision making. This is public law illegality, based upon the concept of abuse of power. Tony Blair succeeded in shifting the responsibility from himself to the attorney general, and to that extent he educated the republicans about the UK constitution. But, when he led them to believe that their text of 4 May 2000 was at least negotiable (by responding positively the following day), he made three legal errors: first, he failed to stress that, in the crown prosecution service's code for crown prosecutors, the evidential stage (the prospects of prosecution) was antecedent to the public interest stage (whether to prosecute); second, he made no reference to the attorney's advice (see below) that an amnesty required legislation; and third, he should have had a better idea – based upon security and intelligence advice – of the scale of the OTR problem.[71] No possible claimant (say a relative of

---

[70]   Sir Bill Jeffrey denied that they were bullied by Sinn Féin. (NIAC, *Report,* Q3322, 19 November 2014)

[71]   Jonathan Stephens noted on 3 May 2000: 'Gerry Adams said that Sinn Fein would give the Government as many names as they could – he did not know how many. It was presumably in our interest to deal with as many of these as possible on a case by case basis but, come July [2000], there needed to be some broadly understood principle for dealing with outstanding cases. Jonathan Powell reminded him that this was all in the context of agreement on the overall sequence. As for the post-July problem, we would look at it.' It was Jonathan Powell and Bill Jeffrey

a victim of the IRA) knew of the 5 May 2000 letter, but, if a judicial review had been brought that summer in the high court (in Belfast or London), the judge – whatever of any contemporary belief in Blair as a peacemaker – would surely have quashed the promise to review OTR cases as unlawful: the prime minister was interfering in the prosecution process, to a greater or lesser extent.

The first written promise of 5/6 November 1999, and the second of 5 May 2000, were to ground two later written promises from Tony Blair to Gerry Adams (chapters 4 and 6). It is now time to look below the level of principals, and to 1999–2000 when the administrative scheme took root in an atmosphere of considerable policy uncertainty.

who raised the number of a dozen cases per month, seemingly in response to Gerry Adams. (Downey case papers, tab 8, pp. 23–35)

CHAPTER THREE

The Administrative Scheme Takes Root, 1999–2000

Gerry Adams wanted the English attorney general to wipe the slate clean in public, on 31 July 2000. The prime minister knew (certainly from December 1999) that Lord Williams of Mostyn QC would be doing no such thing, though the prime minister may not have told his interlocutor this.

Some officials in Whitehall became preoccupied with three distinct issues (following the early release of prisoners): first, the Rita O'Hare case; second, the extradition cases; and third, the review of the wanted to find the not wanted. The three issues bumped against each other in 1999–2000, and the idea of an amnesty came to haunt policy debates as the only solution. The royal prerogative of mercy also emerged, from a most surprising quarter, as a possible way out of the government's dilemma.

Rita O'Hare and Others

Rita O'Hare was from Belfast. She is alleged to have tried to kill a soldier there in October 1971. She was arrested and bailed, and fled quickly to the Republic of Ireland. She has lived openly in Dublin ever since. In 1978, she avoided extradition to the UK. The Irish supreme court accepted the political offence defence in international law. (This did not stop the Irish authorities from imprisoning her for other republican activity.)

Her subsequent career (after imprisonment) included: 1985–90, editor of *An Phoblacht*, the republicans' newspaper; 1990–8, Sinn Féin director of publicity; and 1998 to the present, Sinn Féin representative in Washington, DC. She became, in other words, a leading republican, and advocate of the peace process. Gerry Adams valued her particularly.[72] The date of Rita O'Hare's criminal offence meant she could not avail of the early release provision (which applied only from 1973), not that she ever offered to return to NI to stand trial, and serve only a two-year sentence. From 2004, the European arrest warrant has applied to the Republic of Ireland and the UK. So far as can be ascertained, there has been no attempt to extradite her within the European Union.[73] Nor has there been any attempt by the UK to extradite her from the US, using different laws.[74]

An Irish government press secretary captured her early mentality – regarding entitlement – on the eve of the 1994 IRA ceasefire (which was broken later): 'I watched a small Sinn Féin group, led by Adams, Jim Gibney and … Rita O'Hare, walk calmly through the gates of Government Buildings [in Dublin] to meet the Taoiseach and John Hume. There was a nervous moment as a number of Special Branch men glared at the Shinners, who just looked impassively back. Then, when Reynolds, Adams and Hume emerged together on to the front steps, and the awaiting media crowded round, a security man tried to push O'Hare aside. Shaking herself loose, she turned on me like a flash. "That day is over!".'[75]

Mo Mowlam first met Rita O'Hare, probably at Dublin Castle in February 1998 (in advance of the Belfast agreement).[76] This was a meeting between a UK secretary of state and a fugitive suspect, but the former appears to have adopted a sisterly approach. They hugged. The

---

[72] There is a photograph of Barak Obama, Rita O'Hare and Gerry Adams: Gerry Adams' blog, 16 March 2009.

[73] The NIO declared, on 15 July 2015: 'The Government's position is to support the independence of the judicial authorities [including the national crime agency] in pursuing the extradition of wanted individuals in Europe. We are not the decision makers on EAW cases.' (NIAC, *Second Special Report of Session 2015–16*, HC 345, p. 4)

[74] Danny Morrison claimed in 2003 that there was a 'clear understanding' that the UK would not seek to extradite her from the US: *www.dannymorrison.com.*

[75] *Irish Times,* 26 August 2014 (Sean Duignin).

[76] John Reid's private secretary to William Fittall, 31 May 2001. (Downey case papers, tab 8, pp. 452–6); *Irish Independent,* 4 May 2003.

open meeting would subsequently cause considerable disquiet within the UK state, because of a concern that Mo Mowlam (and others) might have prejudiced any possible future prosecution by alluding to her being let off.

Later that summer, Mo Mowlam was to announce the members of the Patten commission on policing, one of the issues not resolved in the Belfast agreement. On 3 June 1998, according to her private secretary, John McKervill (who made sure he noted the incident), she telephoned Rita O'Hare (seemingly in Dublin): 'The Secretary of State explained to Rita O'Hare the pressures which she [the secretary of state] was under. She related that she had had an earlier call with Martin McGuinness and that he had seemed prepared not to go ballistic over the Commission's announcement.'[77]

In April 1999, Mo Mowlam first raised the case of Rita O'Hare with the then attorney general, John Morris QC. The secretary of state wanted her cleared to return to NI. 'He made it clear', according to Kevin McGinty, the attorney's NI adviser, 'that the alleged offences were serious and that the public interest in prosecution would be strong. Only if that individual's return was to be "the coping stone in the arch" that was the peace process was he likely to be able to conclude that the public interest weighed against prosecution.'[78]

Rita O'Hare was mentioned (though her name is redacted[79]) in the prime minister's letter of 5 November 1999. He told Gerry Adams: 'I understand that the Attorney General would wish to use the discretion he has to review, without commitment, whether the public interest continues to require a prosecution…'. There is little evidence that Lord Williams of Mostyn QC (now the attorney general) had made such an offer.[80] It is, in any case, an inadequate statement of the constitutional

---

[77] John McKervill, memo, 4 June 1998, CAIN website, University of Ulster.

[78] First witness statement, 13 January 2014 (Downey case papers, tab 6).

[79] But not her position: see letter of Peter Mandelson to Lord Williams, 17 May 2000, para 24. (Downey case papers, tab 8, pp. 42–55)

[80] He did see the letter of 5, but not 6, November 1999. The letter of 5 May 2000 was only sent to him on 22 May 2000.

position. Jonathan Powell refers to Gerry Adams visiting Downing Street in December 1999, to complain about a failure to pardon Rita O'Hare.[81] The attorney general, minuting the prime minister and others, on 20 December 1999 (his first apparent involvement), suggested that he was responding instead to an initiative of Barra McGrory, then Sinn Féin's solicitor, about some of his clients, including Rita O'Hare. The attorney general stressed constitutional propriety, on 20 December 1999: 'It is vital that it is understood that this is a prosecution matter, with the decision whether or not to prosecute being held by the Director of Public Prosecutions for Northern Ireland [Sir Alasdair Fraser] subject to my supervision. I may, at the appropriate time, seek the views of ministerial colleagues on the public interest aspect but the decision will, of course, be a matter for the Director ... and me. Our independence from Government is central to the integrity of the criminal justice system.' That was an accurate statement of the law by the attorney general. Further, there had been no instance of the attorney directing in the previous 25 years, so Sir Alasdair Fraser essentially had the first, and last word, on prosecution.

Jonathan Powell mentions Lord Williams twice in his NI book, to the effect that the attorney general said no repeatedly to the prime minister in 2000.[82]

On 17 May 2000 (seemingly responding to an invitation), Peter Mandelson, in a long judicious letter, advised the pardoning of Rita O'Hare, for political reasons.[83] This was the NIO position. He discussed the public interest, from the point of view of the NI secretary of state. But this amounted only to support for O'Hare from: the Irish government and Irish America (which might stymie an extradition request to the US). Those were not relevant public interests, as he could have been advised legally. Ultimately, the secretary of state wrote, if she were convicted in NI, he would have to use the royal prerogative of mercy

---

[81] *Great Hatred*, p. 166.

[82] *Great Hatred*, pp. 180 & 181.

[83] He later changed his mind: private secretary to Mr Brooker, 8 June 2000. (Downey case papers, tab 8, p. 70)

because she would not be entitled to early release. The royal prerogative of mercy was hardly an argument in her favour, but it was the decisive reason given by Pater Mandelson on official advice.

The prime minister and Lord Williams discussed Rita O'Hare in a telephone conversation, on 9 June 2000. Tony Blair was circumspect, though Jonathan Powell had been told the attorney did not need to hear further from the prime minister on her case.[84] The prime minister was keen to state his public interest opinion: namely, no prosecution.[85] Lord Williams – sticking strictly to the code for crown prosecutors – told him that Rita O'Hare passed the evidential stage, that there was sufficient evidence to convict. He was now considering abuse of process (see below), and would only then look at public interest. Again, this was the law.

Lord Williams concluded eventually,[86] as was legally predictable, that there was no basis for dropping the prosecution. He seems to have concluded there had been no abuse of process. As for the public interest, if Rita O'Hare could not make a case, no other IRA fugitive was likely to succeed. Rita O'Hare, therefore, raised the bigger issue of all OTRs.

Abuse of Process

On 20 December 1999, Lord Williams – fifteen years before Downey – had warned: 'it is very important no indication be given to any person which could form the basis of an abuse of process application at a later stage.' He became concerned principally about ministers (mainly Mo Mowlam) and officials (including the UK ambassador in Dublin, Ivor Roberts) dealing with Rita O'Hare. The attorney was concerned to

---

[84]   Note meeting, 30 May 2000. (Downey case papers, tab 8, pp. 60–3)

[85]   Jonathan Powell recorded him as saying: 'The Prime Minister said that the case of [Rita O'Hare] was an extremely important one in the context of the peace process. She was a firm champion of that process and could play an important role in defeating those who wanted to continue violence. She was of great persuasive authority. He believed her case was both important and urgent.' (Downey case papers, tab 8, pp. 71–2)

[86]   Jonathan Powell states he called Gerry Adams with this news on 23 October 2000: *Great Hatred,* p. 181.

investigate the possibility of an abuse of process challenge (which he saw as part of the evidential stage in the crown prosecutor's test).

On 12 April 2000, Jonathan Powell, Bill Jeffrey and Jonathan Stephens travelled to Dublin, for a meeting with the Irish government and Sinn Féin at the royal hospital, Kilmainham. Rita O'Hare attended on behalf of Sinn Féin. At the end of the meeting, according to Jonathan Powell, 'Gerry Adams suggested jocularly that [she] should join us at the next meeting in Belfast. I said it would not be a good idea as it was likely that she would be arrested.'[87] This comment raises a number of questions of fact: one, was Gerry Adams really trying to get Rita O'Hare into NI, incrementally?; two, did Jonathan Powell's advice stop her returning, on the occasion of that next meeting?; and three, would he have advised the RUC of her presence if she had turned up in Belfast, given the delicate state of number 10's relations with the republicans?[88]

To conclude on Rita O'Hare: there was a significant difference between the prime minister and the attorney general; the former pushed his version of the public interest (perhaps too far[89]); the latter, with the NI director of public prosecutions, worked through the evidential stage, abuse of process and the public interest stage – taking into account the views of ministers, but not acceding to their peace process urgings. The rule of law – as was predictable – required her prosecution.

Ending Extradition Cases

This issue grew out of the Rita O'Hare question. Extradition is mentioned in the Blair letters of 5 and 6 November 1999 (probably inaccurately), but not in the promise of 5 May 2000.

The Bertie Ahern letter of 23 December 1999, makes clear that the Irish government would no longer assist in extradition. The attorney

---

[87] Letter to Lord Williams, 23 June 2000. (Downey case papers, tab 8, p. 80)

[88] Gerry Adams brought Rita O'Hare into a second meeting, at Dublin airport, on 27 July 2000. (Downey case papers, tab 8, pp. 133–6)

[89] Jonathan Powell, knowing the attorney's mind, advised the prime minister to get other ministers to write to Lord Williams: note to Tony Blair, 14 July 2000. (Downey case papers, tab 8, pp. 96–7)

general told Jonathan Powell on 30 May 2000 that, at the beginning of 1999 (after the Belfast agreement), the Irish government had refused to respond to letters of request regarding Rita O'Hare.[90]

Extradition became an issue for the NIO on 2 June 2000, when the attorney general wrote to Peter Mandelson about the Sinn Féin list of 36 names (see below).[91] The secretary of state was responsible, the attorney conceded, for the 17 (later 21) escaped prisoners, all of whom would have to be extradited from either the Republic of Ireland or the US. (In 1983, 38 IRA members – including Gerry Kelly – had escaped from the Maze prison: a prison officer died as a result. There were other prison escapes.) Lord Williams offered legal advice to Peter Mandelson: the test for extradition was the public interest (not defined politically); existing cases might have to be reviewed; if the secretary of state favoured abandoning the extraditions, that would have implications for the attorney general decision making; the question of charging for escape had to be considered by the NI director of public prosecutions; the secretary of state could consider the royal prerogative of mercy; but all this would be liable to judicial review.

The attorney general then referred to the OTR issue generally: 'I am seriously concerned that the exercise that is being undertaken has the capacity of severely undermining confidence in the criminal justice system in [NI] at this most sensitive of times. Individual prosecution decisions have to be justifiable within the framework in which all prosecution decisions are reached and I am not persuaded that some unquantifiable benefit to the peace process can be a proper basis for a decision based on the public interest. Conversely it may well be a proper basis for some kind of legislative solution – as it was for the early release provisions in the Northern Ireland (Sentences) Act 1998.'

The reference to a legislative solution is to a statutory amnesty. There is no evidence that Lord Williams was advocating this. He was putting it forward as the only lawful way to achieve what the prime minister was seeking.

---

[90]   Downey case papers, tab 8, pp. 60–3.
[91]   Downey case papers, tab 8, pp. 64–6.

Peter Mandelson accepted the attorney's advice with alacrity, asking officials to report on what commitments had been made regarding extradition.[92] 'He has also suggested that it might be preferable – or indeed unavoidable – to go for a thorough amnesty act.'[93] He told the attorney general as much, in a letter of 27 June 2000. But the NIO seemed to be hoping that the escapees would return, in order to avail of the Northern Ireland (Sentences) Act 1998 (this raising the problem of prosecution for escaping and the possibility of up to two years' imprisonment).

Jonathan Powell advised dropping all extraditions, in a note to Tony Blair on 14 July 2000 (the day after he had passed on preliminary news that Rita O'Hare would remain liable to prosecution). On 18 July 2000, the secretary of state minuted the prime minister, stating he favoured a legislative amnesty but not yet. On extradition, he raised detailed (not principled) objections to the Powell position: 'Most people would accept that there is little point in carrying on spending public money trying to get back from [the Republic of Ireland] or the USA people who would in all probability not have to serve any significant time in prison even if we succeeded.' He was thinking, post extradition, of the royal prerogative of mercy and amending the Northern Ireland (Sentences) Act 1998 to deal with this category of OTRs.

Peter Mandelson recorded his decision eventually in a minute to the prime minister, on 26 July 2000. He would drop extraditions. But it would only be announced later in the summer. He thought the sentence review commissioners could help, the secretary of state now not wishing to amend the Northern Ireland (Sentences) Act 1998. Even so, this policy did not address whether the director of public prosecutions would prosecute for escape.[94] On 28 July 2000, Sinn Féin, in the form

---

[92] He later criticized the prime minister: to Martin McGuinness, on 25 August 2000; and to the attorney general, on 11 September 2000. (Downey case papers, tab 8, pp. 196–200 & 218–20)

[93] Private secretary to Mr Brooker, 8 June 2000. (Downey case papers, tab 8, p. 70)

[94] Lord Williams to Peter Mandelson, 15 August 2000. (Downey case papers, tab 8, pp. 150–2)

of Gerry Kelly, made clear to Jonathan Powell, that the IRA wanted an all clear: 'The escaped prisoners would simply tell them to F-off. They were not going to surrender to the British authorities.'[95]

As the NIO sought to firm up this policy, in August 2000, the term 'administrative scheme' came to be used initially for the 21 extradition cases.[96] William Fittall, the new associate political director, sold the idea of conceding to Assistant Chief Constable Ray White of the RUC, and, among the sentence review commissioners, Sir John Blelloch and Brian Currin, on 16 August 2000.

Peter Mandelson made his announcement on 29 September 2000, by press release (parliament not then sitting). He referred to the public interest. He also referred to the 'anomaly' of extraditees being treated differently from the early release prisoners: 'In view of this and the time that has elapsed, I do not believe that it would now be proportionate or in the public interest to pursue such cases.' The secretary of state then went on to deal with voluntary return to NI. They could approach the sentence review commissioners. He concluded: 'The decision has no implications for the prosecution of other offences where sufficient evidence exists. It is not an amnesty.' Other offences formally included escaping from prison.

The numbers – 21 and ten – were given in an attached question and answer sheet. This document also hinted at the administration scheme (as originally conceived): 'A procedure is being put in place so that those who wish to return to [NI] can notify their intention and be advised in advance of the arrangements which will apply on their arrival.' That procedure appears to have involved the escaped prisoner contacting the NI prison service from abroad; and the latter checking with the RUC (re other offences), with the NI director of

---

[95] Jonathan Powell note, 28 July 2000. (Downey case papers, tab 8, pp. 133–6)
[96] William Fittall to secretary of state, 18 August 2000, annex C. (Downey case papers, tab 8, pp. 162–5) In a meeting, of William Fittall and Douglas Bain, with Gerry Kelly and Siobhán O'Hanlon, at Castle Buildings on 31 August 2000, the term slipped to also cover the unprosecuted OTRs. (Downey case papers, tab 8, pp. 207–14)

public prosecutions (re prosecution for escaping) and with the sentence review commissioners (for an informal indication regarding release). There was no risk of arrest in NI, because the escaped prisoners would simply stay away if they were not given the all clear.

Extradition was abandoned on 29 September 2000. Number 10 has imposed the policy on the NIO. Only 21 OTRs were involved, and ten of those cases – including Rita O'Hare's? – had collapsed already. Once again, the attorney general, Lord Williams of Mostyn QC, had protected the director for public prosecutions in NI. This meant that any of the 21 who returned to NI, might be prosecuted for escaping[97] – their support for the peace process had been judged to be of no legal significance effectively, by the attorney general. But Peter Mandelson was defining the public interest, and the attorney general had always been aware that he could not readily contradict the secretary of state.

To conclude on the extradition cases: this was one element of the OTR problem; number ten of course wanted them dropped; Peter Mandelson took nearly four months in the summer of 2000 to do it; the secretary of state was able to define the public interest (the pointlessness of returning an escaped prisoner to NI only to release him shortly afterwards); as a result, Peter Mandelson as secretary of state made the OTR administrative scheme possible – without him, the prime minister may have remained overruled by Lord Williams, directing Sir Alasdair Fraser.

The Not Wanted versus the Wanted

The not wanted is the administrative scheme as it evolved, in 2000–14. Its origin is in the Blair letter of 5 May 2000 to Gerry Adams (though the letters of 5 and 6 November 1999 seemed to have started a process

---

[97] Sir Alasdair Fraser expressed the view, in a paper of 15 December 2000, that, given he had yet to run the evidential test regarding prison escapes, the prosecution decisions should be made using the public interest test (where he cited the secretary of state's precedent regarding outstanding sentences). A decision was made on 8 January 2001 not to prosecute the Maze escapers: Barra McGrory, written evidence, 6 June 2014, paras 9 & 10.

back in NI, involving Barra McGrory as a solicitor). Thus, Rita O'Hare, extradition and the OTRs more generally were interlinked, initially.

Barra McGrory, in advance of giving evidence to NIAC on 6 June 2014, directed that a note be prepared, based upon the PPSNI's records (not all of which were disclosed in the Downey case).[98]

Seemingly, the attorney general had telephoned Sir Alasdair Fraser, on 5 November 1999 (the day of the first Blair letter). The former suggested prosecution reviews to the latter, though it may only have been of extradition cases. The attorney was acting at the behest of number 10. 'The Director' – in his secret minute of 7 November 1999 as paraphrased by Barra McGrory – 'informed the Attorney General that he viewed the proposal as being fraught with difficulty. The Director pointed out that in any event such cases were kept under continual review by a committee chaired by staff from his Department (a standing committee of representatives from PSNI, Crown Solicitor's Office, DPP [director of public prosecutions] and AG [attorney general] which monitored progress in live extradition cases). The Director pointed out that such an undertaking carried with it an implication that future decisions would be liable to be influenced to the benefit of fugitives. The Director informed the Attorney General that in his view such an undertaking would be damaging to perceptions of the independence of the prosecuting authority and to the administration of justice. The Director observed that it may be preferable to legislate. The Director observed that it was inevitable that the issues they were discussing would become public and it was essential that the Attorney General be willing to explain his approach fully to Parliament.' Sir Alasdair Fraser, it now seems, was the first to suggest the idea of an amnesty, but only as an obstacle to him acting as number 10 was indirectly inviting him to do.

These are the most prescient words in the whole OTR story. One wonders why the attorney general in London even proceeded. And why Sir Alasdair Fraser acceded to whatever he was asked to do subsequently. It is possible that the reference to a standing committee reviewing extradition cases was used to persuade the director to embark upon

---

[98]   Written evidence, 6 June 2014.

a wider prosecution review.[99] In 2000–6, Sir Alasdair Fraser seems to have tried to continue much as before.

Kevin McGinty, of the attorney general's office, wrote later of Sir Alasdair: 'The prosecuting authorities accepted the administrative scheme with some reluctance. In part this was because the actual and perceived impartiality of the prosecution authority was of crucial importance to the maintenance of public confidence and the administrative scheme would only benefit one side of a divided community. The second reason was that it was not usual for an assessment of the evidence to be made in the absence of the individual concerned. The third reason was that where an individual was still wanted, to inform them that they would be arrested if they returned to the jurisdiction could amount to "tipping off". This last concern was mitigated to some extent by the fact that given that an individual's name had been put forward in itself suggested that that individual had cause to believe they were in fact wanted for arrest.'[100]

The attorney general first raised the matter of OTRs with the prime minister – following a telephone call from Peter Mandelson – on 20 December 1999. He was against a review of all outstanding prosecutions concerning terrorists in NI. This is the minute where Lord Williams referred to Barra McGrory having approached his office recently.[101]

The attorney's officials met with the NIO on 18 April 2000, and with number 10 on 2 May 2000.[102] They complained to their official colleagues about the absence of a scheme. David Brooker of the NIO referred to John Sawers, Bill Jeffrey and Jonathan Stephens[103] as the key people. At the latter meeting (2 May 2000), John Sawers was minuted: 'It was difficult for the PM to get a handle on the scale of the problem and [the earlier minutes] would help him understand the complications

---

[99] Barra McGrory, NIAC, *Report*, Q1298, 10 June 2014.
[100] First witness statement, 13 January 2014, pp. 3–4 (Downey case papers, tab 6).
[101] Downey case papers, pp. 10–11.
[102] Downey case papers, pp. 16–19 & 20–22.
[103] The name being misspelled as Stevens.

as well as some of the ways in which the problem may be approached.' The latter meeting referred, for the first time, to a RUC estimate of about 200 cases, which was remarkably close. This number did not filter through to number ten or even the NIO. The RUC figure never appeared subsequently in the policy debates. There was an operating assumption of a much smaller number of cases. On 2 May 2000, officials recommended a public announcement of prosecution reviews by the secretary of state: 'Such a process, even if not resulting in any great number of cases being dropped would have the benefit of allowing individuals to determine where they stood in relation to the prosecuting authorities.' The public announcement was never to take place.

The tentative advice from these officials (including John Sawers) was grabbed immediately by the prime minister, and given in private to Gerry Adams as a promise, on 5 May 2000. It may be inferred that Sir Alasdair Fraser, in communion with Lord Williams, agreed to the proposal of a public announcement. He was, however, to find himself engaged in prosecution reviews, with the police, under the direction of Tony Blair and Jonathan Powell in number 10, from May 2000, without any public acknowledgement that this was happening.

The Hallett report refers to a meeting in April 2000, at which the chief constable, Sir Ronnie Flanagan, was present. No minutes are available. This appears to be the occasion when the RUC decided to play ball. Sir Ronnie stressed the rule of law. But he accepted the idea of answering a suspect's query, as to whether he was wanted. The chief constable proposed the following words: 'On the basis of the information currently to hand the RUC will not arrest you if you return to Northern Ireland.'[104]

The Sinn Féin One List of 19 May 2000

Jonathan Powell referred on 2 May 2000 to processing a dozen cases a month, but Bill Jeffrey later referred to a total of a dozen reviews. The number twelve may have originated with Gerry Adams on

---

[104] Para 4.12.

4 November 1999, but, on 2 May 2000 as noted, he declined to state a figure. It is unlikely he did not know the size of the IRA.

On 19 May 2000, Sinn Féin submitted a list of 36, later 41,[105] names to number 10. Dame Heather Hallett refers to it as 'SF1'. Three days later, Jonathan Powell sent SF1 to the attorney general. This was the beginning of the later administrative scheme (22 May 2000), even though the term was being used elsewhere by William Fittall. The attorney acknowledged receipt on 24 May 2000, uttering the now usual cautions and caveats.

The original 36 names were categorized: there were 17 escaped prisoners outside the UK; ten cases were for the director in NI; six cases were for the director in England and Wales; and three were unknown. Thus, of SF1, while the attorney general was reviewing ten plus six cases, the secretary of state had a role regarding 17 of the original list of names. That composition determined, through Peter Mandelson's decision making, that the administrative scheme would take off. SF1 is also important as regards the attorney's involvement: ten of the cases went to Sir Alasdair Fraser; but the other six went to the director of public prosecutions in England and Wales. There were two relevant jurisdictions within the UK.

Unfortunately, no one in the PSNI was to know about this 2000 precedent, when it came to dealing with John Downey, from 2002, and then again in 2007. And, by that stage, the attorney general was backing out of the administrative scheme.

Of the 41 names on SF1, four would be held to be wanted, with three under review – meaning 34 presumed members of the IRA benefited from the administrative scheme, eventually. That is a very significant proportion. It suggests the following hypothesis: either the authorities were too ready to suspect republicans; and/or the administrative scheme became a process of letting suspects off, almost regardless of the strength of the evidence. There is a possible reconciliation of these two positions: there had once been sufficient evidence (in the 1970s or later), but, over time, it had deteriorated.

---

[105]   Five were added on 16 October 2000.

The prosecution reviews have been paraphrased as follows by Barra McGrory: 'The practice was quickly established whereby in respect of each name on the list the police were asked to review whether the person was wanted for arrest and interview about any outstanding offence; was wanted for arrest and charge for any offence; or was the subject of any outstanding warrant. Meanwhile a check was carried out with the DPP's office to find whether the person was the subject of any live files; ie where a direction to prosecute had issued and the person had not yet been dealt with. Where a live file was identified police were asked to carry out a review of the available evidence.' Later, the idea of a template, namely a series of 16 standard questions, was developed, whereby each fugitive suspect could be assessed.[106] There seems to have been a template for each suspected offence.

The director in England and Wales quickly cleared two, of his six, cases.[107] SF1/2 is believed to be Evelyn (or Eibhlin) Glenholmes,[108] who was suspected of involvement in the 1982 Hyde Park and Regent's Park bombings. SF1/16 is believed to be Patrick McVeigh,[109] who was wanted for a series of other offences in London in 1981–3. These were also failed extradition cases.

On 15 June 2000, Jonathan Powell wrote two letters from number 10. These are reproduced in Hallett at pages 26 to 27. It is extraordinary that the prime minister's chief of staff, and not the attorney general or the secretary of state (or an official on his behalf) sent the letters. They went to Sinn Féin, for onward transmission. Jonathan Powell recalls they were sent to Gerry Adams.[110] It is clear that the English director had some, but insufficient, evidence regarding the second person, Patrick McVeigh, given the different wording of the letter concerning him.

---

[106] Barra McGrory, written evidence, 6 June 2014, paras 5 & 7.

[107] It is interesting that Kevin McGinty recalled the first applicants as Rita O'Hare plus these two. (NIAC, *Report,* Qs527–530, 30 April 2014)

[108] HC, *Hansard,* vol. 388, col. 137W, 1 July 2002.

[109] Barra McGrory, written evidence, 6 June 2014, para 13. This was another failed extradition: HC, *Hansard,* vol. 135, cols. 198–209, 14 June 1988.

[110] Witness statement, undated, para 6: Downey case papers, tab 6.

The number of two grew to four over the summer of 2000. Sinn Féin expressed its annoyance repeatedly at the small number benefiting.

Following the extradition announcement, Peter Mandelson minuted the prime minister on OTRs generally, on 4 October 2000:[111] 'Adams believes that he has firm commitments from you dating from last November and repeated in May, that the OTR issue would be "sorted". The impression created was that we simply needed to resolve a small number of anomalous cases. What we now know is that: there are far more cases than we were led to believe; changing our approach to extradition and reviewing the evidence case by case solves only part of the problem; and legislating for a solution inevitably means an amnesty since we could hardly waive prosecution in respect of fugitives while still keeping open the possibility of prosecutions for everyone else.' The secretary of state's passing reference to an amnesty suggests it would apply all round, contrary to the advice that was to come from Sir Quentin Thomas.

To conclude on the wanted versus the not wanted: this was an inauspicious beginning in the summer of 2000; it raises the question: why did the attorney general even permit the director in NI to begin the review of prosecutions? The answer is that Lord Williams believed it was only a handful of cases, not all the OTRs. He was standing up to the prime minister, but he evidently felt he could conciliate him with a low-key prosecution review as close as possible to what was normal procedure under Sir Alasdair Fraser.

Amnesty

The Belfast agreement – as officials advised at the time – went no further than early release of prisoners. But, suddenly, the idea of an amnesty was thrown into the policy pot. Paradoxically, this was simply as an argument against an administrative scheme: it was not a serious policy proposal from the attorney general, who showed no general interest in NI.

---

[111] Downey case papers, pp. 240–2.

An amnesty was first mentioned by officials, on 18 April and 2 May 2000. On 12 May 2000, Bill Jeffrey advised against the Sinn Féin idea of an announcement on 31 July 2000. When Lord Williams received the unexpectedly large SF1 list of names, he made clear he would not act 'for reasons of political convenience'; on 24 May 2000, he emphasized:[112] 'If the expectation is that the thirty-six persons so far named (and that total may rise) should be free to return to the United Kingdom regardless of the individual circumstances of their case that can only be achieved by a legislative amnesty.'

As noted, he made the same point to the secretary of state, on 2 June 2000,[113] and the latter, through his private secretary, endorsed the idea six days later, to the extent of making it a serious policy option.

On 9 June 2000, on the telephone to the prime minister, Lord Williams made the same point, with Jonathan Powell taking notes.[114] The attorney general raised the question of an amnesty personally with the prime minister, on 29 June 2000.[115]

On 11 September 2000 – following meetings between Peter Mandelson and the attorney general, and then with Jonathan Powell and John Sawers at number 10 – William Fittall, who accompanied the secretary of state, drew up a minute headed 'OTRs and a possible amnesty'.[116]

Again, on 4 October 2000, after the extradition announcement, Peter Mandelson minuted the prime minister: 'An amnesty would raise much more fundamental issues than the early release scheme provided for in the Good Friday Agreement. To confer immunity from prosecution for many of the gravest crimes on the statute book would, in any circumstances be contentious. In the absence of decommissioning, disbanding of the IRA or unequivocal evidence that the "war" really was over, it would probably be impossible to get through Parliament.

---

[112] Downey case papers, pp. 58–9.
[113] Downey case papers, pp. 64–6.
[114] Downey case papers, pp. 71–2.
[115] Downey case papers, pp. 89–90.
[116] Downey case papers, pp. 228–30.

It would also be hard to justify an amnesty in our jurisdiction without parallel arrangements in the [Republic of Ireland].'[117] These were all strong points.

On 6 November 2000, Tony Blair and Peter Mandelson discussed a 'balanced package to keep the process moving forward' (that concept again). The officials present were: Joe Pilling, William Fittall. Jonathan Powell and John Sawers. Part of the package, in advance of a legislative amnesty, was a report to the prime minister from an eminent person. This is the decision which led to the commissioning of the now-retired Sir Quentin Thomas,[118] and ultimately the report *Clean Sheets* in January 2001 (see immediately below).[119]

To conclude on the notion of an amnesty: this was put forward by Lord Williams as the only legal way to do what the administrative scheme was going to attempt; Peter Mandelson, Tony Blair and Sir Quentin Thomas surprisingly grasped at the idea in the second half of 2000, with legislation to follow possibly in the new parliament of 2001–5.

The Northern Ireland Office Considers an Amnesty, 2000–1

The Belfast agreement, on one view, was a political compact, between the UK and the Republic of Ireland, and, separately, the pro-agreement political parties (but not Sinn Féin) in NI.

But the NIO, in purporting to implement the agreement, actually extended it considerably after 1998, through: the September 1999 (Patten) report on policing;[120] and the March 2000 criminal justice review, which was conducted within officialdom.[121] There followed

---

[117] Downey case papers, pp. 240–2.

[118] John Sawers' minute to Peter Mandelson's private secretary was copied extremely widely – and unusually – to: Stephen Lander (security service), Sherard Cowper-Coles (foreign office), Julian Miller (ministry of defence), Richard Abel (cabinet office), Ivor Roberts (Dublin embassy) and Christopher Meyer (Washington embassy). (Downey case papers, tab 8, pp. 248–50)

[119] Downey case papers, pp. 248–50.

[120] Lord Patten, *A New Beginning: policing in Northern Ireland.*

[121] *Review of the Criminal Justice System in Northern Ireland.*

police legislation in 2000 and 2003, and criminal justice acts in 2002 and 2004, while the IRA still refused to decommission.

There is now evidence that some NIO officials, with the knowledge of the secretary of state (Peter Mandelson), considered the possibility of a NI amnesty, for terrorists (including those held to be a continuing public danger). Quentin Thomas was a senior NIO official, 1988–98, and a major architect of the Belfast agreement. He left for the cabinet office,[122] became Sir Quentin, and retired, taking up the position of film censor in 2002.

In late 2000, after the Northern Ireland (Sentences) Act 1998 had been implemented, he was asked to advise the NIO on, essentially, outstanding criminal investigations. In November 2000, Sir Quentin sent a draft scheme to the attorney general's officials. On 1 December 2000, Peter Mandelson sent a draft report to Tony Blair (and the ministry of defence). Sir Quentin reported finally, on 15 January 2001, at 77 pages, his confidential report being entitled: *Clean Sheets: dealing with outstanding criminal cases.*[123] Unfortunately, the terms of reference have been redacted heavily. Nevertheless, this is an extraordinary document, made publicly available exceptionally – courtesy of Mr Justice Sweeney – after 13 years.

Sir Quentin asked, at an early stage, whether the security forces should be included, only to endorse the ministry of defence line of no equivalence with terrorists: 'Despite the difficulties, the better course is to exclude the security forces from any amnesty scheme. This is because the greater public (and British) interest lies in preserving the important political and military asset that the security forces operate within, and in defence of, democracy and the rule of law. It would be wrong and, ultimately, against our own interests to do anything to damage that claim, or to imply an equivalence between the actions of the security forces in resisting the terrorist challenge and the paramilitaries in mounting it.'[124] It is true that the number of unlawful security force

---

[122] Where he became: head of the constitution secretariat.

[123] It has been disclosed in the Downey case papers.

[124] Para 34.

killings was small, and that soldiers and police officers were not meant to go out to kill. But this exclusion of the security forces – to avoid equivalence in ministry of defence minds – was to play later into the hands of the republicans.

Sir Quentin laid out a set of options: one, the continued application of the criminal law; two, abandoning extradition; three, an automatic amnesty for all scheduled offences; four, a selective amnesty for only 'deserving' applicants (as he put it); five, an inhibition on prosecutions for those on ceasefire; and six, the royal prerogative of mercy by way of pre-conviction pardons.[125] Options three, four and five were considered, by Sir Quentin, to be amnesties.[126]

This was an intellectual civil service way of promoting automatic (not selective) amnesty, as is clear from paragraph 89 (with the original emphasis: '... <u>In many ways, if an amnesty were to be introduced in present less than ideal circumstances, Option [five] would offer the best combination of political defensibility, acceptability to republicans and others and administrative convenience.</u> However, its selective and conditional elements may be more apparent than real. <u>If the circumstances for an amnesty were more obviously suitable than they now are it would be better to go for Option [three]</u> (automatic amnesty). This is more straightforward; in practice [it] will not produce a very different result; and [it] will minimise the contamination of the system of justice.'

Interestingly, option five – no prosecution in return for continuing ceasefire – came close to the administrative scheme then developing.

Officials may well protest that there was no amnesty in 2000 or later, but *Clean Sheets* prevents NIO ministers suggesting the government never considered the option because of the views of victims.

The Royal Prerogative of Mercy

The royal prerogative of mercy arose after the amnesty idea, in a theoretical and then a practical way. The royal prerogative of mercy is a little-known constitutional power. Formally, it is exercisable by the

---

[125] Considered further below.
[126] Para 103.

sovereign, but now only on the advice of ministers. Today, it involves a release from prison, and is exercised in a limited number of circumstances. It was to play a role in the OTR story, and became a separate object of criticism.

The Irish Contribution

The Bertie Ahern government in Dublin (1997–2002) was a coalition of Fianna Fáil and the progressive democrats. The attorney general, from July 1999, was Michael McDowell SC, a future leader of the minority party, but then without a seat in Dáil Éireann, the Irish parliament. As senior counsel, and the grandson of Eoin MacNeill (the leading cultural nationalist in 1916, who tried to stop the Dublin rising), he was considered to be strongly anti-IRA. But Michael McDowell was, at this point, principally a legal advisor in a constitutional republic which had separated from the UK in the 1920s.

Presumably remembering his Dublin legal education at king's inns (where barristers trained), Michael McDowell came up with the idea of a pre-conviction pardon in NI law (though he may have been thinking of English law). He seemingly secured an independent Irish legal opinion on the matter. The idea was simply that there was a surviving common law power, whereby a minister could pardon a suspect, in advance of conviction and sentencing. For a constitutional republican like Michael McDowell, this was a remarkably monarchist proposal: the sovereign should simply excuse all IRA members any criminal sanction – it would really be a magic wand solution.

On 29 November 2000, Michael McDowell met Lord Williams in London. He handed over a dossier of legal documents.

On 6 December 2000, UK and Irish officials met in London. They discussed the idea of pre-conviction pardons. The NIO considered the idea a 'blind alley'.

The English attorney general had already sought advice from Philip Sales,[127] junior crown counsel, on the Irish dossier. The attorney evi-

---

[127]   Now Lord Justice Sales.

dently received the advice within days. Lord Williams's written advice of 11 December 2000 (quoted by Peter Mandelson) was: 'since this is a common law power it cannot have become extinct by mere disuse, even though pre-conviction pardons have been obsolete from a very long time ago (probably since the 19th century); but an attempt to revive the power would run a substantial risk of successful challenge in the courts and would constitute a very high risk strategy.'

On 18 December 2000, Peter Mandelson minuted the prime minister, to the effect that he was inclined to say no to the Irish idea.

The Escaped Prisoners

The secretary of state's announcement on 29 September 2000 had not lead to the return of the 21 escaped prisoners. Subsequently, the NI director of public prosecutions decided not to prosecute them for escaping from prison. That followed from his desire not to contradict the secretary of state on the assessment of the public interest.

The first prisoners did not return to NI until 24 December 2000. William Fittall's administrative scheme (see above) had worked apparently. Douglas Bain, of the NI prison service, had a meeting in the Canal Court hotel in Newry. Using his powers as a senior prison officer, he arrested and immediately released at least one returning prisoner. In time, the sentence review commissioners released him, he having already served the two years' minimum before escaping. The release was on licence. Something was working, albeit very slowly.

The administrative scheme had originated on 2 May 2000, in the Irish embassy in London, Jonathan Stephens' official note recording the birth. How did it fare in NI, once the police and the director of public prosecutions, Sir Alasdair Fraser, had agreed to review the prosecution of IRA fugitive suspects?

CHAPTER FOUR

The Administrative Scheme Proper, 2001–5

The question of OTRs first came to public attention in March 2001. This was nearly two years after the story began.[128] However, the administrative scheme was to continue in the background, and remain there through the second Blair government. Paradoxically, the public face of the OTR issue helped obscure the private face.

Devolution On and Off

Devolution had come to NI on 2 December 1999. David Trimble and Seamus Mallon became the first and deputy first minister. However, they were not to hold office for long.[129]

The NI assembly was to be bedevilled by the following suspensions, relating to the failures of the republicans:

- on 12 February 2000, because of the IRA's failure to decommission. This first suspension was lifted on 29 May 2000;
- on 11 August 2001, following the resignation of David Trimble. This second suspension was tactical on the part of the UK government;
- on 22 September 2001, in order to avoid an assembly election. This third suspension was also tactical on the part of the government;
- on 15 October 2002, following the discovery of a IRA spy ring at Stormont. This fourth suspension was to continue through the 2005 general election and beyond.

---

[128] Mo Mowlam had raised the Rita O'Hare case with John Morris QC in April 1999.

[129] David Trimble, 2 December 1999 to 14 October 2002; Seamus Mallon, 2 December 1999 to 6 November 2001, Mark Durkan taking over and serving until 14 October 2002.

Thus, the NI assembly sat only in December 1999 to February 2000, May 2000 to August 2001 and September 2001 to October 2002. The June 1998 assembly elections were followed by postponed elections in November 2003. But there was no devolution for much of the 2001–5 parliament.

The Prime Minister's Chequers Promise, 19 January 2001

Even as the extradition (escaped prisoners) issue was being concluded at the end of 2000, and Sir Quentin Thomas was getting ready to report on an amnesty in January 2001, number 10 and the NIO continued to debate OTRs with Sinn Féin and the Irish government.

On Friday, 19 January 2001, Tony Blair held discussions with Sinn Féin at Chequers. The prime minister gave Gerry Adams a third written promise: 'The Government recognises the difficulty in respect of those people against whom there are outstanding prosecutions for offences committed before 10 April 1998. At present, they face the possibility of extradition or prosecution even though the offences if proven were committed before the key date for the early release scheme under the GFA [Good Friday Agreement]. The Government is committed to dealing with this difficulty as soon as possible, so that those who, if they were convicted, would be eligible under the early release scheme, are no longer pursued.'[130]

A number of comments is necessary. First, this was the third signature promise: 'as soon as possible'. Second, the prime minister was well on his way to eliding the difference between prisoners and OTRs. Third, this private written promise was offered to Sinn Féin as a future public commitment, 'as part of a wider understanding'.[131] That would come on 8 March 2001. And fourth, there was no reference to a legislative amnesty.

Subsequently, number 10 asked for legal advice. Lord Williams came back to legislation only: '... I believe that the text will need

---

[130] Downey case papers, tab 8, attachment to letter of 22 January 2001, pp. 406–7.
[131] Michael Tatham to David Brummell, 22 January 2001. (Downey case papers, tab 8, pp. 406–7)

to be altered, as it might imply that the Government, rather than Parliament, will seek to influence or even prevent the prosecution of individuals. Not only would this be constitutionally wrong, it would not be possible either ... What does concern me is the possible use of such a statement in any abuse of process arguments that may arise at any trial of any individual covered by the statement. [] The refusal to prosecute by either DPP [director of public prosecutions] [in NI or in England and Wales] is, of course, susceptible to judicial review, with the consequential duty of disclosure of all relevant internal documents.'[132]

Number 10 replied the following day (24 January 2001). Events had moved on from the previous Friday. There was now a draft Irish/UK statement. Legislation would be covered by the phrase: 'will take such steps as are necessary in their jurisdictions to deal with this difficulty'.[133] Though there was no reference to legislation, it was stated on behalf of the attorney that he would construe the phrase that way.[134]

This was the day after Peter Mandelson (because of the Hinduja affair) was replaced by John Reid. The attorney general was to be replaced, in June 2001, after the general election. Meanwhile, the administrative scheme continued to progress.[135]

The Irish Government List

Reference was made above to the SF1 list of 19 May 2000, and the 41 names. At some point, the Irish government submitted four names. A great deal less is known about what Dame Heather Hallett calls the 'IG' list. The earliest date noted is: 26 January 2001, for a letter from the director of public prosecutions. All four became not wanted.

---

[132] Lord Williams to prime minister, 23 January 2001. (Downey case papers, tab 8, p. 408)

[133] Michael Tatham to David Brummell, 24 January 2001 (plus undated text); see also, David Brummell to Michael Tatham, 25 January 2001. (Downey case papers, tab 8, pp. 409–10 & 411)

[134] David Brummell to number 10, 25 January 2001, Downey case papers, p. 411.

[135] Attorney general to John Reid, 26 January 2001. (Downey case papers, tab 8, pp. 412–3)

The Prison List of 11 February 2001

That list was followed, on 11 February 2001, by what Dame Heather calls the prison list ('PL'). The PL comprised 14 names. The origin of the PL lies in Peter Mandelson's handling of the escaped prisoners. William Fittall's administrative scheme had been designed to be used by the up to 21 escaped prisoners. A central role was to be played by the NI prison service.

It is believed that, after 24 December 2000, the NI prison service compiled this list, of what became 14 names on 11 February 2001.

Again, looking ahead, Dame Heather shows that Sinn Féin was only told about one name – PL/12 (on 30 April 2008) – being wanted. That does not mean that 13 were declared not wanted. The picture is much less clear. Most likely, while the extradition attempts were abandoned, numbers of prisoners, residing abroad, including in the US, decided simply to stay there, and not return to NI.

The Hillsborough Statement, 8 March 2001

On 8 March 2001, the prime minister and the Irish taoiseach met at Hillsborough, outside Belfast, with the political parties. Gerry Adams had pressed for the Chequers promise of 19 January 2001 to be made public. It was. The two governments promised: 'in the context of the agreement of May 2000 being implemented [which had led to the restoration of the assembly], it would be a natural development of the [early release] scheme for such prosecutions not to be pursued, and would intend as soon as possible thereafter to take such steps as were necessary in their jurisdictions to resolve this difficulty, so that those concerned were no longer pursued'.

William Fittall later commented: 'Behind the circumlocutions what this actually meant was that, in the right context, we were now effectively committed to legislation'.[136] The Chequers timescale of as soon as possible was in the public domain. So also was the elision of

---

[136] 'OTRs – a brief history of crime', 3 September 2002. (Downey case papers, tab 8, pp. 644–52)

prisoners and OTRs, with the concept of 'natural development'. This statement was an articulation of the need for a OTR policy. But there was no reference, by the UK or Irish governments, to the need for a legislative amnesty.

The Sinn Féin Two List of 30 March 2001

On 30 March 2001 (after the Hillsborough statement), Gerry Adams submitted a further 61 names to number 10. Dame Heather calls this SF2. SF2 grew eventually to 143 names, in principally November 2001 and January 2002 – but with names being added in 2003, 2005 and 2006.

With the benefit of hindsight, it is possible to see that 119 letters of comfort (or the equivalent) were issued by the NIO against this list. Again, 119 of 143 is a very significant majority. And it suggests again the following hypothesis: either the authorities were too ready to suspect republicans; and/or the administrative scheme became a process of letting suspects off, almost regardless of the strength of the evidence. Again, it is necessary to make the point about evidence eroding over time.

The Royal Ulster Constabulary

The attorney general in London worked to the director of public prosecutions in Belfast. There was little sight of the latter's relations with the RUC. From May 2000, the police in NI was involved in what would become the administrative scheme. Peter Mandelson recalled meetings with the chief constable, in approximately April/May 2000.[137] On 12 April 2001, William Fittall in the NIO wrote to the chief constable, Sir Ronnie Flanagan (the only such letter in the Downey case papers): 'The RUC kindly carried out a number of checks on the backgrounds and current status of these individuals.'[138]

It is significant that William Fittall reported to the chief constable on the SF1 list of 41 names (after nearly a year). That number was

---

[137]   NIAC, *Report,* Q2999, 4 November 2014.
[138]   Downey case papers, tab 8, p. 447.

now: 24 escaped prisoners; and 17 others who were wanted. Sixteen prisoners had been told they could return, and 12 had done so. Five of the 17 others had got letters of comfort. 'Some of the remaining 20 cases are still being considered,' he wrote, 'though with most of the pre-trial cases the prosecuting authorities have concluded that the evidence and public interest continue to warrant prosecution.' The officials, and in particular the political director, were clearly managing the administrative scheme.

PSNI Guidance

On 19 March 2002, Detective Inspector James Davison, of extradition and disclosure, sent a guidance document[139] to the head of C1 branch (where OTRs was located within the PSNI), dealing with the 'standard of research' in the prosecution reviews.

This was not a legal document. It was a checklist of questions for each reviewer of a OTR's file or files. It was clear the police was working to the director of public prosecutions, 'who [was] personally chairing this review'. They were to start with identity, and then whether the person was wanted. There followed seven general questions. Question one (is the person wanted for questioning?) concluded practically: 'A Senior Officer should consider the merits of the case and confirm in writing whether or not the person is to be sought by PSNI.' Question number six was: 'Does any other Police Service in the [UK] want the person? [] The Director and Crown Solicitor also require this information from the Reviewing Officer, in writing.' The reference to the merits of the case implies that arrest and prosecution were being considered together. Here was the seed of uncertainty. Wanted for questioning should have stopped a letter being issued, whereas the reference to merits means the chances of prosecution became the test. It is conceivable that, given the absence of the administration scheme, the police might have questioned a paramilitary suspect, even if there was little in the way of a case at that point.[140]

---

[139] Downey case papers, pp. 554–7.
[140] This point was made by Barra McGrory: 'I have no doubt that many people

The 2001 General Election

On 4 May 2001, John Reid wrote to the prime minister regarding an amnesty bill in the new parliament. Sir Quentin Thomas was the inspiration. The secretary of state advised: NIO officials should do everything short of drafting a bill; he wanted a selective amnesty, with reversibility; he wanted the security forces excluded; and it might be necessary to use the parliament act to get a bill through the house of lords.[141]

Parliament rose on 11 May 2001. Whitehall went into purdah. The general election was to be held, on 7 June 2001.

On 31 May 2001,[142] an official (name redacted), in the NIO, prepared six copies of a 'policy instruction for the creation of an amnesty for Prisoners on the run'. The reference to prisoners in the title was an error; the term fugitives should have been used. The mistake was due most likely to the emphasis upon the Northern Ireland (Sentences) Act 1998. Two copies went to the attorney general's office. The other four stayed in the rights and international relations division. The amnesty was to be based upon a group of qualifying offences, 'without requiring that an individual confesses to their role in them'. Dissident republicans were to be excluded, and the amnesty was to be reversible if the IRA became a specified organization (that is, broke its ceasefire). 'We are aware,' the drafter wrote, 'of the difficulties of delivering reversibility in practice ...'. The scheme was not to apply to the security forces. John Reid had come out against an immunities commission (like the sentence review commissioners), and officials envisaged immunity being granted during pre-trial processes.

The New Government

John Reid was left in charge of the NIO after the general election. Lord Williams, however, was promoted to become leader of the house

---

received letters saying that they were not wanted who, in ordinary circumstances, the police would have liked to speak to.' (NIAC, *Report,* Q1301, 10 June 2014)

[141] Downey case papers, pp. 448–51.

[142] Downey case papers, pp. 458–68.

of lords (and a cabinet minister). Lord Goldsmith QC – another peer and lawyer rather than politician – became the attorney general.

The Weston Park Proposals, 1 August 2001

Political talks took place at this Staffordshire conference centre on 9–14 July 2001, shortly after the general election. There was no agreement to restore devolution to NI. However, on 1 August 2001 – and facing a deadline of 12 August 2001 for the re-election of the first minister and deputy first minister – the two government published a 22-paragraph set of proposals (plus an accompanying draft statement). The Weston Park proposals were not accepted by the political parties.

Paragraph 20[143] (under proposals on normalization) read in full: 'Both governments also recognise that there is an issue to be addressed with the completion of the early release scheme, about supporters of organisations now on cease-fire against whom there are outstanding prosecutions, and in some cases extradition proceedings, for offences committed before 10 April 1998. Such people would, if convicted, stand to benefit from the early release scheme. The Governments accept that it would be a natural development of the scheme for such prosecutions not to be pursued and will as soon as possible, and in any event before the end of the year [that is, 2001], take such steps as are necessary in their jurisdictions to resolve this difficulty so that those concerned are no longer pursued.'

A number of comments is apposite. First, the Weston Park proposals were agreed by the UK and Republic of Ireland. Second, they were not agreed by the NI political parties. Third, the regional political crisis continued. Fourth, the basis of governmental thinking was the Northern Ireland (Sentences) Act 1998. Fifth, London and Dublin sought to stretch the Belfast agreement to cover IRA members who had not been convicted. Sixth, the two governments simply put the issue on the agenda: 'an issue to be addressed'; and 'to resolve this difficulty'. Weston Park was not a UK commitment to legislate for an amnesty,

---

[143] There is a copy at Downey case papers, tab 8, p. 472.

much less a political agreement that it should be done. However, Sinn Féin had got the OTR problem aired, and there was a deadline of the end of 2001.

The UK government later amended this to 'in any event by March 2002', making the promise tougher but later.[144]

On 23 October 2001 – though it is difficult to read this in the IRA statement – the republicans decommissioned some arms: 'in order to save the peace process we have implemented the scheme agreed with the IICD [independent international commission on decommissioning] in August [2001].' The commission refused to explain the decommissioning: it is believed that it involved the sealing of an arms dump.

The New Attorney General

Lord Goldsmith, with Kevin McGinty, had met John Reid, with Bill Jeffrey and William Fittall, on 11 October 2001 at short notice, to discuss OTRs.[145] John Reid quickly asked Lord Goldsmith if he could be more accommodating of the prime minister. While the attorney wanted to be helpful, he could not – in law – permit a non-legislative solution. Lord Goldsmith referred expressly to the Shawcross two-stage doctrine of 1951,[146] and even alluded to a 'constitutional crisis' if the prime minister gave Sinn Féin what it wanted. Decommissioning would not alter the position. Lord Goldsmith, however, was prepared to accept the administrative scheme continuing. He left the secretary of state a copy of the code for crown prosecutors; one may infer that the new attorney – a commercial lawyer – had read it with interest as part of his brief.

The new attorney followed up with a long letter on 17 October 2001,[147] essentially endorsing the position taken by Lord Williams: 'It

---

[144] William Fittall to David Brummell, 15 October 2001. (Downey case papers, tab 8, pp. 473–4)

[145] Downey case papers, pp. 469–72 & 473–4.

[146] The then labour attorney general had told parliament that, while he supervised the director of public prosecutions, and he and ministers could advise on what the public interest was, the prosecution decision was based essentially on the first, evidential, stage: HC, *Hansard,* vol. 483, cols. 679–90, 29 January 1951.

[147] Downey case papers, pp. 475–82.

would … be an unlawful fettering of my discretion if I were to conclude that all cases falling into a particular category should not be prosecuted and the decision would be susceptible to judicial review in the courts. It would amount to an amnesty, which it is perfectly legitimate for Parliament to decide but which is not something that I can provide by way of exercising prosecutorial discretion.' The existence of this letter, and the content, suggests that the new attorney was trying to make things clear to the secretary of state.

Lord Goldsmith explained to NIAC his lawyer's hesitancy about the administrative scheme: 'in my office, we went along with [it] with a degree of reluctance, and the reason for that was twofold: first of all, because the process risked damaging the perception of justice, and that we were concerned to avoid; secondly, because of the factual inquiries that had to be made, it was a burdensome process. It was particularly burdensome on the office of the [director of public prosecutions], a very fastidious, painstaking man of absolute integrity …. We did the job we were asked to do, he did the job, but it did have a burden attached to it, which added to the reluctance, but there were are; we did it.'[148]

A Legislative Bill

In February 2002, parliamentary counsel produced an immunity from prosecutions bill. This was to be based upon an independent commissioner. He would grant immunity (much as the sentence review commissioners offered early release). 'Private soundings of Trimble revealed that [according to William Fittall], while he would have to oppose any legislation, he might not suffer irretrievable political damage if the scheme included elements of due process, including some kind of determination of guilt and subsequent licensing arrangement.'[149]

David Trimble was first mentioned in advice from Bill Jeffrey to John Reid, on 18 February 2002.[150] On 7 March 2002, David Trimble wrote to the prime minister proposing that the OTR issue

---

[148] NIAC, *Report*, Q2058, 2 July 2014.
[149] 'OTRs – a brief history of crime'. (Downey case papers, tab 8, pp. 644–52)
[150] Downey case papers, pp. 528–34.

be resolved essentially by the sentence review commissioners; there would be charging, guilty pleas, convictions and sentencing but also bailing and early release. This implied an amendment of the Northern Ireland (Sentences) Act 1998, reducing the two-year minimum to 'a notional sentence'.[151]

Surprisingly (given what Sinn Féin had said), the NIO took up the idea of the Trimble scheme. However, a press report of 10 November 2002, referring to the government's dilution of the scheme, led David Trimble to dissociate his party.[152] The policy debate within government petered out, though this may be a function of inadequate disclosure in the Downey case.

Another likely explanation is the replacement of John Reid in October 2002, who went off to chair the labour party. Paul Murphy, who took over as secretary of state, and remained to the end of the parliament in May 2005, was more cautious about responding to number 10 interventions. He told NIAC: 'I have had a look at the documents that have very kindly been sent to me and they may well have crossed my desk, but I do not see my name on any of them, in terms of being copied to me. As I say, I am not saying I did not know about it [the administrative scheme], but I cannot recall certainly it being an issue, in the way it developed into as the years went by. My knowledge of it was pretty slim, if at all.'[153]

William Fittall had concluded his handover note, on 3 September 2002: 'Sinn Fein will continue to harass us over individual cases and, more generally, nurture the issue as yet another grievance. They have a point in claiming that on a number of occasions, promises have outstripped delivery. There was always a very high risk that an Amnesty Bill would be rejected or worse (in business management terms) mauled out

---

[151]   Downey case papers, p. 545. Lord Trimble told NIAC that he had misunderstood the Northern Ireland (Sentences) Act 1998 at the time of the letter. He thought that there was only one two-year period, expiring on 28 July 2000. (NIAC, *Report*, Q785, 13 May 2014)

[152]   Downey case papers, p. 664.

[153]   NIAC, *Report*, Q2321, 15 July 2014.

of all recognition in the House of Lords. In either event, we recognised that the Government would probably have no option but to invoke the Parliament Act. The revised scheme [developed in response to David Trimble] is a touch less hairy. Even so, it seems to be that there would need to be a much more favourable context than looks likely anytime soon for Parliament to be willing to swallow something quite so indigestible. If people could be reasonably satisfied that the IRA was really moving into retirement, that would, of course, be another matter.'[154]

And that was the problem with the administrative scheme. Gerry Adams followed his own constitutional logic: his army would not submit to the rule of law, however benign. Tony Blair, in turn, would not impose the rule of law, in negotiation: it was give/give to Sinn Féin; while the republicans refused to surrender the IRA's arms.

Divide and Rule

After the 2001 general election, Des Browne became a junior minister at the NIO. In the spring of 2002, the NIO tried to speed up the administrative scheme.

On 27 March 2002, Des Browne, in a meeting with the attorney general, proposed changing the question: from assessing the evidence with regard to prosecution; to simply asking whether a OTR was recorded as wanted by the PSNI. 'It would mean that the NIO would be relying on the police, rather than [the director of public prosecutions], to say whether an individual could return.'[155] Lord Goldsmith accepted that the question could be changed, as long as it was made clear to Sinn Féin that the risk for the OTR was greater: there would be less comfort in a letter. He seemed not to spot that changing the question for the PSNI would, effectively, diminish the role of Sir Alasdair Fraser, who was still directly in charge.

The attorney's legal secretary (David Brummell) faxed a letter that day to Sir Alasdair Fraser in Belfast, asking for a response the same day.

---

[154] Downey case papers, pp. 644–52.

[155] David Brummell, Attorney General's Office, to Sir Alasdair Fraser, 27 March 2002. (Downey case papers, tab 8, pp. 586–8)

The latter replied to the former by telephone. During that call (according to a note made on the letter), David Brummell, having checked seemingly with Anita Bharucha, head of the rights and international relations division in the NIO, confirmed 'to the DPP [director of public prosecutions] that the NIO were perfectly [illegible?] for the [director] to speak to the PSNI on a confidential basis about the interpretation of "ON THE WANTED LIST".'[156]

Sir Alasdair Fraser replied in writing to David Brummell, on 4 April 2002. He had spoken in confidence to two senior police officers: 'I am informed that in order to provide a reliable answer, [the police] would follow the present methodology and levels of research.' The director of public prosecutions went on to refer to the absence of a simple wanted/ not wanted listing on the ICIS computer system. The police had to consult also hard copy files, which were distributed throughout NI. An ICIS check recently had failed to find seven or eight out of ten suspects who were found to be wanted. Though Sir Alasdair might have wished to escape the administrative scheme, he told the attorney general, who told the NIO, that the answer was effectively no. The director also told the NIO, indirectly, about the problem with the ICIS computer, which would return to haunt the administrative scheme.

The NIO did not take no for an answer. On 10 April 2002,[157] Anita Bharucha wrote to Detective Chief Superintendent Kennedy of the PSNI, head of C2. She was evidently trying to exclude the director of public prosecutions, despite his supportive comments about the police.

Detective Chief Superintendent Kennedy closed off the option of a lesser question, in her reply of 24 April 2002: 'I have further considered the present methodology used to review the OTR lists. I am satisfied that it would not be possible to report the position in respect of individual OTRs without completing the present checks undertaken by PSNI. [] I believe the present review process, albeit slow, is necessary as the Chief Constable, PSNI, is under an obligation to ensure that all

---

[156] David Brummell, Attorney General's Office, to Sir Alasdair Fraser, 27 March 2002. (Downey case papers, tab 8, pp. 586–8)
[157] Downey case papers, pp. 606–8.

intelligence and factual information in respect of each investigation is thoroughly examined and assessed before a final decision is reached as to whether or not an individual is wanted for arrest and prosecution.'[158] Wanted for arrest and prosecution indicates that no distinction was being made.

The PSNI and DPP stood together in 2002, and defeated the NIO initiative. It would appear that, later, when Operation Rapid was set up by the police alone, this was done through a downgrading of the role of the NI director of public prosecutions.

The Hillsborough Joint Declaration, 1 May 2003

Further political talks took place at Hillsborough near Belfast, on 3–4 March 2003. The UK and Irish governments failed to get political agreement. The conference did not resume on 10 April 2003, as planned. London and Dublin subsequently published their so-called joint declaration on 1 May 2003 (though the date April 2003 remains on the texts).[159] The Hillsborough joint declaration comprised: a 17-page joint declaration, including three annexes, by the two governments; a separate agreement, plus annex, on the proposed independent monitoring commission (which Sinn Féin continued to oppose); and a two-page document entitled proposals in relation to on the runs (which the unionists said they had not supported).

The UK and Irish OTR proposals made reference to: a context of acts of completion, meaning the decommissioning of terrorist weapons; due judicial process and a sensitivity to the position of victims; similar action in the Republic of Ireland; and 'the complete ending of exiling and allowing those exiled to return'. The plan involved: an eligibility body; and a special judicial tribunal (the ordinary courts having already been ruled out). The eligibility body would exercise the powers of the sentence review commissioners, with the Northern Ireland (Sentences) Act 1998 being amended as follows: the reduction of the two-year

---

[158] Downey case papers, pp. 620.

[159] David Cooke drafted this document: Graham Spencer, ed., *The British and Peace in Northern Ireland,* Cambridge 2015, pp. 147–76.

minimum period to zero; and the removal of the requirement of at least a five-year sentence.

The Hillsborough joint declaration went further. First, the Northern Ireland (Sentences) Act 1998 was to remain the statutory vehicle, suggesting continuity. Second, new quasi-judicial institutions were to be grafted on. Third and again, this was the UK and Sinn Féin in the lead, with Irish support and NI opposition.

The Comprehensive Agreement, 8 December 2004

There was a third attempt to restore devolution, during the second Blair government. David Trimble had been eclipsed by Dr Ian Paisley, in the 2003 assembly elections. The two governments sought – again unsuccessfully – to restore devolution, this time with the Democratic Unionist Party ('DUP') and Sinn Féin as the principal beneficiaries. The OTR issue was not included in the so-called comprehensive agreement of 8 December 2004, no doubt because of DUP opposition. But it was not dead – the Weston Park proposals and the Hillsborough joint declaration, certainly according to Sinn Féin, remained on the table.

Who Knew What?

The idea of OTR legislation was made public on 8 March 2001. It did not affect the underlying administrative scheme. It is now clear that the former helped obscure the latter.

Tony Blair, ironically, confirmed this analysis, when he gave evidence to NIAC belatedly: 'My experience in Northern Ireland is that people look at these thing pretty carefully, but I suspect that the people at the time were also concentrating far more on the big question about how to deal with on-the-runs, and the administrative procedure to deal with people who … the prosecuting authorities decided should not be charged, and informing them that they are not going to be charged, was obviously of far less political salience…'.[160]

The following answers to parliamentary questions show that

---

[160]   NIAC, *Report,* Q3686, 13 January 2015. (Tony Blair)

ministers were able to restrict the amount of information released (with relative ease as they stated privately on a number of occasions):

- Jane Kennedy to Harry Barnes, 27 November 2001;[161]
- John Reid to Quentin Davies, 5 December 2001;[162]
- Tony Blair to Nigel Waterson, 10 April 2002;[163]
- John Reid to Quentin Davies, 1 July 2002.[164]

The latter parliamentary answer is, ironically, the closest a minister came in the 2001–5 parliament, to giving even a detail.[165] But the existence of the administrative scheme remained obscured by references to the need for legislation. No minister came out and said: a secret administrative scheme had commenced on 22 May 2000; this was agreed between Sinn Féin and the UK government; the prosecution reviews involved the PSNI, the NI prosecutor, the attorney general's office and the NIO; the following lists – SF1, IG, PL and SF2 – were being processed, with the vast majority receiving NIO comfort letters. These answers did not meet the standard required by the parliamentary authorities.

Ironically, the Irish taoiseach, in his own parliament, on 20 March 2002, had disclosed the existence of an 'administrative procedure'.[166] This, however, was not spotted by the media, and there was no consequential political discussion.

---

[161] Fuller answer given, 11 December 2001: HC, *Hansard*, vol. 375, col. 768W & vol. 376, col. 753W.

[162] HC, *Hansard*, vol. 376, col. 317.

[163] HC, *Hansard*, vol. 383, col. 18.

[164] HC, *Hansard*, vol. 388, cols. 136W–137W.

[165] 'As a result of inquiries received and referred to the prosecuting authorities and the police, 32 individuals have been informed over the past two years that they are not wanted for arrest in relation to terrorist offences. In accordance with the policy announced on 29 September 2000, an additional 25 persons, who had left Northern Ireland without completing their sentences, have been informed since then that they can return to Northern Ireland without serving more time in custody and that the prosecuting authorities and police have confirmed they will not face fresh charges.'

[166] DE, *Official Reports,* vol. 550, cols. 695–6.

Conclusion: Front and Back Doors

Lord Williams had advised on the need for legislation, if Tony Blair was to keep his promises to Sinn Féin. The idea acted as a constitutional brake on the administrative scheme, as envisaged. It was not possible, as some ministers and officials seemed to think, to re-designate most wanted members of the IRA as not wanted, whether moving fast or slow.[167]

The OTR issue warrants its own legal metaphor, particularly with regard to the relationship between the administrative scheme and amnesty legislation: it is that of NI as a house, with a front (legislative) and back (administrative) door. The republicans were still out in the cold. Could they be admitted to the political house? While there was limited public discussion from March 2001 (no legislation being introduced), about allowing IRA members through the front door, ministers and officials worked with Sinn Féin to bring lists of OTRs quietly through the back door, year after year.

Again, the question of legality – in a public-law sense – arises about the 2001–5 parliament years. The administrative scheme, on its own, might not have been strictly illegal. The police and the public prosecution service, it may be assumed, would not have gratuitously stepped over the line – they would not have abused their powers.

But there is a theoretical contrast within prosecution reviews, depending upon the decision taken.[168] If the prosecutor decides to pros-

---

[167] John Reid came close to this position, when he wrote to Lord Goldsmith about the administrative scheme, on 22 January 2002: 'Of course the more cases we can deal with by these means the more we can ease pressure at a later stage.' (Downey case papers, tab 8, pp. 514–6)

[168] This was made clear by an unknown official reporting to Bill Jeffrey on 18 February 2002, about an inspection of the PSNI OTR team: 'We got the impression that the police were proceeding as quickly as possible in the context of the DPP's understandable requirement that every last shred of evidence be followed up and considered before he was willing to provide an answer on an OTR's current status. It was also clear that the CJ [criminal justice] system was simply not designed for the task we were asking of it.' (Downey case papers, tab 8, pp. 523–4. See also, pp. 554–7.)

ecute, the judge or jury may acquit. There is a check on prosecution mindedness. However, if the police and prosecutors decided someone is not wanted erroneously, there is – as Downey proves – little possibility of resisting an abuse of process application. There is an argument that a prosecution review, where there was no possibility of correcting a mistake (that someone was not wanted), might be unlawful in itself: the whole administrative scheme could be vitiated by such a certainty of risk.

On 28 November 2001, John Reid and Bill Jeffrey had had a breakfast meeting with Gerry Adams at Hillsborough. Bill Jeffrey recorded himself explaining the clearing of the next eight names: 'In other words, final checks were going on to ensure that there wasn't a file that had been overlooked, or a police force that was still interested. I hoped this wouldn't take more than a few days or weeks.' This was the Downey mistake, anticipated by the NIO's political director six years in advance.

The idea of an amnesty had been in play in Whitehall from late 1999. It was only after Tony Blair's third and final general election victory in 2005, that it became a practical political proposal; however, it would be undermined by Sinn Féin (the intended beneficiary), because the security forces were to be included.

CHAPTER FIVE

Amnesty: Northern Ireland (Offences) Bill, 2005-6

The government knew that it could only keep its OTR promises with an amnesty. But it was not until Tony Blair's third parliament, and with Peter Hain as secretary of state, that the Northern Ireland (Offences) Bill ('NIOB') was introduced in November 2005. The government was to have its payroll vote, and the support of Sinn Féin (still abstaining from parliament). All other parties opposed the bill, even in NI. Then, in January 2006, with the social democratic and labour party majoring in no amnesty for the security forces, Peter Hain – following the Sinn Féin change of position – was forced to withdraw his bill from parliament. It was a major defeat for the government.

The 2005 General Election

Tony Blair won his third general election, in May 2005. This was to be his last government. Paul Murphy was replaced at the NIO.[169] The new secretary of state, with his anti-apartheid background (and Irish republican sympathies[170]), had already helped Tony Blair unsuccessfully regarding Gibraltar (when a junior foreign office minister). Now, he was faced with getting Dr Paisley and Martin McGuinness to share power in a restored Stormont, in order to end UK direct rule in NI.

Decommissioning

On 28 July 2005, more than seven years after the Belfast agreement, the IRA brought its armed campaign formally to an end. So much is clear from the army council's statement, issued in Dublin: 'All IRA units have been ordered to dump arms.' On 26 September 2005, the independent international commission on decommissioning – in

---

[169] He became chair of the intelligence and security committee in the house of commons.
[170] *Outside In,* London 2012, pp. 312–3.

Belfast and Dublin – announced that the IRA had fully decommissioned,[171] Fr Alec Reid, a catholic priest, and the Rev Harold Good, a methodist minister, being identified as witnesses of the event.

But Sinn Féin did not yet support the PSNI, and policing and justice powers remained to be transferred to NI.

The Bill

In the queen's speech of 17 May 2005, introducing the long 2005–6 parliamentary session, there was no reference to a bill on OTRs.

Then, in October 2005, a junior NIO minister, David Hanson (who had been Tony Blair's parliamentary private secretary) asked John Prescott, the deputy prime minister, for legislative clearance: 'The sensitivity of the policy has meant that it has been kept close, and this approach for clearance [by the domestic affairs sub-committee of the cabinet] comes at a very late stage in the path towards legislation.'[172] John Reid, now the defence secretary, and reflecting a ministry of defence change of attitude about no equivalence, came out against the exclusion of the security forces.

The Provisions of the Bill

The NIOB provided for:

- *one*, certificates of eligibility issued by a certification commissioner (effectively immunity);
- *two*, the non-appearance of OTRs in a bespoke alternative justice system;
- *three*, trials for certified offences by a special tribunal consisting of a retired judge;
- *four*, the release on licence of anyone so convicted;
- *five*, appeals commissioners (again retired judges) to consider certificates of eligibility and licences;

---

[171] Some decommissioning had occurred in October 2001, April 2002 and October 2003.

[172] Letter, 12 October 2005. (Downey case papers, tab 8, pp, 707–8)

- *six*, the ousting of judicial review;
- *seven*, a right of appeal against conviction and sentence to a special appeals tribunal, again comprising a retired judge; and
- *eight*, special prosecutors in the special tribunal and the special appeals tribunal.

The government's amnesty, while provided for in a bill, was located legislatively outside the existing criminal justice system. Nevertheless, the lord chancellor, Lord Falconer, offered retired judges from, not just the NI high court, but also the crown court and county courts in NI. The lord chief justice of NI, Sir Brian Kerr, appears to have been consulted, but his views are not known. This alternative justice system included a provision for the ousting of judicial review, and no appeal to the court of appeal in NI.

The government was to argue – none too persuasively – that this was not an amnesty.[173] It referred to the licensing of offenders in the special tribunal, in their absence. Terrorists would not be walking free. But sending a person to prison would only be lawful, if the offender committed a new offence – outside the category of offences on which the NIOB bites, which is what makes it an amnesty.

The key to the NIOB was: the certification commissioner. This idea was derived from the sentence review commissioners. It is unknown who the NIO had in mind. This commissioner was to control the entry point to the amnesty (a word that was studiously avoided), through the certifying of an applicant as having immunity. This was to be granted after running a checklist: not a supporter of a specified organization; not currently involved in acts of terrorism; not convicted of a serious offence committed after 10 April 1998; but suspected of, charged with or convicted of a qualifying offence (similar to the scheduled offences which had founded the Northern Ireland [Sentences] Act 1998).

There was then to be a special trial, with guilty or not guilty pleas. The former would lead to sentencing, and – through the Northern Ireland (Sentences) Act 1998 – the releasing on licence. The latter might

---

[173] Peter Hain, HC, *Hansard,* vol. 439, col. 1542, 23 November 2005.

lead to acquittal. All this was special: a special prosecutor; a special tribunal; appeal commissioners (to consider certificates of eligibility and licences); and a special appeals tribunal, to deal with conviction and sentencing. While the special tribunal would sit in Belfast, it – uniquely – would have jurisdiction throughout the UK, through the application of NI law to England and Wales and Scotland.[174]

The OTR – as had happened with returning escaped prisoners – would not have to engage personally. He could be represented by a solicitor, when applying to the certification commissioner. 'A statement by the applicant that he does not support a specified organisation would constitute evidence of that fact.'[175] 'The Commissioner [would] consider the information from the applicant and the Secretary of State and reach a determination as to the eligibility of the individual against the criteria set out above.'[176] 'Once someone had been declared eligible, he or she would be free to return to [NI] without risk of arrest for questioning or charge in relation to a certified offence.'[177] 'There would be no requirement upon the defendant to appear before the Special Tribunal, either to give evidence or at the time of sentencing.'[178]

For and Against the Bill

At Westminster, the government had the whipped support of its members of parliament, and – for a time – Sinn Féin. There was an unprecedented alliance against the bill of all other NI and mainland political parties. But the arguments differed.

British parties and the unionists tended to oppose this concession to Irish republicans (and Ulster loyalists). Some were uneasy at the

---

[174] Sch 2 para 4.

[175] 'On the runs terrorist suspects, shape of the scheme', 11 October 2005, para 13. (Downey case papers, tab 8, p. 711)

[176] 'On the runs terrorist suspects, shape of the scheme', 11 October 2005, para 13. (Downey case papers, tab 8, p. 711)

[177] 'On the runs terrorist suspects, shape of the scheme', 11 October 2005, para 18. (Downey case papers, tab 8, p. 712)

[178] 'On the runs terrorist suspects, shape of the scheme', 11 October 2005, para 23. (Downey case papers, tab 8, p. 713)

inclusion of soldiers and police officers, given the perceived equivalence of security forces and their terrorist opponents.

The constitutional nationalists, the social democratic and labour party, who had three members of parliament, were the most vigorous opponents of the bill. But they did not oppose the amnesty for republicans as such. They objected to so-called state killers getting a 'get-out-of-jail card'. The social democratic and labour party caught Sinn Féin out as less anti-British. The republicans were forced to formally come out against the bill, when it was going through its committee stage in the commons. The constitutional nationalists stirred up a storm: few if any soldiers and police officers were likely to be charged with unlawful killings.

Eamonn McCann, a radical journalist, who was involved with the Bloody Sunday families during the Saville inquiry, may have played a role. He was to write, much later, that: 'From the point of view of Republicans, the key moment came when members of the Bloody Sunday families who had been pursuing prosecution of the soldiers responsible for the Derry killings told senior members of Sinn Féin in what may be called no uncertain terms that if they accepted the Bill … they'd be "denounced from the rooftops".'[179]

The Republic of Ireland

The Weston Park proposals and the Hillsborough joint declaration had envisaged the Irish government acting alongside the UK. Bertie Ahern, the taoiseach in 2001 and 2003, remained in office through 2005. However, his justice minister, Michael McDowell TD SC, had not been involved in those earlier negotiations. Further, the Irish government had been forced belatedly to exclude the killers of a police officer, Garda Jerry McCabe, from their early release scheme introduced in 1998 (arguing, with no response from the UK, that the McCabe gang had been excluded from the Belfast agreement: it had not).

On 9 November 2005 – to coincide with the first reading of

---

[179] *Irish Times,* 2 April 2015.

this bill – the Irish department of justice published a press release: 'McDowell confirms that OTR arrangements will not apply to persons wanted for killing of Garda Jerry McCabe'.

The Irish government proposed to rely upon article 13.6 of the constitution, which states: 'The right of pardon and the power to commute or remit punishment imposed by any court exercising criminal jurisdiction are hereby invested in the President, but such power of commutation or remission may, except in capital cases, also be conferred by law on other authorities.' A non-statutory eligibility body would be established. It would determine who were 'qualifying persons'. The eligibility body would then notify the justice minister. The government would advise the president about the granting of presidential pardons.

The press release stated: 'While the approach taken in the two jurisdictions reflect their differing Constitutional and legal frameworks, the net effect is similar viz. persons benefiting from the arrangements would not be imprisoned.' No one pointed to the difference between a UK licence and an (irrevocable) Irish pardon.

There was some Irish discussion of presidential pardons. Article 13.8.1 provides that the president is not answerable in any court (though case law holds that this does not apply to government advice to the president). And article 13.9 states that the president acts only on the advice of the government, unless the constitution provides otherwise. One question was: is an application to the intended eligibility body sufficient to justify a presidential pardon?

The Stages of the Bill

First reading in the house of commons was on 9 November 2005.[180] Second reading followed on 23 November 2005.[181] The bill went then to standing committee B.[182] It met on eight occasions, between 6 and 15 December 2005. No amendments were accepted. The bill never went to the lords. And it never came back to the commons for the report stage.

---

[180] HC, *Hansard,* vol. 439, col. 305.
[181] HC, *Hansard,* vol. 439, cols. 1528–626.
[182] Standing Committee B, cols. 1–378.

Second Reading

Peter Hain opened the debate on 23 November 2005, and David Hanson closed. The secretary of state was soon subjected to a torrent of interventions, including some from his own side. Peter Hain rejected the suggestion of Sir Patrick Cormack, then the chair of NIAC, that there should be pre-legislative scrutiny: 'This Bill is being introduced at this time as part of a sequence of events negotiated by both Governments some years ago.'[183] Paul Murphy was critical of the bill (but voted for it). Ultimately, the government succeeded on a whip, the house voting 310 to 262 on second reading.

There had been a similar vote on the conservative/liberal democrat amendment against second reading (which may be noted since it contains reasons for opposing): '... because it creates an amnesty for terrorist fugitives from justice; because it allows such fugitives to return to [NI] without ever being arrested or questioned by the police about their alleged offences; because it proposes a quasi-judicial process in which those accused of perpetrating terrorist offences will never have to appear before a court or spend any time in custody; because it allows an indefinite period of time for terrorists to take advantage of this procedure; because it treats members of the Armed Forces and the police on a par with terrorists; because it fails to contain an obligation on terrorist organisations to allow the safe return to [NI] of those they have exiled; and because it places the rights of those suspected of serious offences before those of the victims of terrorism in [NI] and throughout the rest of the [UK].'[184]

The Security Forces?

Sir Quentin Thomas has originated the idea of excluding the security forces from an amnesty. Gradually, the 'no equivalence' idea gave way, by the time of the NIOB, to the 'no discrimination' (Peter Hain's words) perspective; what was good enough for terrorists should be

---

[183] Col. 1536.
[184] Col. 1551.

extended to any members of the security forces at risk of prosecution.

The NIOB contained no express reference to the security forces. The key provision is clause 1: offences to which the act applies. This did not follow the Northern Ireland (Sentences) Act 1998 by referring to scheduled offences (in counter-terrorist) legislation.[185] Instead, the offences were defined spatially (the three jurisdictions of the UK) and temporally (before 10 April 1998): they were offences 'in connection with terrorism and the affairs of Northern Ireland (whether committed for terrorist purposes or not)'. The parenthesis extended the terrorist amnesty to members of the security forces. This was admitted quietly, in the explanatory notes accompanying the bill.[186]

Peter Hain was open about inclusion through clause 1, in his second-reading speech. He then became caught up in a discussion about paratroopers on bloody Sunday in 1972, then the subject of the Saville inquiry. Mark Durkan, the leader of the social democratic and labour party, intervened. He was the member of parliament for Foyle. Later, he made clear that he opposed republicans, loyalists and state forces all benefiting from the amnesty. He promised amendments in committee, limiting the NIOB to OTRs only. That was the point, though Mark Durkan might not have known it, when the fate of the bill was sealed.

Battle was joined in standing committee B, in the morning and afternoon of 6 December 2005, when clause 1 was considered. Laurence Robertson, later the chair of NIAC, proposed to leave out the security forces parenthesis: 'whether committed for terrorist purposes or not'. It is not clear that everyone understood its significance. And there was a clear divide, among opponents of the NIOB, between no equivalence supporters and no discrimination supporters (though they did not follow the secretary of state in using the term). The committee divided 16 votes to 13 (including all the NI members voting against) in opposing the Robertson amendment. The security forces remained in.

Peter Robinson, of the DUP, had proposed a new clause 2,

---

[185] Northern Ireland (Sentences) Act 1998 s 3(7). Members of the security forces (not that there were any in prison) were eligible for early release.

[186] Para 4.

including those who had combated terrorism in NI (presumably when in uniform). This was lost, 18 votes to eight, on 15 December 2005, at the tail end of standing committee B. The loss of the clause did not exclude the security forces from the NIOB.

The Withdrawal of the Bill

On 11 January 2006,[187] Peter Hain, in a statement to the house of commons, announced the withdrawal of the bill. The issue, he said, would have to be revisited by legislation, possibly in the autumn. He indicated the government had been thinking of possible amendments.

The reason for withdrawal – elicited by members' questions – was Sinn Féin's opposition, and in particular a threatened republican boycott of the alternative justice system. It is a measure of the republicans' seriousness that, faced with new labour delivering on its OTR promises, it permitted the government to withdraw the bill, because it did not want the security forces to also benefit. Sinn Féin, of course, had the secret administrative scheme, from which it alone benefited. The question in January 2006 was: would number 10 continue with the administrative scheme? The answer was to be surprising: instead of abandoning it, the NIO would reconstruct it in the form of the PSNI's Operation Rapid.

---

[187] HC, *Hansard,* vol. 441, cols. 287–91.

Sir Alasdair Fraser QC (27.03.06) © *Pacemaker Press*

Lord Williams of Mostyn QC (06.05.97)
© PA Archive/Press Association Images

Lord Goldsmith QC (04.06.07) © Pacemaker Press

Peter Hain (22.01.07) © Pacemaker Press

Sir Hugh Orde (03.01.08) © Pacemaker Press

Sir Bill Jeffrey receiving his knighthood from Prince Charles (19.03.08) ©
PA Archive/Press Association Images

CHAPTER SIX

The PSNI's Operation Rapid, 2007–10

No amended OTR legislation ever appeared. At some point in 2006, Sir Alasdair Fraser fell ill. In the NIO, Mark Sweeney breathed new life into the administrative scheme. On the public stage, events speeded up: first, in January 2007, Sinn Féin came out in support of the PSNI; second, Stormont was restored in May 2007, under Dr Paisley and Martin McGuinness; and third, in June 2007 – as had been anticipated – Tony Blair handed over to Gordon Brown. The first public event led, by reciprocity, to the PSNI establishing secretly Operation Rapid on 7 February 2007. Though few realized it, this was the 2002 speeded-up process (which the PSNI and Sir Alasdair Fraser had then prevented). Operation Rapid – supposedly randomly named[188] – was to be the administrative scheme operating in a transformed political context, with the NIO working much more directly with the PSNI.

After the Northern Ireland (Offences) Bill

Sinn Fein stopped the NIOB, because of the inclusion of the security forces. The government seemed relieved to escape the onslaught from all other parties.[189] But the administrative scheme was not abandoned. Sinn Féin knew that, and so did the government, but most other observers remained in the dark.

On 23 January 2006 (twelve days after the withdrawal of the bill), Mark Sweeney, head of the rights and international relations division in the NIO,[190] had a meeting with a senior PSNI officer (whose name

---

[188] Peter Sheridan's staff officer, Detective Sergeant Gillian Ferguson, obtained the name within the PSNI. She emailed Norman Baxter on 5 February 2007: 'Thought the Op name was good given the history!'. (Hallett, *Report*, para 5.20)

[189] Peter Hain, NIAC, *Report*, Q1775, 18 June 2014.

[190] He occupied this post between May 2004 and November 2007.

is redacted)[191] in Belfast. The former was (as he wrote later) 'working on a single list which brings together all of the information we have, including the prison list, so that we can go forward from here on a shared basis'.[192] Mark Sweeney was working to Kevin McGinty, in the attorney general's office. The senior PSNI officer replied on 31 January 2006. He wrote – proposing a round-table meeting (which was not what Mark Sweeney envisaged): 'I am copying this reply to the Director of Public Prosecutions for Northern Ireland as the review of the OTR lists to date has been undertaken at his request and all correspondence/ results are replied to his office. It would be important that the NIO, PPS, AG [attorney general]'s Office and PSNI are all in agreement as to what exactly is the position in relation to all persons named on all lists.'[193] That was the way it had been done in 2000–6.

On 27 February 2006, Lord Goldsmith reported to Peter Hain on the reinstated administrative scheme (though he may not have had a full picture): 'Some cases could not be traced on the information available and despite requests for further information from Sinn Fein, through the [NIO], this was not forthcoming and work on the lists came to a halt in early 2004. However, prompted perhaps by the introduction of the [NIOB], or its withdrawal, some additional information was recently provided and the Director and police have recommenced their review.'[194] It is interesting that he did not make clear whether it was the introduction, or the withdrawal, of the NIOB, which led to the resumption of prosecution reviews. It is significant that he did not advise that, parliament having rejected a statutory amnesty, the prime minister was now in an even more difficult legal position.

On 22 March 2006, Mark Sweeney signed four new comfort letters. He sent them, via Gerry Kelly at Connolly House. And, despite the legal risk of assisting fugitives,[195] he mentioned the names of

[191] T/D/Superintendent, CJI Branch. (Downey case papers, tab 8, pp. 722–6)
[192] Letter, 27 January 2006. (Downey case papers, tab 8, pp. 722–6)
[193] Downey case papers, pp. 727–32.
[194] Downey case papers, pp. 733–4.
[195] On 25 September 2006, Kevin McGinty emailed Jim Davidson of the PSNI:

three IRA members who were still wanted, including John Downey![196] If Mark Sweeney did not recall this refusal, the NIO's schedule or spreadsheet most certainly recorded John Downey's lack of OTR success in 2002–6.

Peter Sheridan of the PSNI (who was to be responsible officially for Operation Rapid), in his published written evidence to NIAC, has listed a series of meetings, initiated by the attorney general's office on 5 April 2006. For reasons difficult to understand, none of the following is documented in the Downey case papers:[197]

- 25 May 2006: first meeting in the royal courts of justice in Belfast (where the attorney general's library was located);
- 9 June 2006: second meeting at the same venue (see further below);
- 17 October 2006: chief constable (by video from NIO at Stormont) in meeting with the secretary of state in London;
- 30 November 2006: PSNI (Hugh Orde and Peter Sheridan) meet Sinn Féin on OTRs;
- 7 December 2006: Peter Sheridan and David Mercer (also of the PSNI) meet Barra McGrory.

Political talks had resumed at St Andrews in Scotland, on 11 to 13 October 2006 (this was the occasion when Bertie Ahern led a celebration of Dr and Baroness Paisley's fiftieth wedding anniversary). The agreement, of the UK and the Republic of Ireland, at St Andrews, was to lead, with fits and starts, to devolution being restored. However, in the sixteen pages of text issued – the so-called St. Andrews agreement

---

'the nature of the review is NOT to give indications that an individual is wanted. What [we] are doing is giving an indication that an individual is not wanted.' (Written evidence, Peter Sheridan, 26 May 2014)

[196] Downey case papers, pp. 735–6.

[197] The PONI, in its report of 20 October 2014, records: 'Other than electronic notes of the June 2006 meeting my investigation has not had access to minutes from the other meetings.' (para 4.30) Norman Baxter told NIAC that the PSNI gave him a copy of those minutes, in advance of his appearing before the committee. (NIAC, *Report*, Q88, 2 April 2014)

– there is not one reference to OTRs as a public policy issue. There was certainly no reference to the administrative scheme. Sinn Féin knew about it: the DUP evidently did not.

In the 17 October 2006 London meeting referred to above, which also included the attorney general, OTRs was brought back on to the agenda. Peter Hain stated he wanted to try and speed up the administrative scheme. The chief constable, with the support of the attorney general, stated that it had to proceed properly, as it had been doing. Sir Jonathan Phillips, the NIO permanent secretary, who was also present, recalled this as a meeting to consider speeding up the administrative scheme.[198]

Meanwhile, following the meeting on 7 December 2006, David Mercer wrote to Barra McGrory. At that point, the PSNI envisaged interviewing OTRs – either voluntarily or on arrest - about specific incidents. Barra McGrory rejected this, on 19 December 2006: 'I simply cannot imagine fugitives presenting themselves for interview at the Serious Crime Suite in Antrim or anywhere else on such a basis.'[199] Thus, before Operation Rapid was established, the PSNI knew it would not be interviewing: it was to engage only in a desk exercise for each OTR. There was no possibility of questioning suspects.

The Prime Minister's Fourth Promise, 28 December 2006

On 28 December 2006 (from Miami), and engaged in telephone shuttle diplomacy on the NI question, Tony Blair wrote again to Gerry Adams. There was no promise of another bill, and an amnesty (which remained the position of the government). Instead, he was working on 'expediting the existing administrative procedures'. The prime minister concluded: 'I have always believed that the position of these OTRs is an anomaly which needs to be addressed. Before I leave office I am committed to finding a scheme which will resolve all the remaining cases.'[200]

---

[198] NIAC, *Report,* Q3470, 19 November 2014.

[199] NIAC, *Report,* Q155, 2 April 2014.

[200] This letter is quoted in para 74 of Mr Justice Sweeney's judgment. It is not clear from where he obtained it. It must have been disclosed late.

The 2006 labour party conference, it had been remarked, was Tony Blair's last in number 10. The actual departure date was related to his poor relationship with Gordon Brown. But, after the St Andrews agreement, and working with Dr Paisley and Martin McGuinness, the prime minister seemed to hope he could solve NI (with devolution restored), in time to launch his legacy as a peacemaker in one country.

The legality of this fourth written promise follows from the comments in chapter 3 on the first two promises (the third is dealt with in chapter 4). Tony Blair knew he needed legislation. But he was not even alluding to it after the NIOB. He was offering Gerry Adams a complete administrative solution, based upon the false – republican – idea of an anomaly. Lord Williams of Mostyn and, to a lesser extent, Lord Goldsmith had advised the prime minister, on many occasions, that that was not acceptable to them as law officers: the fourth written promise was simply unlawful and unconstitutional. It is not possible to construe 'resolve all the remaining cases', as meaning only the continued review of outstanding cases one by one (with no predetermined outcome). A possible defence, that the prime minister intended only to consider the problem further, and was therefore not promising anything, is difficult to substantiate given the wording of the letter.

NIAC asked Jonathan Powell about the relationship between this fourth letter and the setting up of Operation Rapid. He did not know. But he attributed significance: 'clearly, if the Prime Minister writes a letter like that he does not just do it out of the blue. It is something that he has agreed and agreed with the [NIO], who will then go about implementing it and making sure what he has promised happens, to the best of their ability.'[201]

The Sinn Féin *Ard Fheis*

On 28 January 2007, in Dublin, Sinn Féin, at an *ard fheis* (conference), voted to support policing in NI.[202] The return to the OTR

[201] NIAC, *Report*, Q2564, 8 September 2014.
[202] The text of the resolution included 'Support for the PSNI and the criminal justice system'.

issue made this possible. And the Sinn Féin vote, in turn, would lead to the restoration of devolution in May 2007.

The PSNI (Sir Hugh Orde and Peter Sheridan) had met Sinn Féin, on the OTR issue, on 30 November 2006. They met them again, on 24 January 2007 (four days before the *ard fheis*). Once Sinn Féin reciprocated, in Dublin on 28 January 2007, the way was open for a serious review of all OTR files. Sinn Féin support for the police was effectively rewarded through Operation Rapid. It was more than a cynical deal: there was also relief. The PSNI was no longer formally unloved by republicans. Their job could only get better and better. Police officers were now invited to do the NIO's bidding. It is difficult to distinguish such administrative coaxing by civil servants from the PSNI's leadership response to republican recognition of the police. Norman Baxter (who was to be in everyday charge of Operation Rapid) recalled that Peter Sheridan's female staff officer – who seemed keen on the administrative scheme – asked him frequently: 'Can you not get these people off the list'; 'Can you not find them a way back to the jurisdiction?'[203] This was the back door of the NI house, and certainly not a ploy (on the part of the staff officer) to make OTRs susceptible to police investigation once back in the jurisdiction. She was evidently a protestant, working for a catholic boss, and a new NI might be beckoning.

Staffing the Administrative Scheme

The administrative scheme had comprised initially – in 2000 – a detective inspector and a detective constable. In 2001, an additional seven detectives (under a detective sergeant) joined the review team. Later that year, the RUC became the PSNI. In April 2002, this team was disbanded: it was replaced by one made up of six retired police officers returning as civilians. This review team was then disbanded, in September 2003. There was an interlude of a number of months (to which Lord Goldsmith may have been referring). In April 2004, a review team was reinstated, with an inspector in charge of two retired

---

[203] NIAC, *Report,* Q35, 2 April 2014.

police officers. In January 2007, these two officers joined what was to become Operation Rapid, and a third retired police officer was brought in to manage them. There was considerable turnover, and it is not clear who, if anyone, in the PSNI, was directing these officers.[204]

The Leadership of Operation Rapid

Peter Sheridan was ultimately responsible for Operation Rapid (under Sir Hugh Orde). In February 2006, he had been appointed assistant chief constable, crime operations department. In that position, he had a number of responsibilities – the administrative scheme, it is important to note, was only one: 'I had 1,400 officers under my command. I was running live operations at that time … On-the-runs was that much of my day [gesture], if it came into my day's work at all. I had delegated responsibility to Norman Baxter, and his team got on with that job.'[205] It is clear that Peter Sheridan was not going to get involved in Operation Rapid in any way: his job was to sign off on behalf of the PSNI.

Peter Sheridan, however, took part in the 2006 planning meetings. Significantly, he did not attend at the royal courts of justice, on 9 June 2006. He sent District Inspector Jim Davidson to represent the PSNI. There are rather strange draft minutes of this meeting.[206] Mr Justice Sweeney did not see the minutes of the 9 June 2006 meeting, in any form. Kevin McGinty disclosed them to NIAC as flag 17, to his witness statement of 25 April 2014. However, these appear to be extracts only. Mark Sweeney told NIAC he was not 'Mr XX' from the NIO, but then went on to speculate about the minute taker (also unidentified).[207]

Kevin McGinty and Katie Pettifer of the NIO (not the home office as Peter Sheridan believed[208]) were present on 9 June 2006. There was

---

[204] Private information.

[205] NIAC, *Report,* Q230, 2 April 2014.

[206] These are quoted in Hallett, *Report,* para 5.4, but the status of the one-page document is not discussed.

[207] NIAC, *Report,* Q3921, 19 January 2015.

[208] NIAC, *Report,* Q17, 2 April 2014.

also another NIO official, whose name is not given in the minutes. This meeting may be crucial for understanding the so-called Downey mistake. The PSNI – after Patten – was very much NI bound. This jurisdiction accounted for much, but not all, of the troubles violence. The minutes read in part: 'Mr McGinty asked the group to determine who was best placed to confirm the Mets interest in any individual, Ms Pettifer replied that she would be content to make these enquiries but [and?] that it may be inappropriate for the Home Office to act in this manner. Mr Davidson stated that the PSNI could check with the Met but that additional enquiries would have to be made [by the metropolitan police service] to determine why the individual was wanted and if evidence existed in relation to the incident. Mr McGinty accepted it would probably fall to the Attorney General's office to make these enquiries, he accepted the Met would have to be persuaded of the necessity of responding to these enquiries. [] (**ACTION 2** – Kevin McGinty to confirm with the Metropolitan Police if individuals are wanted, why they are wanted and what evidence exists in relation to the incidents.)'

Kevin McGinty explained to NIAC that he was offering to help in only one case, not agreeing a division of labour with the PSNI.[209] That case could be SF2/41, who was wanted by the metropolitan police and was sent a comfort letter on 10 January 2007. Lord Goldsmith told NIAC that the attorney general's office could not access the police national computer: 'Mr McGinty believes that [the action point] related simply to a specific issue and not a general responsibility – or a specific name or names and not generally taking on the responsibility.'[210] Whatever of Kevin McGinty's attempt to explain away these strange minutes, the document appears to have blindsided Peter Sheridan. He read the minutes subsequently, and thought that a clear division of labour had been agreed as between NI and England and Wales. Operation Rapid, from the first, was not to be clear about what it was doing. That was the responsibility, partly of Sir Hugh Orde as the chief

---

[209]   NIAC, *Report,* Qs647-8, 30 April 2014.
[210]   NIAC, *Report,* Q2083, 2 July 2014.

constable, but mainly of Mark Sweeney, who had reinvigorated the administrative scheme after the defeat of the NIOB.

The second most important figure is Norman Baxter, who, in April 2006, as a detective chief superintendent, was appointed head of C2 branch, which dealt with serious crime. He too had other duties. He was still in charge of the 1998 Omagh bomb investigation, for example. But he was to be assigned day-to-day responsibility for Operation Rapid. C1 branch had handled extradition etc, but it was unable to take on Operation Rapid because of redundancies. Significantly, Norman Baxter did not attend the 2006 planning meetings. He first heard about an administrative scheme on 8 January 2007, during a working lunch with Peter Sheridan. Neither he, nor the assistant chief constable, knew that the RUC/PSNI had been involved from 2000. Norman Baxter was not at a meeting on 12 January 2007, where, he claims, the minutes record the Peter Sheridan direction to consider NI offences only. On 2 February 2007, he discussed Operation Rapid with Peter Sheridan, one to one. Pressure of work may account for a great deal of non-communication, aside from any need-to-know police philosophy, but there was already a long chain between Mark Sweeney and Norman Baxter. The latter did not want political interference. The former had his secretary of state's bidding to do, while seeming to continue respecting police operational independence.

On 9 January 2007, someone in the PSNI had informed assistant chief constable Drew Harris (in charge of criminal justice) that OTRs were now a priority: 'Due to the renewed progress on the political front the NIO are pushing strongly to: a. Have the outstanding reviews completed as soon as possible b. To resolve the instances of approx 54 OTR's who, following review, are listed as wanted by PSNI for arrest and questioning in relation to serious terrorist offences.'[211] This seems pretty clear: it was the NIO which pressed the PSNI to look again at wanted cases. 'I would say that', Norman Baxter told NIAC, 'there was a culture within the [NIO] to ensure that republicans were not

---

[211] Hallett, para 5.13. The author is not identified.

prosecuted.'[212] Norman Baxter may not be representative of other senior PSNI officers of the time. However, a pointless hue and cry has been raised, about the fact that Operation Rapid went back over previous cases. That is what it was told to do, by the NIO. The Operation Rapid team did not know what had gone before. And, in a sense, it wanted a standard review of all cases. That was a sign of thoroughness, in a context where the NIO did not brief the PSNI officers in charge.

There is evidence that the much delayed Sean Hoey judgment, of 20 December 2007, reinforced the need to look again at rejected cases.[213] Norman Baxter may have expected serious judicial criticism, and that is what the police would get regarding their investigatory competence.

The Terms of Reference

Norman Baxter appears to have drafted the terms of reference, shortly after his one to one with Peter Sheridan. On 6 February 2007, the latter, as assistant chief constable, signed the eight paragraphs. He made no significant changes, no doubt trusting a subordinate officer with considerable experience. Peter Sheridan implies that the PSNI's human rights lawyer approved the terms of reference.

The terms of reference can only be understood in the context of Operation Rapid. The PSNI and PPSNI worked together to mount prosecutions. But the police was responsible for investigations; an officer had the power to arrest on reasonable suspicion, in order to question a suspect pending possible charging. The police also collected the evidence, but the PPSNI applied the code for crown prosecutors: the evidential stage, and the reasonable prospect of conviction test; and the public interest stage, with little likelihood of abandonment for serious crime. Operation Rapid produced two significant departures from the norm: first, the PSNI was not charged with arresting and questioning suspects (far from it); and second, it appeared to be taking over responsibility for the code for crown prosecutors, and trying to apply the

---

[212]   NIAC, *Report,* Q71, 2 April 2014.
[213]   Barra McGrory, written evidence, 6 June 1014, para 29.

reasonable prospect of conviction test itself. Sir Alasdair Fraser, after all, was no longer around (he attended the 6 June 2006 planning meeting), and those acting in his place were different prosecutors.

That is a hypothetical explanation for Norman Baxter's original three-stage test in the terms of reference, formally for arrest but actually not to prosecute (note the three alternatives): '[1] existing evidence, the integrity of which would withstand a legal challenge within a judicial process in [NI]; or [2] reasonable suspicion of committing serious crime in [NI], such suspicion being based upon a standard which meets current Human Rights standards; or [3] being unlawfully at large having escaped from custody or failed to return to prison from parole or having failed to surrender to a court as a condition of the granting of bail.'

This is admittedly a legal dog's breakfast, but then police officers are not judges or lawyers. Limb [1] is about evidence, but also prosecution. Limb [2] is the more familiar arrest power, with a perhaps gestural reference to human rights (necessary in the upper reaches of the PSNI in 2007). And limb [3] is about other arrest powers, exercised by police officers frequently. Norman Baxter was, it might be argued, seeking to legally dignify what he believed needed to be done – namely let off as many 'bad guys' as was administratively possible. He may not, with the benefit of hindsight, have liked it. But he was doing what he believed Sir Hugh Orde wanted. People in organizations, particularly in senior management, negotiate such dilemmas all the time.

On 15 February 2007, Peter Sheridan sent the terms of reference to Hilary Jackson, then the 'director political'.[214] This was a retitling of the political director post in the NIO. Hilary Jackson had no comments to make, so far as is known.

This is the way a later secretary of state – Theresa Villiers – explained the administrative scheme to parliament, on 27 March 2014 (after the John Downey case): 'Sinn Fein submitted a list of individuals who believed that if they returned to the UK, they might be arrested by the police in connection with terrorist offences committed before the 1998 Belfast agreement. The names were then checked by the police,

---

[214] Hallett, *Report*, pp. 220–1.

and in some cases by the Public Prosecution Service. If that checking process concluded that the lack of evidence available at the time meant that there was no realistic prospect of a successful prosecution, the individuals concerned were in most cases informed that they were no longer wanted by police in a letters signed by a [NIO] official.'[215] The secretary of state was referring only to Operation Rapid: it is obvious that the police, in the absence of the PPSNI, were doing the prosecutor's job, even if – as police officers – they concentrated on a OTR being wanted or not wanted for questioning.

Norman Baxter's View of the World?

Some senior police officers may have developed theories about state power, which is more usually associated with republicans and their intellectual supporters. Alternatively, paranoia, and other mental states, make conspiracy theories attractive to some people.

On 11 November 2009, after retiring from the PSNI, Norman Baxter gave evidence to NIAC, on the Omagh bombing.[216] Asked to explain a reference to political interference in policing, he blurted out a story about the NIO having 'an extremely unhealthy interest' in OTRs. That was years before the John Downey case, but it was the first public airing of Operation Rapid (not that the name was used). Norman Baxter was guided back to the subject of that inquiry, by his questioner. But he then interjected with a story about Martin McGuinness, who had been stopped by the police on a particular occasion, telephoning Mo Mowlam as secretary of state to secure his release.[217] He was alleging political interference in policing.

Giving evidence to the OTR inquiry on 2 April 2014, Norman Baxter returned to a theme of the NIO 'cross[ing] the boundary of what was constitutionally correct'.

On 8 March 2007 – as he recounted to NIAC during the OTR

---

[215] HC *Hansard,* vol. 578, col. 559, 27 March 2014.

[216] *The Omagh Bombing: some remaining questions,* 4th report of session 2009–10, HC 374, 16 March 2010.

[217] Ev 49.

inquiry – when he was in charge of Operation Rapid, he was the senior investigating officer for two arrested republicans: Gerard McGeough and Vincent McAnespie. (The former was convicted and sentenced in 2011, but, under the Belfast agreement, he was released in 2013. It is not thought that either of them received a comfort letter.) Interestingly, Norman Baxter said that they were arrested within Operation Rapid.[218] He stated that, at 21.10, the duty senior officer[219] (taking over from Sir Hugh Orde) telephoned him. (Norman Baxter may then have been in London, to where he had travelled with Detective Superintendent Hanley.) Apparently, Gerry Adams, hearing of the arrests, had telephoned someone (Jonathan Powell?) in number 10; the prime minister's office had then telephoned the PSNI; Norman Baxter believed, either then or subsequently, that he was being asked to release two arrested republicans. He did not, of course, do so.[220] And that fact alone may help shape an interpretation of what might have happened, whether it was a number 10 conspiracy or simply an assistant chief constable warning that the Sinn Féin president was looking out for the two IRA suspects.

The number 10 interfering story excited considerable interest, and there are those who have criticized Norman Baxter's recollection and/ or interpretation. Sir Hugh Orde was very dismissive, and the assistant chief constable could not be identified. (In fact, the duty officer may have been of lesser rank.) Norman Baxter, it may be stated in passing, has not helped his own cause. He declined to answer questions from Dame Heather Hallett, possibly on legal advice for which the PSNI was paying.[221] On 4 November 2014, Drew Harris told NIAC that the PSNI investigation had come to an end, with Norman Baxter again declining to engage.[222] True or not, the story does reveal what

---

[218] NIAC, *Report,* Q84, 2 April 2014.

[219] Hallett, *Report,* p. 70 produces evidence that this may have been the head of C3, but then goes on to assume it was an assistant chief constable.

[220] NIAC, *Report,* Q36 –Q39 (2 April 2014).

[221] Para 5.57; Private Information.

[222] NIAC, *Report,* Q3103, 4 November 2014. Also, Q3110, 4 November 2014.

the head of Operation Rapid thought – accurately or not – about the peace process in 2007. It therefore has a bearing on interpreting the Operation Rapid document trail, even if Norman Baxter was obviously reacting badly to being blamed for the Downey mistake.

Operation Rapid Established

On 7 February 2007, Norman Baxter chaired a gold meeting of Operation Rapid, at Ladas Drive in Belfast. The administrative scheme was to be moved to Clogher police station in Co. Tyrone, 59 miles from the capital (and close to his home).[223] There were to be six members: acting Detective Chief Inspector Neal Graham, the senior investigating officer; Detective Sergeant William Foster, responsible for intelligence matters; Detective Sergeant [Name?] Leonard, in charge of forensics; and three civilians (retired police officers): Paul McGowan, Robert Brewster and Howard (Robert) Ming.

The minutes, later amended by Norman Baxter, record: '[Norman Baxter] stated that Mr McGrory, Solicitor, who acts on behalf of OTR's, had requested information about the current legal status of his clients. Under article 3 of the ECHR … all persons have a legal right upon request to be informed if Police require them for questioning. He stated that Police were therefore obliged to review all those cases and determine the current status of these persons … Where it was established that no current legitimate basis existed to have a person arrested, this information would be passed to ACC [assistant chief constable] Crime for onward transmission to their Solicitor. Alternatively, if reasonable grounds still existed to suspect a person of committing a specific terrorist offence when balanced against Human Rights considerations, a firm recommendation would [be] made to have these persons remain circulated as wanted for interview…'.

It is clear that, at the beginning of Operation Rapid, it was seen as self-contained within the PSNI. There is no reference here to the PPSNI, much less the NIO – or the distant attorney general in London.

---

[223] Hallett states incorrectly that it was based at Ladas Drive: para 5.36.

The end user is perceived to be Barra McGrory. That is crucial. Norman Baxter had heard about Barra McGrory from Peter Sheridan. He had already drafted the terms of reference, and they echo here in the idea of wanted versus not wanted. But where did the idea of article 3 come from? There is no such human rights law, article 3 of the European convention on human rights dealing with torture and ill-treatment. The minutes may bear competing interpretations: one, this was something Barra McGrory had said, or implied, on or after 7 December 2006;[224] alternatively, the idea came from Norman Baxter, with or without support from the PSNI human rights advisor.[225] When Sir Hugh Orde gave evidence to NIAC, on 9 April 2014, he said there was such an article 3 obligation.[226] That was legally incorrect. Unfortunately, NIAC did not receive written or oral evidence from the PSNI's human rights advisor.

A PSNI press officer (Ken Devlin) had attended the gold meeting, on 7 February 2007. This was in case of any press queries about OTRs. A press release was drafted.[227] It was requested by Downtown Radio, but unsurprisingly – given the anodyne content – it was not used. The PSNI did not seek to announce Operation Rapid.

Report Number One

On 3 March 2007, Norman Baxter (in circumstances which are

---

[224] According to Peter Sheridan, he and David Mercer, a legal advisor, met Barra McGrory on 7 December 2006. The solicitor and the lawyer subsequently exchanged letters. I have not seen those letters. Barra McGrory hesitantly denied it was him. (NIAC, *Report,* Qs1391–2, 10 June 2014)

[225] Norman Baxter told NIAC he received 'legal advice'. (NIAC, *Report,* Q13, 2 April 2014)

[226] NIAC, *Report,* Q314, Qs319–20 & Qs327–8.

[227] The text reads: 'As a result of information made available to the [PSNI], officers from Crime Operations Department are conducting a review of individuals wanted for serious terrorist crime dating back a number of years. Inquiries are at any early stage but Police are working to determine whether there remains a lawful basis for arrest, having regard to current human rights legislation. Where evidence exists, and meets required standards, it remains the role of police to bring those responsible for crime before a court, regardless of their current whereabouts.'

unknown) went to Cambridge university law library. One presumes he was in the city on other police business. He, according to a later note, 'conducted [a] review to ascertain [the] jurisprudence with regard to "reasonable grounds for arrest" post Human Rights Act 1998'. His interest in human rights law is commendable. Several days later (on 6 or 9 March 2007), he drafted a report number one for Peter Sheridan. This contained a list of the first eight names, who were to become not wanted. Seven of them, on earlier review, had been listed as wanted. This document of ten pages is strange: what was the head of C2 branch doing drafting it? Under 'general', he wrote: 'Operation Rapid is a review conducted within the statutory parameters of the [PSNI] and is not the subject of political intervention or influence.' Norman Baxter cannot have believed that. He then included the terms of reference in the document. This was then followed by near six pages on 'law and jurisprudence'. It is difficult to avoid the conclusion that Norman Baxter, who perceived there was political interference, was trying to investigate the constitutionality of the administrative scheme. He may have been doing this, unconsciously. Norman Baxter may have had the right instincts, but he lacked the legal training in this specialized area. By being alert to human rights concerns, he constructed – perhaps inadvertently - a legal edifice of rationalization; if the government was going to exonerate the terrorists, Norman Baxter would be the police officer to legally justify the administrative scheme. That way, he could do his job, or at least be seen to be doing his job, properly.

One can only speculate about what may have been going on in Norman Baxter's head. There is no need to discuss his legal analysis at length. There is clear awareness of police powers in NI. He discusses *O'Hara v Chief Constable of the RUC* [1997] 2 WLR 1, but makes 'reasonable grounds for suspecting' too high a hurdle. The arrest power is then confused with the putative article 3 right of OTRs to know if they are wanted. Article 6 (right to a fair trial) is then dragged in. It is a diversion to criticize Operation Rapid for making legal errors, because the administration scheme came first and report number one simply sought to dignify it legally. The question is: what did the members of

Operation Rapid do? It is unduly legalistic to suggest: wrong legal test led to too many OTRs being declared not wanted. Most likely, the Operation Rapid team ran the arrest test: after all, that was their day job. However, given the absence of Sir Alasdair Fraser, it is likely that the prosecutor' code was also applied, perhaps in a less clear way. Above all, the political momentum in 2007 probably explains Operation Rapid.

The Regina v Hoey Judgment, 20 December 2007

Norman Baxter, in charge of the Omagh investigation, also appears to have been influenced by the judgement of Mr Justice Weir, in the NI crown court, on 20 December 2007. Sean Hoey had faced a total of 58 counts for 13 terrorist incidents, including Omagh. The trial began in September 2006, and lasted 56 days. Mr Justice Weir (giving judgement eleven months later) acquitted the defendant, largely because of the prosecution's reliance upon low copy number DNA, in a context where the police and army had not properly handled forensic samples.

This added to the feeling that it might not be so easy to prosecute successfully republican terrorists whose crimes had been investigated by the PSNI. The case helped tip the scale away from wanted and towards not wanted.

Operation Rapid's Decisions

Attention has come to focus on, what might be called, Operation Rapid's productivity, particularly under Norman Baxter, in 2007–8. It is important to remember three dates: Sinn Féin came out in support of the PSNI on 28 January 2007; the NI assembly was restored on 8 May 2007; and Tony Blair resigned as prime minister on 27 June 2007.

In the twelve months from March 2007, Operation Rapid found the following numbers of OTRs to be not wanted:

- 2007:
  March..8
  April 20
  May 17
  June 4

```
July ........................................................ 0
August ................................................... 0
September ............................................. 10
October ................................................. 0
November .............................................. 0
December ............................................... 0
```

- 2008:
```
January .................................................. 0
February .............................................. 19
```

That was 78 in 12 months, certainly the most productive year, in the period 2000–14. Most of these came from the SF1 and SF2 lists (the SF3 list not being submitted until May 2008). Obviously, Operation Rapid explains the figure. But so too does the focus on the PSNI rather than the PPSNI. And one cannot avoid the political context: Sinn Féin support for the PSNI, the restoration of Stormont and the imminent departure of Tony Blair.

John Downey

The story of John Downey is dealt with separately below, in closer focus, in chapters 8 and 9. He was one of the 17 in May 2007, Norman Baxter making the first of two reports that month on 10 May 2007. He had been preceded, in March and April 2007, with 28 not wanted decisions. There was a dynamic there.

The Various OTR Lists

The following lists have been introduced in chapters 3 and 4:

- SF1, 19 May 2000, 36 (later 41) names;
- IG, no date (before 26 January 2001), four names;
- PL, 11 February 2001, 14 names; and
- SF2, 30 March 2001, 61 (growing to 143) names.

These lists bring the total of applicants to 202. Of those, at least 157 became not wanted. There is one final list.

The Sinn Féin Three List of 19 May 2008

This list is distinct, because it arose out of the Operation Rapid planning. On 7 December 2006, Peter Sheridan, accompanied by the PSNI lawyer, David Mercer, met Barra McGrory. The two latter subsequently exchanged letters. Dame Heather Hallett refers to this list as 'SF3': she characterizes it as comprising names submitted by P.J. McGrory & Co, on behalf of its client, Sinn Féin.

According to appendix 5 of her report, SF3 comprised 35 names. They were submitted between: 19 May and 7 August 2008; with follow ups in 2009, 2010 (one), 2011, 2012 and even 2013 (one).[228]

The success rate was 24 out of 35.[229] But, it must be stressed, members of SF3 remained under review when the administrative scheme collapsed eventually. Again, the following hypothesis is suggested: either the authorities were too ready to suspect republicans; and/or the administrative scheme became a process of letting suspects off, almost regardless of the strength of the evidence. Or, as I have suggested twice above, evidence decays with time.

Operation Rapid: Changes at the Top

Peter Sheridan – after 30 years as a police officer - retired as assistant chief constable of the PSNI, towards the end of 2008. He became chief executive of Co-operation Ireland, on 1 January 2009. Norman Baxter retired the same year, in November 2008. He did not take up a public position, subsequently.

Drew Harris became assistant chief constable crime operations, seemingly as early as 16 September 2008. Norman Baxter was replaced, as head of C2 branch, by Detective Chief Superintendent Derek Williamson. This was also in advance of his retirement. The senior investigating officer of Operation Rapid became Detective Chief Inspector Justyn Galloway.

---

[228] The figure above of 202 plus 35 gives 237. This figures contains nine duplicates. Removing them, gives the OTR total of 228 applicants.

[229] The figure above of at least 157 plus 24 gives 181. This must contain duplicates. The accepted figure for not wanted is 178.

On 25 November 2008, Detective Chief Superintendent Williamson, having sought legal advice, was told that Operation Rapid could relax its prohibition on intelligence gained from detainees, as it might permit arrest. This point raises the question: why did Norman Baxter not seek legal advice when he was in charge (if he did not)? Detective Chief Superintendent Williamson also reviewed the terms of reference, making manuscript amendments. The new terms of reference are not available, but the change amounted to half a page on 'reasonable suspicion'. More significantly, Detective Chief Superintendent Williamson wrote to (seemingly) the new assistant chief constable, Drew Harris: 'I have had a recent meeting with the Director of Public Prosecutions Service and he agrees that the "standard tests" are being applied and should be applied to the review of material both by the PSNI and by the PPS. I have also met with the [NIO] and neither those meetings nor any material made available to me detract from my view that the attached Terms of Reference are necessary…'.[230]

The problem continued. The PSNI and the PPSNI were under political pressure, mediated through Sir Hugh Orde in the case of the former. There was no clear distinction between arrest and prosecution; both bodies were working to find that they did not have enough evidence to proceed against as many OTRs as possible.

The long period of labour government was to come to an end in 2010. Did the David Cameron coalition continue the administrative scheme? The answer – embarrassingly for the conservatives – is yes, though it must be admitted that things were running down.

---

[230] Quoted in Hallett, *Report,* para 5.60.

CHAPTER SEVEN

The Administrative Scheme Wanes, 2010–14

The high point of the administrative scheme was 2007–8. However, it continued after Peter Sheridan and Norman Baxter retired from the PSNI, during the government of Gordon Brown. Why was the administrative scheme not devolved to NI, in April 2010 (when Gordon Brown was still in office)? Important questions also arise regarding the years 2010–14, during which Operation Rapid continued under conservative ministers. What did Owen Paterson do, as conservative secretary of state, in 2010–12? What did his successor, Theresa Villiers, also a conservative, do? And was the administrative scheme closed down definitively, following the Downey abuse of process judgment of February 2014?

Final Figures

The five OTR lists – SF1, IG, PL, SF2 and SF3 – were discussed above. The remaining statistics are, by year (the numbers referring to NIO notifications to Sinn Féin):

2009:	21
2010:	11
2011:	1
2012:	3
2013:	0
2014:	0[231]

The declining numbers do not exonerate government policy and practice, even after Gordon Brown gave way to David Cameron, because of the important principle (political non-interference in prosecution). The administrative scheme, however, – with 35 names in the

---

[231]   Hallett, *Report,* para 5.66.

SF3 list of May 2008 – withered slowly on the vine: it wound down in uncertainty. The coalition government was responsible for the issuing of twelve letters, in 2010-12. Following the arrest of John Downey on 19 May 2013, the PSNI stopped Operation Rapid. There were still names in the system. The coalition government continued to deal with whatever came through, up to – and even beyond - the Downey judgment of 25 February 2014.

The final statistics of the administrative scheme are: 228 applicants to be declared not wanted; and at least 187 being notified, either with a comfort letter to Sinn Féin or the exercise of the royal prerogative of mercy. That was a success rate of 82 per cent, an extraordinary figure for criminal liability. The decisions were based upon admissible evidence, and not upon terrorist intelligence. The high proportion of non-prosecution decisions makes the administrative scheme effectively the grant of immunity.

The Devolution of Policing and Justice Powers

Gordon Brown and his Ministers

Unfortunately, the Downey case papers do not continue much beyond July 2007. One has to avoid inferring that nothing happened on the policy front.

Gordon Brown replaced Tony Blair in June 2007. He certainly never abandoned the administrative scheme. However, it is unclear whether he knew about it. Gordon Brown had once been the leading modernizer in his party, and he did not – as prime minister – undo everything done by his predecessor. But NI, frankly, was not a major issue for him, after the restoration of the assembly in May 2007. Almost from the time he became prime minister, he had the global financial crisis of 2008 to deal with.

The secretary of state for NI, throughout the Brown premiership, was Shaun Woodward. He certainly knew about the administrative scheme. It must be inferred that he was not troubled by it. This is based upon his defensive public comments, following the Downey judgment.

Baroness Scotland QC was the attorney general, for the entirety of the Brown premiership. Unlike Lord Williams of Mostyn and Lord Goldsmith, there is no record of her having given legal advice. That does not mean she did not do so.[232] However, there is nothing in the public domain to suggest that she was uncomfortable with Operation Rapid. By June 2007, the administrative scheme had been running for over seven years, and Operation Rapid was apparently working better than the earlier scheme.

Devolution, 12 April 2010

The devolution of policing and justice powers completed devolution to NI after the Belfast agreement. Three main points may be made. First, ministers, officials and others have sought to portray the administrative scheme as benign, even as normal, and certainly legal. Second, part of the royal prerogative of mercy, on its way to the minister of justice in NI, David Ford, was expressly reserved to London, namely its granting to terrorists. And three, the most likely relevant function devolved, was 'prosecution' – after all, the administrative scheme was referred to as prosecution reviews. It does not fit readily into a different function, namely the 'criminal law', which may be excepted on the ground of national security.

There may have been a security service input into the PSNI, but that does not make the administrative scheme a matter of national security. Blankets may put out fires, but that does not justify the invocation of national security to, reserve the administrative scheme to London, and/or decline to tell the minister of justice in NI that it existed. Nick Perry, about to be transferred from the NIO, to head up the new department of justice in Belfast, told NIAC: 'the Ministers who had responsibility for this issue had decided that it would not devolve. They took that decision, I believe, on the basis of legal advice and the Law Officers supported that advice. ... I was told that functions being

---

[232] Shaun Woodward told NIAC he discussed the administrative scheme with her. (NIAC, *Report,* Q344, 9 April 2014) He also referred to a 'rather thick file' of documents from his time as secretary of state. (NIAC, *Report,* Q366, 9 April 2014)

carried out by the political directorate were not a problem.'[233]

The devolution of policing and justice powers is a matter of law, in particular the effect of amendments to the Northern Ireland Act 1998. To which function did Operation Rapid belong? And was that function designated for Belfast or London? It was not a question for ministerial decision. However, the NIO obviously interpreted the law, to justify its apparent reservation of the power and duty in London. Nick Perry suggests that the question asked was: did the functions of the political directorate have to be transferred? The answer was clearly no. But that raises the question of whether the political directorate could continue with the administrative scheme. Obviously, it feared having to disclose its existence to David Ford, and his anticipated hostility to such a scheme.

Evidence

NIAC heard in public in Belfast from Nick Perry, David Ford and John Larkin QC on this issue, and also in public in London from Owen Paterson and Dominic Grieve QC.

Nick Perry was private secretary to Mo Mowlam and then Peter Mandelson, as secretary of state. He remained in the NIO, travelling between Belfast and London. By 2010, he was in charge of the devolution of policing and justice. He knew about the administrative scheme, but he told NIAC he had never seen a comfort letter.[234] He saw it as a public interest question, which it was not (it was a matter of insufficient evidence). In April 2010, he moved to the new department of justice as permanent secretary. He believes the NIO took legal advice, about the administrative scheme being reserved in London.[235] But he also suggested that he did not know the administrative scheme continued after devolution: 'I was not aware until the outcome of the Downey case that the scheme continued to operate after devolution.'[236] That became

---

[233] NIAC, *Report,* Qs1025 & 1043, 9 June 2014.

[234] NIAC, *Report,* Qs998 & 1043, 9 June 2014.

[235] NIAC, *Report,* Q1025, 9 June 2014.

[236] NIAC, *Report,* Q969 (see also Q1050), 9 June 2014.

his reason (aside from an argument about change of government[237]), for not discussing the matter with David Ford, his new minister in Belfast.

David Ford became the minister for justice on 12 April 2010. He evidently knew nothing of the administrative scheme.[238] It is another matter entirely, what he would have done if it had been devolved (and Nick Perry had argued that it should be allowed to run down quietly). He says he would have refused to touch it.[239] David Ford declined to disclose the legal advice he received after Downey.[240] He was clearly opposed to the administrative scheme: 'The reality is: it was [the NIO's] scheme. They implemented it. They bear responsibility for it morally. You are almost suggesting that I should somehow take over and try to sort out the mess that they have created.'[241] But NI's minister of justice did not articulate the key question: if the administrative scheme had been legally devolved to him (regardless of whether he wanted it), then the NIO had no power in law to continue with it.[242]

John Larkin QC also declined to disclose his legal view of the administrative scheme, as being a devolved or reserved function. He cited the law officers' convention of not disclosing the content of advice, and even whether it existed.[243] But that is only a convention, and Lord Goldsmith QC disclosed his opinion on the legality of the Iraq war, in March 2003, admittedly a much more important matter.[244]

Owen Paterson gave an interesting answer to NIAC regarding devolution: 'When we came in there was still great uncertainty about devolution of policing ... I cannot remember a single person at that time suggesting that we should have handed over this issue to the very

---

[237] The Whitehall convention about officials not discussing business with succeeding ministers was applied, to devolution from London to Belfast. (NIAC, *Report*, Q1207, 9 June 2014) The two are related but not the same thing.

[238] NIAC, *Report*, Q1186, 9 June 2014.

[239] NIAC, *Report*, Q1200, 9 June 2014.

[240] NIAC, *Report*, Q1198, 9 June 2014.

[241] NIAC, *Report*, Q1222, 9 June 2014.

[242] NIAC, *Report*, Q1205, 9 June 2014.

[243] NIAC, *Report*, Qs1623-1638, 10 June 2014.

[244] Advice to the PM, 'Iraq: Resolution 1441', 7 March 2003.

new devolved Minister, but, after two years when his position was stable and settled and it was all working well, we were really getting [some]where.'[245]

Dominic Grieve was asked, in June 2012, to advise the NIO on whether the administrative scheme had been devolved.[246] He hinted, albeit not too clearly, that it had left the NIO: 'It can be argued, and perfectly clearly argued, that, if somebody wishes to get a letter of the type that we have been looking at, post-2010, then the place to go is to write directly to the only two entities that could actually respond, because there is no filter channel through the [NI] Executive, which would be the DPP and the police.'[247] But he also seemed to suggest that the power had not arrived in the DOJ. And, apparently developing a legal justification for what had happened, he concocted a new role for the NIO as post-boy. But this surely was to confuse two things: namely the power having been devolved to Belfast; and the minister, David Ford, being opposed to exercising it. It would appear that the NIO, confronted with David Ford's likely opposition, simply allowed Operation Rapid to continue while acquiescing in the absence of ministerial accountability in London. Dominic Grieve's legal analysis does not even record that it was the NIO which continued to issue the letters. Regarding all the letters from April 2010, a particular – devolution – legal doubt must hang over them, separate from general legal concerns about the administrative scheme.

The conclusion on the devolution of policing and justice powers is: on 12 April 2010, Operation Rapid, within the PSNI, became the responsibility of the department of justice in NI; it therefore follows that the NIO lost any legal powers it had exercised. Clearly, Nick Perry should have told David Ford. Equally clearly, he did not. Ultimately,

---

[245] NIAC, *Report,* Q2671, 10 September 2014. See also, Q2791, 10 September 2014.

[246] NIAC, *Report,* Q2166, 2 July 2014.

[247] NIAC, *Report,* Q2204, 2 July 2014. He did go on to refer to national security, and the DPP in NI consulting him as advocate general. See also, NIAC, *Report,* Qs2220, 2224, 2226–2230, 2 July 2014.

it was the responsibility of the NIO: it should have tabled the issue in advance of devolution.

However, what civil servants in London did on devolution day became obscured by the change of government shortly afterwards, in May 2010.

The Conservatives in Office

Owen Paterson MP

David Cameron took over at number 10 in May 2010. He, as noted above, appointed Owen Paterson as secretary of state for NI (the minister of state was Hugo Swire MP). The new secretary of state had occupied the shadow post for nearly three years, and came to office interested and experienced.

Evidence

Owen Paterson told NIAC that, when he was shadow secretary of state, Shaun Woodward never told him about the administrative scheme. He received a briefing when he became secretary of state, in May 2010. But his recollection was that other issues effectively excluded it from consideration. He adopted a policy of continuing with the existing names. When, in the summer of 2012, it looked like Sinn Féin might produce a further list, the secretary of state began to have second thoughts.

In July 2012, Owen Paterson had one of his regular meetings with Gerry Adams at Leinster House in Dublin, the latter having stopped abstaining at Westminster to be elected to Dáil Éireann, which he attended. The president of Sinn Féin complained again about OTRs. Owen Paterson appears to have indicated that he should now pursue the matter in Belfast: 'I am increasingly coming to the conclusion that, following the devolution of policing and justice functions to the Northern Ireland Assembly, there is little that I can do to take the issue forward.'[248] This begs the obvious question: why had he not said this

---

[248]   Letter, [?] August 2012.

in May 2010? And, if he was correct in July 2012, what did that say about the unlawful exercise of powers reserved by London?

Dominic Grieve, who was briefed in writing when he became attorney general, told NIAC that he was not aware that the administrative scheme was continuing in May 2010.[249] Owen Paterson raised the issue with him in June 2012, on the fringes of a cabinet meeting. The attorney general provided advice subsequently to the secretary of state.[250] He too declined to tell NIAC what he advised, but it was consistent with previous attorneys 'which was to express reservations about of the operation of the scheme and its effect, particularly on prosecutorial decision-making…'.[251]

It is known that, on 18 July 2012, Dominic Grieve wrote to Owen Paterson, 'flag[ging] up a concern that Westminster should no longer be involved in the process in the light of the devolution of justice.' In a later letter, of December 2012, the attorney general stated he no longer wished to be involved in the administrative scheme.[252]

Theresa Villiers MP

Owen Paterson was promoted to environment, in September 2012. His successor as secretary of state was Theresa Villiers, a former member of the European parliament, who had become a transport minister in 2010. Her ministers of state were successively: Mike Penning; Andrew Robathan; Dr Andrew Murrison.

Shortly after being appointed, Julian King briefed Theresa Villiers on the administrative scheme. She stated she agreed with Owen Paterson's decision: 'There was … a recognition that, if we had cases already in the system, they could continue to be dealt with. We would not take on new cases…'.[253] Asked about telephoning David Ford,

---

[249] NIAC, *Report*, Q2160, 2 July 2014. See also, NIAC, *Report*, Q2235, 2 July 2014.

[250] NIAC, *Report*, Q2162, 2 July 2014.

[251] NIAC, *Report*, Q2163, 2 July 2014.

[252] Barra McGrory, written evidence, 6 June 2014, para 34.

[253] NIAC, *Report*, Q2419, 3 September 2014.

Theresa Villiers said: 'I am afraid it did not [occur to me], and that is something I do regret.'[254] Echoing Dominic Grieve on grey areas in devolution, she went on: 'I would emphasise that there was no question of [the administrative scheme] being devolved to the Department of Justice. All we were doing was advising Sinn Féin to go directly to the devolved police and prosecuting authorities.'[255] The power, or rather duty, had to be in Belfast or in London. It seems that the NIO, having lost it, nevertheless acquiesced in Operation Rapid continuing, without ministerial accountability.

On her second appearance before NIAC, on 19 January 2015, the secretary of state went further: 'As Heather Hallett put it, you would have to be a very astute observer to fit together all the pieces in order to get a clear idea of what was happening. I completely agree … that it should have been handled more transparently by the previous Government. I regret that I did not discuss it with the Ministry of Justice when I was first briefed about it.'[256]

The End of the Administrative Scheme

The arrest of John Downey at Gatwick in May 2013 quickly came to the attention of the PSNI. That is when the NI police learned first about the NIO letters to OTRs.[257] Assistant chief constable Drew Harris told NIAC: 'I also … learned, and was very shocked to learn, of the weight that may be placed in one of those letters … I returned to the office and sent a direction to my own staff, but I sent communications to the Northern Ireland Office: because of the uncertainty around the legal challenge, because of the risk now of abuse of process, because it went so far past the Good Friday Agreement – this was 2013, so

---

[254] NIAC, *Report,* Q2420, 3 September 2014.
[255] NIAC, *Report,* Q2421, 3 September 2014.
[256] NIAC, *Report,* Q3847, 19 January 2015.
[257] It is incorrect that the PSNI learned of the NIO letters, in December 2011. A member of PPSNI told one member of the PSNI. There was no formal notification, by the NIO: Northern Ireland policing board, minutes, September 2014 (question re Hallett).

some 15 years later – we were now withdrawing and suspending our role in that.'[258]

The Downey judgment, as noted, became available on Tuesday, 25 February 2014. The secretary of state – in a written statement to the house of commons – asked for more time to consider 'its full implications'. There were some not quite accurate admissions: an administrative scheme from around September 2000; around two hundred applicants; around three quarters succeeding; the fault of labour (which did not disclose fully to parliament), but not the coalition parties; not immunity and certainly no amnesty; new applicants had been referred to the devolved authorities in NI. John Downey was credited with carrying his letter (inaccurately). No claim was made about the significance of the judgment. But the NIO blamed particularly police officers: 'The judge concluded that the error had been made by officers of the PSNI' (which he did not do).[259]

The following day, Theresa Villiers took NI questions (immediately before the prime minister's weekly slot). The secretary of state continued to blame the PSNI: 'there [should be] a thorough investigation into the grave mistake of the PSNI which, I am afraid, led to the outcome in the case yesterday.' Peter Hain was unapologetic, having helped bring NI (as he put it) 'from the hideous horror and evil of the past to the position where old enemies have now governed together for seven years…'.[260]

After prime minister's questions, the attorney general, Dominic Grieve QC MP, made a statement. There had been an urgent question from Laurence Robertson, the chair of NIAC. There were questions for an hour. In his earlier written statement, the attorney had stated that there would be no appeal of the Downey judgment.[261] His oral defence of government policy ranged more widely.[262]

David Ford had not been amused to have the administrative

---

[258] NIAC, *Report*, Q703, 7 May 2014.
[259] HC, *Hansard*, vol. 576, cols. 16WS-17WS, 25 February 2014.
[260] HC *Hansard*, vol. 576, cols. 248-9, 26 February 2014.
[261] HC *Hansard*, vol. 576, col. 19WS, 25 February 2014.
[262] This statement is considered further in chapter 11.

scheme foisted upon him. He met the secretary of state (earlier than arranged) in Belfast, on the evening of 26 February 2014: 'I can say that we had a robust exchange, and the Secretary of State apologised … for wrongly implying that my Department was responsible for the scheme.'[263]

The secretary of state laid a further written statement on 28 February 2014, announcing there was to be a review. Theresa Villiers clarified that, in May 2010, the coalition government had agreed to continue the administrative scheme, for the names already handed over by Sinn Féin. However, she signalled its imminent demise: 'We will take whatever steps are necessary to make clear to all recipients of letters arising from the administrative scheme, in a manner that will satisfy the courts and the public, that any letters issued cannot be relied upon to avoid questioning or prosecution for offences where information or evidence becomes available now or later.'[264]

The NI assembly debated the Downey judgment, in a special sitting on Friday, 28 February 2014. Peter Robinson, the first minister, proposed a motion, which 'expresse[d] disgust at the heretofore deliberately hidden actions of the British Government and Sinn Féin…'. It referred to 'the gross injustice to the many victims who will suffer further because of these shameful actions…'. The motion was passed by 58 votes to 27. Unionists and the alliance party voted for: Sinn Féin alone voted against; and 13 members of the social democratic and labour party actively abstained by voting in both lobbies! David Ford, speaking as a party leader, indicated that the administrative scheme had never been devolved: a senior NIO official had told him that morning that London would continue to handle the last five cases in the pipeline.[265]

On 7 March 2014, in a speech in Belfast to European journalists, Theresa Villiers stated: 'so far as this government is concerned, the [administrative] scheme is over.'[266]

---

[263] Committee for justice, 3 April 2014, p. 2.
[264] HC, *Hansard*, vol. 576, cols. 38WS–40WS, 28 February 2014.
[265] *Official Report*, vol. 95, no. 5, pp. 1–26, 28 February 2014.
[266] NIO, transcript, 7 March 2014.

There was a third written statement from the government, on 25 March 2014, further disclosing details of the administrative scheme: 228 applicants in total; 45 (not 38) pending cases in May 2010; and twelve comfort letters issued by the government, up until December 2012. The NIO seemed preoccupied with the Hallett inquiry: because she referred to 'work to reconcile the different information held by the Northern Ireland Office, the … PSNI … and Sinn Fein to determine the actual numbers dealt with by the scheme.'[267] It is significant that the NIO did not even mention the PPSNI. It is remarkable that the NIO was continuing to work with Sinn Féin on the matter.

Backbenchers in the house of commons secured a debate on the Downey judgment, on Thursday, 27 March 2014. Theresa Villiers responded for the government: 'The scheme and the era of side deals [an echo of Mark Durkan MP] that undermined confidence in the political process must come to an end, and we now need to look forward.[268]

Dame Heather Hallett reported on 17 July 2014. Subsequently, on 4 September 2014, the NIO established a OTR policy oversight board, chaired by the permanent secretary. This was to implement the recommendations in her report. One thinks of horses and stable doors. The board comprised all the actors in the administrative scheme, but now with a determination to deal with the consequences. The department of justice in NI was given observer status.

It was to be Tuesday, 9 September 2014 – with an oral statement on the Hallett report – before the secretary of state told the OTRs holding comfort letters that they were worthless: 'those who have received such statements now know in clear terms what position the Government takes. They now have fair and clear warning that such comfort as they may have derived from the statements can no longer be taken. There is no continuing basis for any reliance on the past statements. This scheme is at an end. [] All those who sought or received statements through the administrative scheme should take note of this statement today. I have deliberately made it in the public setting of Parliament,

---

267 HC, *Hansard,* vol. 578, cols. 15WS–16WS, 25 March 2014.
268 HC, *Hansard,* vol. 578, cols. 558–63, 27 March 2014.

recognising and intending that it should be widely publicised as a result. I will take further steps to disseminate it. I will be drawing it to the attention of each of those who made requests on behalf of named individuals, reflecting the channels through which the communication of the original letters was made. In these ways, I can be confident that fair and proper notice will have been given to those affected by this statement, including those to whom letters were sent under the scheme.'[269]

The version of the oral statement on the NIO website began with the byline: 'Villiers addresses Hallett recommendations and tells individuals who received letters through the OTR scheme that they can not rely on them.' Whatever of the syntax, the message was clear.

It is debateable how widely this parliamentary statement circulated.[270] The secretary of state referred obliquely to Gerry Kelly. It is unknown whether he passed on whatever the NIO sent him.

One detects the hand of government lawyers in this statement to parliament, on 9 September 2014. The letters were essentially revoked. But can one make a promise, and then withdraw it? That question remains.

It is possible to identify the end of the administrative scheme as 9 September 2014. But the consequence of further Downey-type abuse of process applications requires returning to the Downey case in detail.

---

[269] HC, *Hansard,* vol. 585, cols. 780–1, 9 September 2014.
[270] The well-known Nuzhound daily selection of press stories on NI shows very little reporting of the secretary of state on 10 September 2014: *www.irishcentral. com/news/thenorth.*

Rights and International Relations Division

Northern Ireland Office
Political Directorate
Rights and International
Relations Division
11 Millbank
London
SW1P 4PN

Mark Sweeney
Head of Division
Northern Ireland Office

Gerry Kelly MLA
Sinn Féin
51-55 Falls Road
Belfast
BT12 4PD

July 07

'ON THE RUNS'

You have previously been in correspondence with the Northern Ireland Office about a number of individuals who are currently on the run but want to return to Northern Ireland and wish to be informed of their status if they were to do so.

Following investigations made by the relevant authorities in Northern Ireland I can now confirm that the necessary checks have been completed on ten more individuals.

On the basis of the information currently held, in respect of the following ten individuals, there is no outstanding direction for prosecution in Northern Ireland, there are no warrants in existence nor are they wanted in Northern Ireland for arrest, questioning or charge by the police:

- [102] John Anthony Downey, DOB 19.01.1952, Creeslough

Rights and International
Relations Division

I enclose a letter informing each of the position. As we do not have an address for these individuals, I would be grateful if you would ensure that these letters are passed on to them.

Yours sincerely,

Mark Sweeney
Head of Division

Northern Ireland Office
Political Directorate
Rights and International
Relations Division
11 Millbank
London
SW1P 4PN

Mark Sweeney
Head of Division
Northern Ireland Office

Rights and International Relations Division

Mr John Anthony Downey
Via Gerry Kelly

July 2007

The Secretary of State for Northern Ireland has been informed by the Attorney General that on the basis of the information currently available, there is no outstanding direction for prosecution in Northern Ireland, there are no warrants in existence nor are you wanted in Northern Ireland for arrest, questioning or charge by the police. The Police Service of Northern Ireland are not aware of any interest in you from any other police force in the United Kingdom. If any other outstanding offence or offences came to light, or if any request for extradition were to be received, these would have to be dealt with in the usual way.

MARK SWEENEY

CHAPTER EIGHT

John Downey: Wanted Republican

John Downey denies any involvement in the Hyde Park, and Regent's Park, bombing of 20 July 1982. He admits to being an Irish republican, still. He was convicted of IRA membership, in the Republic of Ireland. And the police in NI treated him as a criminal suspect, for a series of serious terrorist offences there in the 1970s.

John Downey's Background, 1952-82

John Anthony Downey was born in Kilrush, in Co. Clare, on 19 January 1952: 'I was born into a very Republican family ... and my father, Stephen, had been a member of the IRA since he was sixteen when he joined up to fight the Black and Tans in 1920. He later fought against "the free Staters" in the Civil war ... I took a lot of my value[s] and beliefs from my father as I grew up and my mother, Mary, and her uncles were also involved in the war against the black and tans.'[271]

He too was sixteen, when NI exploded in 1968. He watched the troubles from Co. Clare, on a black-and-white television. John Downey admits to joining the IRA, seemingly when it re-formed in 1970: 'I felt that I could not ignore the situation in the north and pretend that my fellow Irish men and women had nothing to do with me. I could see, at that time…, that nothing was going to be accomplished by peaceful means and we had to fight fire with fire'.[272]

On 28 February 1974 (when he was 22 years), John Downey was accused of being a member of the IRA. This took place in the Republic of Ireland. He was convicted on 21 May 1974, and sent to Portlaoise prison for, it is believed, two years.

He was arrested, for a second time, again by the Irish police. This

---

271 *Donegal Democrat*, 13 March 2014.
272 *Donegal Democrat*, 13 March 2014.

time, John Downey was acquitted of IRA membership by an Irish court, on 4 October 1976. There were further arrests.

Sean O'Callaghan – born in Tralee, Co. Kerry in 1954 – had a similar background: he joined the IRA in 1970 in the west of Ireland. He rose to become head of southern command (in 1985). But, following the killing of Lord Mountbatten in 1979 in Co. Sligo, he had become an unpaid informant for the Irish police. In his book, *The Informer*, published in 1998 (after serving eight years in prison), he refers to John Downey twice: as a frontline operator in the IRA's English department, in 1982; and, in 1983, when he, and then John Downey, were declared wanted by the metropolitan police.[273]

The Hyde Park Bombing, 1982

John Downey was, and remains, a prime suspect for the Hyde Park bombing of 20 July 1982. (A former suspect, Gilbert 'Danny' McNamee, was arrested in NI in 1986, and convicted at the Old Bailey the following year. His finger prints were on a circuit board, used in the car bomb. The prosecution did not disclose that a Dessie Ellis, then in prison in the Republic of Ireland, was suspected of being the bomb maker. Following a referral from the new criminal cases review commission, Danny McNamee was released by the court of appeal in England and Wales in 1998, the non-disclosure making the conviction unsafe.)

The Downey case papers include, at tab 7, 312 pages – running from July 1983 to July 1995 – during which the law officers considered extraditing him from the Republic of Ireland. The English attorneys general (all conservative MPs) were: Sir Michael Havers (1979–87); Sir Patrick Mayhew (1987–92); and Sir Nicholas Lyell (1992–7).[274] The Irish attorneys general were: Peter Sutherland (1982–4, Fine Gael); John Rogers (1984–7, labour); and John L. Murray (1987–91, Fianna Fáil). If there was consistency between the English attorneys, there was

---

[273] Pp. 143 & 154. Downey's lawyers, however, only referred to the latter reference, citing a paperback edition of the book.

[274] The former died on 1 April 1992. Lord Mayhew died 25 June 2016. The latter died on 30 August 2010.

more variation in Dublin: Peter Sutherland was evidently anti-IRA, John Rogers was more a rule-of-law man, and John L. Murray – who would be chief justice in 2004–11 – was identified with a governing party which styled itself 'the republican party'.

Why Was John Downey Not Extradited?

John Downey lived openly in the Republic of Ireland. In 1986, he moved to Creeslough, in Co. Donegal. Two years later, he started an oyster business. A number of evidential issues was involved in his possible extradition from the Republic of Ireland.

First, two NCP[275] parking tickets, for Portman Square and the Royal Garden hotel (where the car carrying the bomb had been parked), bearing John Downey's finger prints. The metropolitan police got a lead on 13 August 1982. However, it was unable to trace two (or three) Nigerian attendants. There was also a changing legal background, regarding the admissibility of such business records. This evidential problem, however, appears to have been overcome by June 1987.

Second, his finger prints. John Downey's finger prints were taken by the Irish police in 1980. Despite police cooperation between London and Dublin (including the idea of a sham arrest), there was a host of legal issues to be considered in both jurisdictions. But it took until September 1988, before the metropolitan police could confirm that the parking tickets bore John Downey's finger prints.

Third, extradition between the Republic of Ireland and England and Wales. This was a variant on the question of extradition to NI. It was a long-running sore in UK-Irish relations. However, there was no Irish legal case on soldiers killed in England and Wales.

Under the council of Europe's 1957 convention on extradition, there was a so-called political offences defence. Irish courts equivocated about the extradition of IRA terrorists to mainly NI, the apogee of this being: *Finucane* [1990] IR 165. By then, the council of Europe's 1977 convention on the suppression of terrorism, had limited the defence

---

[275] National car parks.

– in international law only. The Republic of Ireland did not sign this convention until 1986, and it did not ratify it until 1989. But it was given domestic effect with: the Extradition (European Convention on the Suppression of Terrorism) Act 1987, which came into operation in the Republic of Ireland on 1 December 1987.

The English attorney general and the director of public prosecutions of England and Wales, with other departments in the background, dithered over seeking to extradite John Downey after 1982. On the one hand, there were the above two evidential problems. On the other, there was the 1985 Anglo-Irish agreement to bed in, and the fear that the Irish state would continue to be uncooperative. Officials in London kept waiting for Irish supreme court decisions, in the hope of a jurisprudential breakthrough. The Evelyn Glenholmes's case did not help: nine warrants had been issued (twice) by the metropolitan police in 1984; in March 1986, an Irish court dismissed the case because the warrants should have been re-sworn in London. Towards the end of the decade, the English attorney general became concerned about the delay since the Hyde Park bombing. On 21 November 1989, Sir Patrick Mayhew decided finally not to proceed with extradition: '… at present relations with the Irish authorities regarding extradition were good and he did not wish to jeopardise those good relations by putting forward a case in which the Irish Attorney General could quite legitimately decide that the warrants should not be backed.'[276]

There was an underlying problem with the finger prints. The Irish police held these, but it was not acting against John Downey. The UK needed to be able to mount a *prima facie* case in the Republic of Ireland, according to the Irish courts. It faced a double bind. It was thought that it could not use the Irish finger prints. But the UK needed to extradite John Downey, in order to take his finger prints in London, to use in a prosecution there. It would not obtain extradition in order to obtain what it needed in the first place.

John Downey's extradition file was put away in the attorney general's office in November 1989. It was not considered again, until after

---

[276] Note of conference, 21 November 1989. (Downey case papers, tab 7, pp. 280–1)

his arrest in May 2013. He appears to have remained outside the UK, until he was sent his letter in 2007.

The Wanted Suspect

In May 1983, the metropolitan police – issuing an artist's impression (based upon a photograph!) - indicated that John Downey was wanted. His name and status were added to the police national computer, on 29 May 1983. His entry then read: 'suspected ans[sic] wanted for conspiracy to Murder on or before 20th July 1982'.[277] The reference to conspiracy, and the period before the Hyde Park bombing, is extremely important as regards jurisdiction, namely England and Wales versus NI.

John Downey's name went to the home secretary, when, following the Brighton bombing on 12 October 1984, Sir Leon Brittan made a statement to the house of commons, on 22 October 1984.[278] Among his notes is a paragraph on the clear up of terrorist crimes, which includes the following: 'A man, who is understood to be living in the Republic of Ireland, is wanted by police in connection with the Hyde Park bomb attack in July 1982, and the preparation of a case for his extradition is in hand. (See separate note on Downey).'[279]

John Downey was associated with the Hyde Park, and Regent's Park, bombing in a number of press reports. The sources appear to have been from within the metropolitan police. On 21 October 1984, the *Sunday Times* – which had been following John Downey in the Republic of Ireland – revealed him as a key suspect. There were follow-up stories, in the same paper, in June 1985, March 1986 and October 1987. On 23 January 1986, the *Daily Telegraph* referred to John Downey, in a story associating him with Sean O'Callaghan: the latter being referred to as 'the jackal'. In June 1987, the (short lived) *London Daily News* published two articles on John Downey.

---

[277] Report exhibited to witness statement, DS Stephen Walker, 15 January 2014.
[278] HC, *Hansard*, vol. 65, cols. 435–9, 22 October 1984.
[279] This separate note is not in the number 10 file: PREM 19/1632, National Archives (Kew).

John Downey continued to be wanted by the metropolitan police, through the 1990s. For a short while, 29 August to 31 October 1994, his name was missing from the police national computer. With extradition having not been pursued, he was safe as long as he did not enter NI, or Great Britain. John Downey looked to his personal security. He, and a handful of others, know whether he was, and is, telling the truth about Hyde Park, or not. Given the staying of his prosecution, one may only speculate. It is a respectable republican response to deny criminal liability, partly out of continuing defiance of the UK.

The Administrative Scheme

There are two aspects to John Downey's involvement in the administrative scheme, from 2000. The first is that the PSNI continued to list him as wanted. The second – more decisively – is that Operation Rapid gave him the all clear, in June 2007. A range of NI crimes was in issue, little attention being paid to the Hyde Park bombing.

John Downey Joins the Scheme, 10 January 2002

John Downey has no difficulty explaining away his IRA career of the 1970s, 1980s and probably 1990s. He does it with the republican concept of a peace process: 'From all sides war is ugly. I became involved in the strategy, when it became apparent that our political aims could be achieved through peaceful means.'[280] In other words, he remained loyal to Gerry Adams and Martin McGuinness: the republicans' strategy shifted from violence to politics, though the IRA remained in charge of Sinn Féin. If John Downey had not remained within the republican movement, he would not have been eligible *de facto* for the administrative scheme. Gerry Kelly was the gatekeeper.

John Downey was not on the SF1 list, of 19 May 2000 – in the first 36 to 41 names, collected by Gerry Kelly. He was, however, on the SF2 list, which went to the NIO on 30 March 2001, and was added to until as late as August 2006. John Downey is revealed, in the Hallett

---

[280] *Donegal Democrat*, 13 March 2014.

report, as SF2/102, his date of application being 10 January 2002 (as part of a batch of 25 names on a single sheet, which was called SF list 6 by the NIO initially).

John Downey Fails, 2004–6

Appendix 5 of the Hallett report reveals the following consideration of his case:

- 14 September 2004: PSNI tells PPSNI, wanted in NI;
- 26 September 2005: NIO tells Sinn Féin, under review;
- 31 January 2006: PSNI tells NIO, wanted in NI;
- 8 February 2006: PPSNI tells attorney general's office, wanted in NI;
- 27 February 2006, attorney general's office tells NIO, wanted in NI;
- 22 March 2006: NIO tells Sinn Féin, wanted in NI.[281]

It is not clear why the NIO relented in September 2005, by referring to review. There is also a problem with why the PSNI wrote direct to the NIO, in January 2006. The picture is otherwise clear: John Downey made his application on 10 January 2002; on 22 March 2006 – over four years' later – Sinn Féin was told he was wanted in NI.

The PSNI had six possible cases against John Downey, the intelligence (and evidence) on each comprising a template. These had been compiled first in 2003. The following is ascertainable from police records, the templates being presumably chronological:

- Template 1: ?
- template 2: 25.08.72: Enniskillen: killing two Ulster Defence Regiment soldiers;[282]
- template 3: 21.09.72: Co. Fermanagh: killing Thomas and Emily Bullock;

---

[281] One of three names.

[282] The deaths of James Eames and Alfred Johnston are given as 25 and 27 August 1972 respectively, in David McKittrick et al., eds., *Lost Lives,* Edinburgh & London 2007, p. 255. On 28 May 1985, the DPP directed no prosecution in the absence of additional evidence.

- template 4: ?
- template 5: ?
- template 6: 20.07.82: Hyde Park.

According to RUC special branch records, John Downey had first come to attention in 1971, in the Fermanagh/Donegal area. Special branch knew about Hyde Park. He was last heard of in 1996, his whereabouts being surprisingly unknown. This makes for a terrorist career of 25 years.

There is no doubt that the PSNI knew about Hyde Park. A redacted copy of template 6 is available in the Downey case papers, attached to an assessment form.[283] The police national computer appears to have been accessed on 30 April 2002, by the PSNI.

Very significantly, when the PSNI wrote to the PPSNI, on 14 September 2004, it stated: 'this person is sought for arrest and interview in relation to a number of serious terrorist offences.'[284] These were NI offences. It did not, though it evidently knew about Hyde Park, refer to a crime which was the responsibility of the metropolitan police.

And when the attorney general wrote much later to the secretary of state, then Peter Hain, on 27 February 2006, the letter stated simply: 'Downey is wanted for arrest and questioning in respect of serious terrorist offences.' This came from the PSNI. There was no reference to the metropolitan police, and the Hyde Park bombing.

Conclusion

The conclusion is stark, regarding John Downey's two failed attempts, in 2002–6, to get an OTR letter. The PSNI knew all about Hyde Park, since it listed it as template 6. But it was concerned principally with template 2 (Enniskillen, 1972), and questioning John Downey on it plus the other four NI templates. The small number of people involved, all assumed that the PSNI was referring only to being wanted in NI; they included at the time: Sir Alasdair Fraser;

---

[283] Downey case papers, tab 8, pp. 681–94.
[284] Letter, 14 September 2004. (Downey case papers, tab 8, p. 702)

Mark Sweeney (of the NIO); Kevin McGinty; Lord Goldsmith; and Peter Hain.

Not one of them expected the PSNI to deal with Hyde Park, and the NI police did not. But all that was to change, when John Downey was shifted from wanted to not wanted by Operation Rapid. Then, the question of template 6 and the Hyde Park bombing exposed the poor design of the administrative scheme.

CHAPTER NINE

John Downey Gets a Letter, 20 July 2007

The evidence regarding the John Downey letters reveals a more complicated, and surprising, picture than so far revealed. The general factors have been considered in chapter 6 on Operation Rapid. More particularly, the police team, led by Peter Sheridan and Norman Baxter, conducted themselves as their predecessors had done, in 2000–6. If we need to blame someone for the Operation Rapid mistake, it is undoubtedly Mark Sweeney, head of the rights and international relations division of the NIO. He is liable for criticism principally because: one, he did not invite the metropolitan police (whose job it was), through the attorney general's office, to review John Downey's prosecution for the Hyde Park bombing; and two, he did not send his draft John Downey letter to the PSNI in advance, for Norman Baxter to check. His reason, in each case, related to the difficulty of civil servants becoming involved in criminal justice: the NIO sought to use the more compliant PSNI to do two jobs.

John Downey

Did the PSNI know that John Downey was wanted for Hyde Park? The answer is incontrovertibly yes. But a distinction needs to be made: the PSNI, and everyone else involved, was concerned about John Downey being wanted in NI; the police in NI, in 2002–6, knew that John Downey was on the police national computer as wanted by the metropolitan police. But its non-inclusion of template 6 in their assessments (chapter 8) – unnoticed by anyone at the time – was not deleterious then to the conclusion that he was also wanted for alleged NI crimes.

John Downey, it may be recalled, went on the police national computer on 29 May 1983. With the exception of the August-October 1994 dropping off, he remained on it to, and through, July 2007. His entry read: 'Wanted for murder, if arrested inform S O 13. Evidence is by way of fingerprint.'[285]

John Downey was not in the first Operation Rapid batch of eight cases, which led to report number one of 6/9 March 2007. However, his file appears to have been considered later that month, by the NI team.

The Metropolitan Police Email of 13 April 2007

On the morning of 13 April 2007, Howard (Robert) Ming, one of the three civilian members of Operation Rapid, called a detective constable, Pam Bahia,[286] in New Scotland Yard. He was inquiring about four IRA members believed to be wanted in England and Wales: two (including John Downey) were wanted for the Hyde Park bombing;[287] and two were wanted for other offences.

The telephone call may not have been conclusive, because, at 12.04, Howard Ming emailed the four names, asking for confirmation. At 12.27, Pam Bahia replied: 'As confirmed that Downey is shown as wanted. At present [name redacted] appears to be not shown as wanted. [] I will check the other two [names redacted] and let you know. Just for your information they have been already checked and could not find them in the "register". I will check with another office.'

This was not a straight answer, suggesting the question was not easy. However, in the case of John Downey, he was shown as wanted. That was the clear message conveyed electronically across the Irish sea on 13 April 2007.

That same day, presumably Howard Ming updated template 6 in John Downey's file. Significantly, he noted: 'No case papers are available in Northern Ireland.' He concluded: 'Should Downey be arrested in Northern Ireland for offences here we would [be] duty bound to inform S O 13. New Scotland Yard.' The implication was that Downey would be tried for NI crimes, if any. Howard Ming's answer, however, did

---

[285] Quoted in updated template 6, 13 April 2007. (Downey case papers, tab 8, pp. 760–1)

[286] In SCD6, presumably part of SO15, the counter terrorism command.

[287] The identity of the other is not known.

not address the crucial question: would the PSNI arrest John Downey (if found in NI), solely to hand him over to the metropolitan police? There was a serious jurisdictional problem beckoning.

The PSNI Assessment of 7 May 2007

On 7 May 2007, Neal Graham at Clogher police station, Operation Rapid's senior investigating officer, completed John Downey's assessment. He would have reviewed the full file of six templates.[288] The assessment deserves to be quoted fully (after redaction), as indented below:

> A review has now been completed in respect of [John Downey], with due consideration being given to the agreed Terms of Reference.
>
> All the Templates in relation to Subject are based on intelligence, and relate to the following
>
> …
>
> ≥ Bomb at Hyde Park, London – 20.7.82
>
> **REVIEW OF EVIDENCE**
> Having carefully considered all the above templates, the following considerations are now given
>
> …
>
> + In respect of template 6, this relates to a Bombing in England on 20.7.82. I have reviewed the papers and can find no evidence that would indicate that Subject is wanted by the PSNI for this offence. He is still wanted by the Metropolitan Police subject to any further new evidence.
>
> + In respect of the other templates, there is no evidence or material that can provide sufficient grounds to have the Subject circulated at this time.

---

[288] Tom Little's disclosure report, of 30 January 2014, in the Downey case papers (tab 2), indicates the work Neal Graham did on 2 May 2007. He took a day over templates 1 to 5. His manuscript copy of template 6, between 17.40 and 17.51, was appended to DI Eamonn Corrigan's witness statement of 24 January 2014.

RECOMMENDATION

1. That Subject is listed as 'NOT WANTED' by the PSNI at this time.

2. That clarification be sought from Metropolitan Police as to the current position with their circulation of Subject.

This is the key decision-making document, based upon the six completed templates of 2 May 2007. Unfortunately, templates 1 to 5 have been redacted, though two of these are identifiable.

A number of points may be made. One, the author was Neal Graham. Two, the exercise was about the circulation of John Downey as wanted, 'at this time'. There was a passing reference to the terms of reference: 'due consideration'. But the legal test was: 'sufficient grounds'. Three, the reasons regarding templates 1 to 5 have been redacted. We simply do not know why the PSNI changed its mind, from 31 January 2006.[289] The reason appears to have been the loss of fingerprints between the two dates, for template 2: the 1972 Enniskillen bombing. The phrase 'All the Templates ... are based on Intelligence' was not quite correct (templates 2 and 6 referred to fingerprints). Four, as regards Hyde Park, it is not clear what papers Neal Graham reviewed. The fatal decision, however, is contained here: '[I] can find no evidence that would indicate Subject is wanted by the PSNI for this offence.' Why would John Downey be wanted by the PSNI when the metropolitan police had him on the police national computer? Five days earlier, Neal Graham, noting the London reference to conspiracy to murder, had written: '1. ... It is not known where the Conspiracy was carried out. [] 2. There is no evidence on file that would give me grounds to consider circulation by or on behalf of the PSNI for any offence

---

[289] It is possible that the prosecution, concerned about disclosure, did not appreciate this central question: it was misled by the idea of a PSNI mistake regarding Hyde Park. Tom Little wrote on 30 January 2014: 'If required in relation to the Templates 1 – 5 Neal Graham could have called for the Police papers as they were Northern Ireland matters. Although I had sight of some of those matters in October 2013 I remain of the view that they are not relevant to the abuse of process issues.' (p. 3)

within the jurisdiction.' Six, Neal Graham's second recommendation, regarding the metropolitan police, was not actioned by any member of Operation Rapid.[290]

The Operation Rapid Meeting of 9 May 2007

Two days later (9 May 2007), Norman Baxter reviewed eleven[291] cases with Neal Graham, including John Downey's. This is the Clogher meeting, where the head of Operation Rapid gave John Downey a clean bill.

That is contained in a document dated 10 May 2007, being essentially his third report to Peter Sheridan.[292] This time, there was no law. There was a list of nine names (with inadequate referencing of numbers), all of whom were held to be not wanted. John Downey was singled out for separate treatment, as number 43. Norman Baxter wrote: 'The above person is a native of the Republic of Ireland and is a citizen of the Irish Republic. He has not resided in Northern Ireland and remains resident in his native district. He is not currently "on the run" from his home. I have reviewed his case and there is no basis in my professional opinion to seek his arrest currently for any offence prior to the signing of the Good Friday Agreement. [] The above person should be informed that he is not currently wanted by the PSNI for offences prior to the Good Friday Agreement 1998, but it should be borne in mind that should new properly assessed and reliable intelligence or new evidence which has been judged to retain its integrity emerge which creates reasonable grounds to suspect his involvement in offences then he will be liable to arrest for any such offence which may have been committed during this period.'

Three points need to be made about this Operation Rapid report. First, Norman Baxter completely misunderstood 'on the run' (John

---

[290] Tom Little, disclosure report, 30 January 2014, pp. 4–5.

[291] Norman Baxter recalled nine cases.

[292] Again, things are not clear. The first eight names are dated March 2007. Twenty followed in April. And there were 17 in May. Norman Baxter's third report contains the numbering of those releases: from 33 to 43 (the latter being John Downey).

Downey was on the run from England and Wales). He made the same mistake in the case before: number 42 was residing within NI, and was therefore not on the run! Second, it was only implied – through not being wanted by the PSNI – that John Downey was not prosecutable in NI. There is simply no reference to Hyde Park in this document. However, he made clear that he was applying the legal test of: 'reasonable grounds to suspect'. Three, though Norman Baxter does not state how John Downey was to be informed, he made clear – again seemingly drafting for Operation Rapid – that the official promise was limited to existing evidence; there could be 'new properly assessed and reliable intelligence', or 'new evidence which has been judged to retain its integrity'.

Norman Baxter explained his thinking in oral evidence to NIAC on 2 April 2014. He thought the PSNI would pass information to Barra McGrory (and therefore John Downey). He was alert to the point about not informing OTRs that they were wanted (which others disregarded). Thus, he was against telling John Downey that he was wanted by the metropolitan police: 'For me to send a letter to Mr Downey saying that he was wanted in London would not only have been unlawful, but would have been betraying the victims of Hyde Park.'[293] This is a credible explanation from Norman Baxter. However, it fails to take account of the fact that the NIO (unknown to Norman Baxter) was looking to the PSNI to include any offences in England and Wales. It also fails to take account of why he could not share this information with Peter Sheridan; presumably, he might have feared that the assistant chief constable – rubber stamping his work – would have told Barra McGrory about Hyde Park.

Peter Sheridan Takes a View

On 6 June 2007, Peter Sheridan wrote to the PPSNI; he addressed his letter to W.R. Junkin as (acting) director. It concerned only John Downey. He did not know John Downey was wanted by

---

[293] NIAC, *Report*, Qs 17-19, 2 April 2014.

the metropolitan police, because Norman Baxter had not included this in his third report. Presumably, Peter Sheridan had signed a batch of similar communications the same day. This was the decisive letter as regards John Downey.

It referred to 'the present review', not Operation Rapid, and supplied 'information', not a judgment. Peter Sheridan simply adopted the erroneous point about John Downey not being on the run. The key sentence was: 'Enquiries indicate that John Anthony Downey is not currently wanted by the PSNI.' It is believed that 'enquiries indicate' was particular to this letter. The word 'currently' was no doubt deliberate. Not wanted by the PSNI is the point of the letter. The conclusion is incontrovertible: the PSNI never claimed that John Downey was not wanted by the metropolitan police. The double negative is necessary to rebut the predominant view that the PSNI did not pass on relevant information which it held. Norman Baxter and his colleagues knew: Peter Sheridan did not. That was the institutional response of the PSNI. The police officers in NI assumed that the NIO was dealing separately with England and Wales. Peter Sheridan was not prejudiced on 6 June 2007, when he wrote to the PPSNI. If he had told the NI prosecutor about Hyde Park, the latter would also most likely have proceeded as he did, assuming the attorney general's office was looking after England and Wales.

The Northern Ireland Prosecutor Decides

Peter Sheridan's letters did not reach the acting director, until 12 June 2007. The acting director listed the ten names (including John Downey's), and asked a member of his staff to 'check against the files and information held in this office'. Thereafter, the staff member was to draft letters for the Attorney general's office and Peter Sheridan, 'in accordance again with the manner in which we have written in like cases recently.'

Whatever this was, it was not the administrative scheme overseen by Sir Alasdair Fraser, in 2000–6. It was in fact Des Browne's failed idea of 2002, to have the PSNI ask and answer a lesser question about being wanted or not. The PPSNI would then simply check if there was a live prosecution file held by it.

The Northern Ireland Office Intervenes

After John Downey's name, as one of ten, had left the PSNI, the NIO suddenly raised a systemic point about the administrative scheme. This had not been clarified seemingly in the 2006 planning meetings (chapter 6). Nor had it arisen from Peter Sheridan sending the terms of reference to Hilary Jackson, on 15 February 2007. The systemic point is a major criticism of the officials running the administrative scheme, waiting to be revealed. Kevin McGinty raised this point on 7 June 2007, in a letter to the NIO, following receipt of the first 25 Operation Rapid names.[294]

On or before Monday, 11 June 2007, Hilary Jackson (then director political) had apparently telephoned Peter Sheridan.[295] The call was taken by Detective Sergeant Gillian Ferguson, who is described as the assistant chief constable's staff officer. While the police is quasi-military in this sense, Gillian Ferguson would be the equivalent of a chief executive's personal assistant in civilian life.

On 13 June 2007, at 10.54, Gillian Ferguson emailed Norman Baxter: 'could you please advise in writing that all checks with outside forces have been carried out in relation to the subjects under review by your team prior to them being sent to PPS. Hilary Jackson has requested this in writing.'

Behind the obvious query lurks a problem. The PSNI had carried out a review, and passed its conclusion on to the NI prosecutor. But it could neither review the metropolitan police's evidence (taking Downey as an example), nor could the PPSNI have contributed its bit to the administrative scheme. There was a major piece missing from the jigsaw. The NIO had failed to factor in the metropolitan police, and the director of public prosecutions for England and Wales. And this

---

[294] Memorandum, Sir Jonathan Stephens, 19 January 2015.
[295] This appears to have been initiated by Kevin McGinty in the attorney general's office.

after their involvement from the beginning of the scheme (chapter 4 above): it will be recalled that it was the director of public prosecutions for England and Wales who, clearing two of his six cases quickly, had led Jonathan Powell to write the first two letters of 15 June 2000 from number 10, to Evelyn Glenholmes and Patrick McVeigh.

It is no defence on Hilary Jackson's part, to imply that the PSNI had been intended to encompass these tasks. It could not encroach on the metropolitan police's patch (it could cooperate), and it had no powers to deal with the director of public prosecutions for England and Wales. The attorney general was now taking a back seat. The NIO, of course, was also in difficulty, which is why it assumed the PSNI was doing the job it (the department) could not do directly. The NIO could not go to the home office, to contact the metropolitan police. And it could not go to the director of public prosecutions for England and Wales: they were a jurisdiction apart. But Hilary Jackson's communication suggests the NIO may not have been entirely confident about the alternative PSNI route to the metropolitan police and the English director.

Norman Baxter, having received the email, forwarded it, at 12.15, to Neal Graham. There is no evidence that Hilary Jackson's query captured his imagination. He wrote simply: 'Can you please confirm.' Norman Baxter did not see the lurking problem. But, to properly assess the evidence, he was simply forwarding an email in an age, no doubt even in 2007, of information overload. He may have made a mistake. But it should not have become the hanging offence it has become.

The following morning, at 09.52, Neal Graham forwarded the email to Paul McGowan (who may not have been in Clogher), another of the three civilians in Operation Rapid.

Paul McGowan replied to Neal Graham, on 14 June 2007, at 14.37, with a long email. They appear to have spoken. This email is of major significance. Paul McGowan was evidently familiar with practice up to 2006. Operation Rapid, outside its terms of reference, also consulted ICIS, the PSNI's superseded computer system (which stayed live to 2010).[296] ICIS was built by the police; it was not bought in. Paul McGowan reported that Operation Rapid accessed the police national computer through ICIS: 'Sample checks carried out today have revealed that ICIS cannot be relied on in this respect.' Five of ten names (almost certainly including John Downey) did not show up on the police national computer accessed through ICIS. This was a general point about going straight to the police national computer, which should have been done. It had no implications for the John Downey case, which Paul McGowan appears to have discussed with Neal Graham that day. This point need be laboured no further. Neal Graham was advised to tell the NIO that: Interpol had not been checked; the police national computer checks through ICIS were clearly flawed; and 'It appear[ed] that requests to Interpol [would] require provision ... of significant information, including reason or justification for the check...'.

Neal Graham forwarded this email at 15.03. He endorsed the Interpol point: 'This will also put additional pressure work on the Team and take away from the thrust of the Terms of Reference which only related to persons wanted in Northern Ireland.' The problem with Interpol was simple: the PSNI did not want to reveal what it was doing; because it knew that Interpol (in France) would be punctilious about requests for information.

Norman Baxter replied at 15.39, with three paragraphs of guidance affirming the status quo.[297] (At 15.52, Neal Graham directed no change.) Norman Baxter appears to have missed the point about the police national computer through ICIS. But this has no implications for the John Downey case. However, he articulated possibly a NIO version of what the PSNI was doing: 'Is X wanted for arrest by the police service of [NI] for an offence[s] pre the Good Friday Agreement or circulated as wanted for arrest by an external force and the exist[a]nce of reasonable grounds (within the UK) or a European Arrest Warrant.'

---

[296] The RUC/PSNI used: 1980s to 1999, crime information recording system (CIRS) plus PACIFIC; 1999-2006, integrated criminal information system (ICIS); and from 2007, NICHE, from Niche Technology Inc. in Canada.

[297] Neal Graham forwarded this email on 18 June 2007 to Gillian Ferguson.

The issue arose again on 20 June 2007. At 11.17, Paul McGowan emailed Neal Graham, suggesting an approach to Interpol. He even drafted a request, nervously revealing the existence of the administrative scheme. This certainly reveals that wanted by the PSNI related, not to NI crimes, but to police arrest powers: 'It is incumbent upon the PSNI to determine if those individuals can legitimately be considered as "wanted" persons and remain subject to arrest in [NI] for offences committed there or anywhere else.'

Neal Graham forwarded this to Norman Baxter, at 15.02. The former may have been in touch with Peter Sheridan, or Gillian Ferguson: 'I NOW UNDERSTAND that we will NOT be carrying out the INTERPOL CHECKS at this time.' This was for information only, and there was no reply. It is also clear that the Interpol question muddied the water where lurked the separate jurisdiction of England and Wales.

It is not entirely clear that Hilary Jackson, overseeing the administrative scheme, was communicating clearly in June 2007 with the PSNI (regardless of whether it was proper), concerned as it was with criminal intelligence going on evidence and a lawful test for what it was doing.

On 27 June 2007, Peter Sheridan wrote to Hilary Jackson. He appropriated text from Norman Baxter's email of 14 June 2007 (which had gone only to Neal Graham but had been forwarded to her later). This letter is not accurate. The acting chief constable, or his staff officer, had not spotted that there might be a problem regarding checks with the Republic of Ireland police (An Garda Síochána). Peter Sheridan seems to have been excluded from the debate about Interpol. Norman Baxter's missing of the point about the police national computer through ICIS was also passed up. And the PSNI was stated to be acting consistently, on the basis seemingly of some staff continuity among civilians.

The PSNI was in difficulty. Not knowing John Downey was wanted by the metropolitan police, Peter Sheridan had told the PPSNI on 6 June 2007 that he was not wanted by the PSNI. But, in his letter to Hilary Jackson of 27 June 2007, he put forward a different account of Operation Rapid, namely one where they had checked whether he was wanted in NI, any other part of the UK, or in any other country.

The Northern Ireland Prosecution Decision

Also on 27 June 2007, the PPSNI wrote to Kevin McGinty about eight OTRs, including John Downey.[298] W.R. Junkin simply reproduced the content of Peter Sheridan's letter of 6 June 2007 (including the erroneous point about not being on the run). The only value added was the information that the PPSNI's one file on John Downey was closed.

Wednesday, 27 June 2007, it may be recalled, was the day of Tony Blair's resignation as prime minister, after he answered questions in the commons. The Downey mistake happened on his watch (in the form of the PPSNI letter). This was also Peter Hain's last full day as secretary of state for NI. So, the Downey mistake – following the rule of ministerial accountability in the NIO for Operation Rapid[299] – may be attributed to Peter Hain, if his officials are to be excused their indirect responsibility.[300]

On 11 July 2007, Kevin McGinty, operating now as a post box only, forwarded the PPSNI's information[301] to Katie Pettifer, of the rights and international relations division of the NIO. John Downey was close to getting his letter.

It is clear that the NIO was keeping an OTR schedule, which appears to be the basis of the appendix 5 table or spreadsheet in the Hallett report.

Mark Sweeney Takes a Belated Interest

On the morning of Wednesday, 18 July 2007, Mark Sweeney, as head of rights and international relations, called Gillian Ferguson. The lurking problem, referred to above, was about to break through. He

---

[298] There seems to have been a second letter, with two additional names.

[299] Sir Jonathan Stephens told NIAC: 'At all times, Ministers were aware of the scheme and it was clearly operating with their consent and under their directions.': *Report*, Q2383, 3 September 2014.

[300] This is something Peter Hain denied, by referring to the 20 July 2007 date: NIAC, *Report*, Q1751, 18 June 2014.

[301] It referred to ten names.

wanted to know if Operation Rapid – on the basis of Peter Sheridan's letter of 27 June 2007 – had been checking outside NI. She promised to get him an answer. This was extraordinarily late in the day. And the query reveals that the administrative scheme had become little more than a NIO drive for numbers. Mark Sweeney emailed at 12.52: 'Sorry to make a meal of this: it just helps us to keep our records in order at this end.' Mark Sweeney got the email address wrong: *gillian.ferguson@psni.pnn.gov.uk*, when it should have been: *gillianferguson@psni.pnn.police.uk*.

He sent the email successfully, on 20 July 2007, at 10.19. One infers he had been on the phone. He was pressing: 'if you could come back asap on this it would be much appreciated'.

She did, at 10.38. And she paraphrased Peter Sheridan's letter to Hilary Jackson: 'our review team conduct all searches through our own computer system ICIS, the Police National Computer (PNC) and checks with An Garda Siochana. This is the process conducted for all individuals reviewed prior to any letters being sent from this office and this will continue to be the case.' She confirmed that this applied to the ten names (including John Downey) in the 11 July 2007 letter. Mark Sweeney acknowledged, at 10.41.

There is a trail of inevitability: from Norman Baxter's email of 14 June 2007 (later forwarded to Gillian Ferguson); to Peter Sheridan's letter of 27 June 2007; to Gillian Ferguson's email of 20 July 2007. Mark Sweeney had started this, on or before 11 June 2007, with the Hilary Jackson overture to Gillian Ferguson. And he had concluded it fatally on 20 July 2007 at 10.41. He had custody of the administrative scheme, and he was about to make a historic mistake.

Norman Baxter told NIAC, regarding Mark Sweeney's telephone call to Gillian Ferguson on 20 July 2007: 'That is a breach between the Executive and the police. That is political interference in policing. Is that a criminal offence? I suspect not, although there is an offence of malfeasance in public office. It just should not happen.'[302]

---

[302] NIAC, *Report,* Q73, 2 April 2014.

The OTR Letters

On 20 July 2007, Mark Sweeney signed off on ten more OTR letters. He signed each letter, but did not seemingly photocopy or scan them. The ten original letters were then sent (either by fax or post) to Gerry Kelly, at Sinn Féin's principal office, on the Falls Road in west Belfast. The NIO appears to have a copy of the signed covering letter, which would be consistent with it being faxed to Sinn Féin.[303] So why does it not have a copy of the John Downey letter signed by Mark Sweeney?

Mark Sweeney wrote to Gerry Kelly: 'On the basis of the information currently held, in respect of the following ten individuals, there is no outstanding direction for prosecution in [NI], there are no warrants in existence nor are they wanted in [NI] for arrest, questioning or charge by the police'.

One of the ten was John Downey. His personal letter (also sent to Gerry Kelly), like the other nine, included an additional phrase: 'The Police Service of Northern Ireland are not aware of any interest in you from any other police force in the United Kingdom.'

This inconsistency has been missed totally, to date.[304] Peter Sheridan had written, on 6 June 2007, that John Downey was not wanted in NI. Mark Sweeney's letter of 20 July 2007, to Gerry Kelly, says nothing more. It is his letter to John Downey, of the same date, which contains the crucial additional sentence. Whatever checks had been done on John Downey (and they were inadequate), had not been done on the other nine – yet a standard letter to these ten OTRs.

Gerry Kelly presumably got his covering letter, and the ten letters. Most likely, Gerry Kelly retained the ten letters. Did Gerry Kelly spot the inconsistency between the covering letter and the ten individual ones? Certainly, when John Downey was to be arrested, in May 2013,

---

[303] Letter, Sir Jonathan Stephens, 13 January 2015, to NIAC; NIAC, *Report*, Q3988, 19 January 2015.

[304] Mr Justice Sweeney referred to the two letters in paras 122 and 123. He did not comment on the different information. Hallett, *Report*, paras 6.66 to 6.69 does likewise. She does not point to the inconsistency.

he was not carrying his letter, and seemingly did not possess it. It emerged subsequently, that John Downey referred initially to a home office letter. The metropolitan police contacted this English department immediately. They later contacted the NIO. That department, upon request, forwarded copies of the office copy electronically. Later, a copy of a signed version was sent to the metropolitan police.[305] The source is interesting: it was John Downey's lawyers, seemingly assisted by Gerry Kelly.[306] The conclusion is: Gerry Kelly has been most likely holding John Downey's original letter since just after 20 July 2007.

This late revelation clears up a strange passage in Hallett, paragraph 6.68: 'We have been able to establish that the original – of which I have seen a copy – does in fact contain the handwritten signature.' There follows a copy of the letter from which the signature appears to have been deleted. We now know this cannot have come from the NIO, because it did not copy it. The source can only be Gerry Kelly.

The important role played by Gerry Kelly, which the prosecution was unable to explore in the Downey hearing (because of no live evidence), is also illustrated by another case: Gerard McGeough. As noted in chapter 6 above, he was arrested by Norman Baxter on 8 March 2007, within Operation Rapid.[307] He applied for a stay of his prosecution in the Belfast crown court, on the ground of abuse of process: R v Terence George McGeough [2010] NICC 33. This application included the first consideration of the administrative scheme in a court of law. Gerard McGeough claimed that, as an on the run in July 2000, he gave his name to Gerry Kelly, for onward transmission. He believed, on the basis of what Gerry Kelly said, that he secured immunity at the point of giving his details.[308] He maintained this position, even

---

[305]   Letter, Assistant Commissioner Mark Rowley to NIAC, 2 January 2015.

[306]   NIAC, *Report,* Qs 3848–3851, 3895–3911, 3933–3934 & 3988–3990, 19 January 2015. (Mark Sweeney & Theresa Villiers)

[307]   The judgment details that the investigation was reopened on 14 February 2007 (para 2(x)).

[308]   Para 13. Gerard McGeough went a great deal further: he relied upon the evidence of William Smith, a loyalist leader, who described Mo Mowlam, in Castle Buildings in March/April 1998, as effectively promising terrorists immunity,

though there was a NIO letter of 22 January 2003, stating he was one of six applicants who was still wanted.[309] He, through Gerry Kelly, was refused a comfort letter. In cross-examination, Gerard McGeough claimed: Gerry Kelly never told him about this; and, in January 2003, he, having left Sinn Féin, was not on speaking terms with Gerry Kelly.[310] Gerry Kelly, evidently, was only in the business of helping those who remained loyal to Gerry Adams.

The Downey mistake may be readily brought together: Peter Sheridan's letter of 6 June 2007, stating that he was not wanted by the PSNI (without any elaboration); the inaccurate letter of 27 June 2007, which certainly widened the meaning of 'wanted'; the Gillian Ferguson email of 20 July 2007, affirming this latter letter; Mark Sweeney's letter of the same date to Gerry Kelly, which clearly referred only to being wanted in NI; and finally, his letter to John Downey, which added gratuitously the phrase about not being wanted by any other police force in the UK.

The most likely explanation for the mistake is: Mark Sweeney knew from 2006, that John Downey was wanted by the metropolitan police (he after all was keeping a schedule); but he only made general inquiries to the PSNI about Operation Rapid; he used Peter Sheridan's inaccurate letter of 27 June 2007 to draw the particular conclusion that John Downey was no longer wanted by the metropolitan police. That is where the mistake was made. He should have asked, if he had not been concerned about constitutional proprieties, why the PSNI changed its mind, between 31 January 2006, when Downey was wanted, and 11 July 2007, when he was told – through the PPSNI and the attorney general's office – that Downey was not wanted.

There is another way of articulating this NIO mistake: if Mark Sweeney had sent his draft John Downey letter to Gillian Ferguson, she would have sent it to Operation Rapid: Norman Baxter would then

---

presumably as an extension of the early-release provision which made it into the Belfast agreement. (para 14)

[309] Para 15.
[310] Para 15.

have seen that the draft was incorrect, and would have been able to advise Mark Sweeney; no letter would have gone out to John Downey (he was still wanted). Mark Sweeney is responsible for his non-action, and Norman Baxter is not. Norman Baxter would then also have seen that the letter was not going to Barra McGrory, and he might have been more open about Hyde Park with Peter Sheridan.

Who Was to Blame?

This question is not simple. If Tony Blair had not made his four written promises to Gerry Adams, there would have been no administrative scheme lasting fourteen years. If Peter Hain had not decided to speed up the administrative scheme in late 2006, there would have been no Operation Rapid. If Sir Alasdair Fraser had not fallen ill, the administrative scheme would have proceeded as before. If Sir Hugh Orde had said no to Peter Hain in late 2006, again there would have been no Operation Rapid. And if Sinn Féin had not come out in support of the PSNI in January 2007, there would have been little police willingness to do the NIO's bidding by turning wanted into not wanted.

It is possible to criticize Norman Baxter. He knew John Downey was wanted by the metropolitan police, at least from 13 April 2007. So did Neal Graham. The latter's assessment of 7 May 2007, was endorsed by Norman Baxter on 10 May 2007. Peter Sheridan signed off on it, on 6 June 2007. On 13 June 2007, Norman Baxter did not appreciate the significance of the email from Gillian Ferguson. However, Mark Sweeney was in charge of the administrative scheme, and he should have ensured that Operation Rapid was comprehensively mounted. Norman Baxter again slipped up on 14 June 2007, but his failure to grasp the point about the police national computer through ICIS had no effect on his knowledge that John Downey was wanted by the metropolitan police. Norman Baxter's email of 14 June 2007 contained an expanded version of the PSNI review, which was not correct, but it was Peter Sheridan who paraphrased him in the letter of 27 June 2007 to the NIO. Ultimately, this was a collective failure of the PSNI, for which the chief constable must accept some or all responsibility. Within that collective failure lies Norman Baxter's decision to hide the Hyde Park bombing from Peter Sheridan. Did the former fear that the latter might blurt out that Downey was wanted by the metropolitan police in the anticipated reply to Barra McGrory?

The NIO should not be permitted to hide behind police skirts. Operation Rapid – in the absence of Sir Alasdair Fraser – became a NIO-directed operation. True, the chain of PSNI to PPSNI to attorney general's office to NIO formally remained. But the attorney general's office let the NIO take over the driving. It is significant that, in John Downey's case, the NIO told Sinn Féin, on 26 September 2005, that there was to be a review, and that, on 31 January 2006, the PSNI wrote directly to the NIO. Mark Sweeney was in poll position in the NIO from then, and he showed himself particularly interventionist as regards police decision making. The telephone and emails were his weapons of choice. He reserved letter writing seemingly for OTRs, through Gerry Kelly. And there is no evidence of coordinating the various bodies properly, after Operation Rapid was set up by the PSNI. His fatal intervention of June-July 2007, deserves the searchlight of investigation. Mark Sweeney – at the level of officialdom – warrants some, if not all, of the blame for the inaccurate John Downey letter of 20 July 2007: he orchestrated the administrative scheme, and he could have – deploying the analytical skills of a senior official – detected that the PSNI was working in the dark outside its normal range. Ultimately, Mark Sweeney told Gerry Kelly one thing on 20 July 2007, and went on to tell his ten correspondents with undisclosed addresses, something additional – which, at least in the case of John Downey, the police, and the NIO, had known to be inaccurate for some considerable time. That is a big responsibility for one man to bear.

The secretary of state, Theresa Villiers, who had blamed the PSNI on 25 February 2014, may have modified her position somewhat, by the time she spoke to NIAC on 3 September 2014: 'if the scheme had been gripped and managed properly … the mistake might never have been made. It would have been clearer who was doing what and who was responsible for what. If risks had been addressed properly, there was every possibility that that mistake, if it had been made, would have been picked up and remedied.'[311] She could be talking about Mark Sweeney making the mistake, and Norman Baxter not being given an opportunity to correct him. But the NIO declined to go as far as to admit it had got it wrong at the time of the Downey judgment. It also declined to refer particularly to Mark Sweeney. The secretary of state went on to say: 'Yes, it would not be fair to say that this issue is solely down to a mistake that was made at the PSNI, because they were operating within a scheme that was sanctioned by Ministers and was flawed. The responsibility lies with Ministers too.'[312]

The Downey Mistake Discovered?

There were two occasions, subsequently, when the PSNI discovered that Peter Sheridan's letter of 6 June 2007 ('not currently wanted by the PSNI'), interpreted in the light of his letter of 27 June 2007 (Operation Rapid's wide range of checks), had become incorrect on the occasion of the latter general statement. However, the issue – on both occasions – was one or more of the suspected five NI offences (which had led to the change of position), though the Hyde Park bombing got a passing mention.

On 28 February 2008 (perhaps having heard from the historical enquiries team), Neal Graham apparently re-ran part of his assessment of John Downey.[313] It relates to one NI offence, perhaps template 2 or 3. The earlier assessment, of 7 May 2007, had recommended not wanted for five NI offences. Neal Graham recommended: 'Having reviewed all the available evidence in this matter, I am satisfied that there is currently no grounds to have Subject circulated for any offence in [NI]. He is not resident in the jurisdiction at this time and would appear to be domiciled in the ROI [sic].'

---

[311] NIAC, *Report,* Q2487, 3 September 2014.

[312] NIAC, *Report,* Q2487, 3 September 2014. This was repeated in answer to an urgent question regarding Gareth O'Connor's inquest: HC, *Hansard,* vol. 591, col. 737, 27 January 2015.

[313] Compare Downey case papers, tab 8, pp. 762–3 & 789.

One, July 2008: Enter the Historical Enquiries Team

On 7 May 2008, a Philip Danby, of the PSNI's historical enquiries team, emailed, at 08.58, a Eric Calderwood of C3, who forwarded the message to Paul McGowan, the Operation Rapid civilian. It appears that the historical enquiries team was discovering the administrative scheme, seemingly for the first time. Philip Danby asked about a not wanted note regarding John Downey, of 7 June 2007, on a crime not hitherto disclosed: the killing of Thomas and Emily Bullock, in Co. Fermanagh, on 21 September 1972 (possibly template 3). Paul McGowan confirmed that not wanted for this Co. Fermanagh crime was the decision of the head of C2, namely Norman Baxter.

On 23 July 2008, Paul McGowan spoke to the historical enquiries team (he may have initiated the call). He made a manuscript note on his email of 7 May 2008 (obviously in hard copy): 'HET have located adhesive tape that was crucial evidence re template 1 [actually 2] and will seek to reinstate "Wanted" alert.' Template 2 is the two Ulster Defence Regiment soldiers killed in Enniskillen on 25 August 1972.

He emailed Neal Graham and Gillian Ferguson the same day, at 14.43. Paul McGowan was concerned about a particular point, namely the absence of a caveat about fresh evidence in Peter Sheridan's letter of 6 June 2007, and what the PSNI could now do regarding John Downey: 'presumably because Downey was not considered to be OTR, there was no caveat in the letter issued to the PPS[NI].' This was still the OTR concept confusing the police. He went on to refer to the adhesive tape found by the historical enquiries team: 'It is probable that they will have a SIO [senior investigating officer] create a new wanted alert in respect of the murders concerned.' The ball was now in the historical enquiries team court.

Gillian Ferguson asked, on 25 July 2008, at 10.30, for a report for Peter Sheridan. She made the mistake of asking two people, Paul McGowan and Neal Graham. No report as such ensued; however, there was a flood of forwarded emails, surely a way of sharing, if not passing, responsibility.

On 28 July 2008, at 14.41, following a conversation with Neal

Graham, Paul McGowan emailed him: finger print branch had told the historical enquiries team in February 2008, that it had relocated the adhesive tape (used in the two Ulster Defence Regiment soldiers' killing in August 1972). It had been mislaid when Norman Baxter had done his assessment of 10 May 2007, so had not been relied upon. Though then a civilian, Paul McGowan raised for the first time, in the John Downey case, the possibility of a NI abuse of process application given Peter Sheridan had referred to Downey being simply not wanted for the NI offences.

Neal Graham forwarded this version of the adhesive tape story to Norman Baxter and Gillian Ferguson, on 29 July 2008, at 10.04, referring to the re-discovered adhesive tape as 'new evidence'. He recommended the appointment of a senior investigating officer to review the material in liaison with the PPSNI. Nothing happened.

At 11.04 the same day (possibly having spoken), Paul McGowan emailed Neal Graham about Hyde Park. It was copied to Gillian Ferguson (but not significantly to Norman Baxter). Paul McGowan stated that the historical enquiries team was also aware of Hyde Park. He wrote: 'I have checked PNC [police national computer] and the Met wanted alert for murder is still on the system.... The report from then Head C2 to ACC Crime Ops and the subsequent letter to the DPP do not state that Downey is wanted by the Met.'

This was an important revelation, on 29 July 2008, that Norman Baxter had not told Peter Sheridan about the Hyde Park bombing in his 10 May 2007 report. Both senior officers were preparing that summer to retire (retirement being a major theme of the Patten policing reforms). Norman Baxter had already stood down as head of C2. Neither Peter Sheridan nor Gillian Ferguson took up the point.

On 4 August 2008, at 11.34, Norman Baxter acted on Neal Graham's email of six days' earlier. He emailed Derek Williamson, his successor as head of C2: he was for reopening the two Ulster Defence Regiment soldiers' case; he did not suggest how this might be done, and may have thought that the historical enquiries team would do it now that it had been informed of the fresh evidence.

The buck regarding John Downey stops with Derek Williamson. Much later (29 July 2010), his successor as head of C2 – explaining Operation Rapid to two new staff officers - wrote: 'HET [historical enquiries team] later reported to Op Rapid that Fingerprint Bureau had located previously missing evidence (a piece of adhesive tape that held a fingerprint of the suspect that was located on the firing pack of the device that killed [a soldier]. On this basis D/C/Supt Baxter asked D/C/Supt Williamson (then incoming head of C2) to appoint an SIO [senior investigation officer] to liaise with HET on the case. However, this was not done.'[314]

The prosecution in the Downey case relied upon a witness statement of detective inspector Corrigan of the PSNI.[315] He had been asked by the metropolitan police what, if anything, was done in 2008 regarding the Downey mistake. His answer is abrupt: 'In summary it appears that there was no additional action taken as this information was known at the time of the letter being sent to [the NI prosecutor].'

Two, October 2009

This was a relatively minor incident. Apparently, there were metropolitan police officers attached to C3. They had circulated seventeen names. Operation Rapid, in C2, checked the names, confirming, on 21 October 2009, that John Downey was not wanted by the PSNI, but he was wanted by the metropolitan police.

The juxtaposition of findings is not new, and is indeed unremarkable. However, the Operation Rapid intellectual mistake was again clear. John Downey was not wanted in NI, for any NI crime. However, he could be arrested in NI, for the Hyde Park bombing. He was extraditable, not to NI, but to England and Wales (though this was simply a transfer between UK jurisdictions). The PSNI was concerned principally with NI crime (and thus the letter of 6 June 2007), but it never properly grasped how, if at all, the metropolitan police was factored

---

[314] Email, Tim Hanley to Jeanette McMurray & Robin Dempsey: Downey case papers, tab 8, pp. 798–9.
[315] Downey case papers, tab 6, 21 January 2014.

into the administrative scheme.

All this was to be explored in the court of Mr Justice Sweeney, to where we now turn; the abuse of process application was to be a personal success for John Downey, who claimed the victory, and his lawyers, but a disaster for ministers and officials, none of whom was keen to accept any blame during the ensuing firestorm.

CHAPTER TEN

John Downey and Abuse of Process

John Downey knew of his letter of 20 July 2007, though he never personally received it. However, he relied upon it (or Gerry Kelly's interpretation) in following years, by travelling to and through NI to Great Britain. He was arrested at Gatwick airport on 19 May 2013, and, on 17 January 2014, his trial began at the Old Bailey in front of Mr Justice Sweeney (a jury not being sworn). His defence argued for a stay of the prosecution as an abuse of process, for four reasons: one, the passage of time since the offence, namely 32 years (unfair trial); two, likely early release under the Northern Ireland (Sentences) Act 1998 after two years; three, the Mark Sweeney letter of 20 July 2007; and four, these three reasons taken cumulatively. The defence lost on one and two; as is now well known, it succeeded on the OTR comfort letter. The prosecution was stayed seemingly forever.

John Downey's Reliance?

In the absence of oral evidence from Gerry Kelly, about what he might have said to John Downey (and the latter to him), one is limited to a statement from the successful defendant. The *Donegal Democrat* interviewed him after the collapse of the trail: 'John shakes his head when asked why his arrest and subsequent proceedings took place in London – he still feels at a loss as to why it happened and how it was allowed to happen …. "As far as the letter is concerned this was an arrangement between the British and Irish Government and my arrest was a breach of the agreement reached between the British and Irish government."' John Downey is legally incorrect, and no such argument had been presented on his behalf. However, this is an exaggerated constitutional understanding of the Belfast agreement among some, including those who perceived that there is now joint sovereignty or joint administration in NI.

John Downey must be taken to be referring to the 2001 Weston Park agreement (though he never sought to rely upon it from 2002).

Whether John Downey was involved in Hyde Park or not (a question his legal team prevented being considered by a jury), he most definitely knew that, from 29 May 1983, the metropolitan police had posted him as wanted (this was the reason for the arrest at Gatwick). This fact (namely John Downey's knowledge), which should have figured in Mr Justice Sweeney's assessment, was not given the weight it deserves, or any weight. The point is simply that: a person who knows he is wanted by the police, cannot be surprised that an investigation might lead to a prosecution, it being up to a jury to convict or not.

John Downey knew he was wanted. What then of the letter? He never perceived it as related to his guilt or innocence. He did not worry about the text. But he did believe the IRA, with the support of the Irish government, had extracted a promise from the UK government: that promise was to the effect that he was free to travel to and through NI to Great Britain. Paradoxically, he respected what Tony Blair had said, because Gerry Adams and Martin McGuinness vouched for the promise.

John Downey started to travel the world, or at least parts of it: summer 2008, to Canada (from Dublin), with his wife, to visit a son and grandchild;[316] visits to loyalist prisoners in NI, on 4 April and 7 November 2009; visits to Great Britain (where his daughter was at university), in February, March and April 2010, April and November 2011, July 2012 and January 2013; these English visits included a holiday on the Norfolk broads; a visit to NI in 2012, for a hunger-strike commemoration; and two visits to Corrymeela, Co. Antrim, in November 2012 and March 2013; he was arrested at Gatwick in May 2013, on his way to Greece.

---

[316] He disclosed to the Canadians he was a suspect: 'I was named in some British newspapers as being responsible for the Hyde Park & Regents Park bombings in 1982, which I strenuously deny. No warrant was ever issued by the British authorities to have me extradited and I understand from contacts which have taken place between the British and Sinn Fein that they, the British, have no further interest in me.'

Though John Downey was prepared to see only a UK conspiracy,[317] the common travel area explains his safe travelling and eventual, if not earlier,[318] arrest. Trips to NI, and to Great Britain, are within the common travel area. This is a survival of the pre-1922 UK. It was only when John Downey booked a flight from the UK to Greece, that the national border targeting centre, in Manchester (part of the UK's border force), detected his advanced passenger information, and alerted Sussex police (which contacted the metropolitan police). The flight was out of the common travel area. He was arrested on 19 May 2013, and produced in a magistrates' court three days later (being granted bail later in the summer).[319]

John Downey proceeded towards trial in the crown court. The CPS instructed Brian Altman QC, leading Tom Little. Stuart Baker of the CPS was in the background. John Downey went to Gareth Peirce, who specializes in terrorism cases, Irish and Islamic. She instructed Henry Blaxland QC, leading Mark Summers.

Abuse of Process: the Facts

In September to November 2013, Tom Little carried out a conventional disclosure exercise, covering: the crown prosecution service; the attorney general's office; the NIO; the PSNI; the PPSNI; the ministry of defence; and the cabinet office. The defence's abuse of process application began, on Friday, 17 January 2014, using this unanalysed material. 'It became apparent at an early stage [noted the judge] ... that there had been no investigation, as such, instituted by the prosecution into

---

[317] 'I am told that the reason for my arrest was that I had come up on the Police National Computer (PNC). I had been in and out of Birmingham airport on numerous occasions. I'd also been in Stansted and then on that last day they decided to arrest me. I refuse to believe that if I was on the PNC that I would have gone through all those airports including Derry and Belfast, because that is within their jurisdiction, without being picked up.' (*Donegal Democrat,* 13 March 2014)
[318] In July 2012, he flew to Birmingham airport, *en route* to Faro in Portugal, without being detected.
[319] NIAC, *Report,* Qs2836–7, 22 October 2014.

the precise circumstances [of] ... the letter dated 20 July 2007...'.[320]

Tom Little, at the request of the court, reviewed the attorney general's office disclosure, over the weekend of 18-19 January 2014, and discovered that one relevant letter had been overlooked.

The application continued on Monday, 20, Wednesday, 22 and Friday, 24 January 2014. The prosecution started the *canard* of the PSNI making a mistake about Hyde Park, which was never totally dispelled. At the prompting of the court, the prosecution arranged for the PSNI to disclose more on the 2008 discovery.[321] Tom Little returned to Belfast on Wednesday, 29 January 2014, and further PSNI documents were disclosed the following day. There was a further hearing on Friday, 31 January 2014, during which the court heard final oral submissions. On Tuesday, 2 February 2014, the prosecution and defence provided written submissions on abuse of process. It is not known whether there is a transcript of the five-day application, but the judgment gives the impression of considerable shadow boxing.

It is extraordinary that the defence, and then the prosecution, argued about the administrative scheme, without any objective narrative of the process based upon adequate disclosure.[322] There were no expert witnesses. There were no witnesses of fact. The defence sought to argue that the letter of 20 July 2007 was a sacred promise. The prosecution tried to counter that, partly by textual analysis of the content. It is to

---

[320] Judgment, para 10.

[321] Witness statements, DI Eamonn Corrigan, 21 & 24 January 2014, based on interviews with Norman Baxter.

[322] Tom Little, for example, had thought the Operation Rapid minutes of 12 February 2007, not important: 'When I previously read those I did not regard them as being relevant. As the ambit of Operation Rapid with its focus on Northern Ireland has become of significance it seems to me that these Minutes may be relevant and I have been provided with them.' That was written on 30 January 2014. Peter Sheridan told NIAC on 2 April 2014 that Gareth Peirce had asked him to help the court: 'Then he [DI Eamonn Corrigan] called me back to say that a solicitor [barrister?] who was doing the disclosure on behalf of the Metropolitan Police said that I was not to get access to the letter that I wrote, or the documents. I have to say I found that completely bizarre...'. (NIAC, *Report,* Q124, 2 April 2014)

the credit of Mr Justice Sweeney, that he was able to construct a narrative for his own purposes, which led him to his decision. However, he never claimed to be producing even the first draft of history of the administrative scheme.

The defence had prepared a 60-page skeleton argument, by 3 January 2014. It is surprisingly pro-Sinn Féin, using a great deal of republican terminology: 'the defendant [John Downey] and Sinn Fein had no reason to believe that the written assurance was anything other than it purported to be. On the contrary, the timing of the assurance was such as to positively lead both to believe that the closure of his files had been the result of public interest considerations [which is incorrect]. The defendant had been refused an assurance in 2006 as had two other persons. In May 2007, the Republicans believed that the OTR issue was being used as a negotiating tool by the Unionists. That resulted in a showdown meeting between Paisley, Adams and McGuinness. At that meeting, the impasse was breached and the process of decommissioning began. On 8 May 2007 the new Executive was sworn in. The defendant's assurance letter was issued immediately afterwards. Those events and that chronology would have led any recipient to proceed on the basis that the trigger for the assurance had been the political breakthrough.'[323] This is an unusual submission for a court of law: it simply imposes a Sinn Féin theory on extraordinary facts being disclosed exceptionally. John Downey's counsel were struck correctly by the change in assessment, from 2006 to 2007. But they completely misunderstood the administrative scheme, by believing there had been a public interest test re-run, and that the new public interest was Sinn Féin supporting the police and entering the power-sharing administration at Stormont (those factors were obviously important, but they were not legally reasoned to a conclusion).

The prosecution produced a 55-page skeleton argument, but not until 16 January 2014 (it having been shown to the attorney general). It advanced the theory of a letter issued in error: 'the defence are quite wrong to conclude that given the defendant was still circulated

---

[323]   Para 127.

as "wanted" up to and including July 2007, "the assurance indicates that a decision was made that he was no longer 'wanted'". No such decision was ever made by anyone, and there was simply no decision taken about the sufficiency of the evidence as a precursor to the sending of the letter, and there was no "deliberate decision to revoke the defendant's 'wanted' status." … there was no error in his remaining circulated; the error had been granting the defendant the letter. Indeed, had there been any decision to revoke his "wanted" status based on a decision that the case did not meet the evidential test, or that there was no or no sufficient evidence to meet the test, then, if it had happened as the defence seek to infer, the prosecution would be obliged to disclose it now. There is no disclosure to make about this.'[324] This is an important distinction, between the letter and the metropolitan police wanted status. However, the prosecution went on to make an intellectual error of its own: it failed to see the inconsistencies of the PSNI in terms of the flawed structure of the NIO's administrative scheme. The prosecution had its back to the wall, by 16 January 2014. Following Tom Little's return to Belfast, on 29 January 2014, it was in an even more difficult position.[325]

Witnesses?

The parties agreed that the abuse of process application should proceed on submissions only. The judge noted of 17 January 2014: 'they were agreed that no witnesses would be called by either side and … I should decide any disputed factual issues (of which there were relatively few) on the papers.' This was remarkably complacent, or cautious, conduct on the part of the prosecution. Mr Justice Sweeney noted of 31 January 2014: 'Final oral submissions were then completed – during

---

[324] Paras 114–5.

[325] Dominic Grieve told NIAC: 'What I had not been aware of at the beginning … was it was clear there had been a mistake, but the compounding of the mistake by the fact that no action had been taken on it was not something I was aware of at the start. That only emerged as we started looking at the information available.' (*Report*, Q2202, 2 July 2014)

which it was re-confirmed that neither side intended to call any live evidence.'[326] One understands the defence's aversion to cross-examination, and indeed judicial investigation – but why did the prosecution agree simply to written evidence?

The prosecution relied upon Kevin McGinty, who produced two witness statements (on 13 and 21 January 2014) and the short note on 'The On the Run Scheme'.[327]

The defence had an impressive *galerie*: Gerry Kelly (13 mentions in the judgment); Jonathan Powell (ten mentions); and Peter Hain (13 mentions). While the former's involvement in an important IRA trial is understandable, few have asked what the two latter were doing helping John Downey, which they evidently did.[328]

Gerry Kelly (on 3 January 2014) did not assert that he gave John Downey his letter: 'I confirm that Mr Downey was made personally aware immediately of the receipt of his letter and its contents. The confidentiality of these communications has been maintained by Sinn Féin for each of the individuals involved.' He appeared content to allow Gareth Peirce to write official disclosures into his witness statement. Thus, the republicans' points' man on OTRs was spared having to impart any information: 'I do not exhibit to this statement the lengthy record of communications with the British government and others retained by Sinn Féin.' However, he uttered words which the judge noted in his judgment:[329] 'The Court will be aware from the presence of Sinn Féin MPs at the hearings to date in this case, as well as the presence of the Irish Government, of the importance that is attached to the firmness of each of the building blocks of the peace process in the North of Ireland and the reliance upon the assurances given, by all parties to those agreements, to those assurances being honoured by those who gave them.'

---

[326] Judgment, paras 9 & 17.

[327] Downey case papers, tab 3, described as a brief.

[328] Peter Hain told NIAC he was threatened with a witness summons (Qs1702, 1798 & 1817, 18 June 2014). There was no oral evidence during the abuse of process hearing!

[329] Para 80.

Jonathan Powell was strategic: 'In the book [*Great Hatred, Little Room*] I made clear my view that the most challenging part of the peace process in Northern Ireland, as in most other peace processes, is its implementation. Agreements are necessary precisely because the two sides do not trust each other and agreements by themselves do not establish trust. It is only when the two sides actually implement what they have promised to do that trust begins to be created as part of a process of peace building. If either side reneges on its undertakings or fails to implement what it has promised to do, trust can be fatally undermined.'

Peter Hain (on 30 January 2014 – late in the application) was proud to identify the administrative scheme with his time in the NIO (2005–7): 'The proposed legislation was in due course laid before the House, but it was not passed. I do not set out here the different objections that led to its abandonment. It was in this context that the already ongoing administrative scheme, although begun as a temporary measure, because the mechanism by which all of the "On The Run" applicants were enabled to have their position clarified.' Note the use of the word 'all', but also 'clarified'. Peter Hain was alert to blaming the PSNI and exonerating the NIO, and this passage was quoted by the judge in his judgement.[330]

Sweeney J accepted without hesitation the 'powerful evidence' of Gerry Kelly, Jonathan Powell and Peter Hain, seeing 'no significant conflict' with Kevin McGinty's.[331] The defence evidently deployed its witnesses well, judging by the tone of the final judgment.

Abuse of Process: the Law

John Downey succeeded on the newer jurisdiction (after fair trial), which has been developing since the mid-1990s: the offending the court's sense of justice and propriety test (alternatively, the affront to public conscience test).

The attorney general for NI, John Larkin QC, made the point

---

[330] Para 139.
[331] Para 171.

to NIAC that article 2 of the ECHR was not considered in the judgment.[332] This is very much a NI argument since 2001, namely the relatives' article 2 rights to a proper investigation of all violent deaths. There is only a passing reference to the relatives in the John Downey case (see below). The Hyde Park relatives were, of course, denied a trial, and the revelations which might have come from one.

The Judgment of Mr Justice Sweeney

Mr Justice Sweeney's judgment, handed down on 21 February 2014, runs to 57 pages, as noted, and 181 paragraphs. That is short by modern standards, even after a five-day application. It is all the more remarkable, when one considers that he was dealing with fifteen hundred pages of official documents, which had been disclosed in different tranches.

The judgement has two main narrative sections: overview of the background, paragraphs 18 to 82; and the defendant and the administrative scheme, paragraphs 83 to 141. These contain the judicial summary of the official documents. It is necessary to make a point about each. First, Mr Justice Sweeney made no general finding of fact regarding the administrative scheme. He did not ask the questions: was it lawful?; or were aspects of it unlawful (in a public-law sense)? He simply set the scene for John Downey. The second point is: the treatment of this particular OTR was more forensic, but, again, there was no general finding of fact in this section regarding the attribution of responsibility.[333]

Readers are fortunate in that the *ratio decidendi*[334] of Mr Justice

---

[332] NIAC, *Report,* Q1618 & Qs1661–2, 19 June 2014.

[333] As the defence made clear in its closing written submissions, it was blaming the state, not the police or the civil service: 'The Crown is an indivisible entity when acting in the discharge of its duties as a public prosecutor (see *Blackledge* [1996] 1 Cr. App. R. 326). It is therefore not relevant to the court's assessment of the merits of the application to attribute responsibility for the error in the issuance of the assurance letter. The responsibility is that of the State.' (2 February 2014, para 9)

[334] The point on which the judgment turns: alternatively, the principle which becomes part of the common law.

Sweeney's judgment is to be found in one paragraph with the reasons in a second. Paragraph 173 contains 32 key findings of facts, some by (generous) inference, showing what evidence – essentially, the existence of the administrative scheme – led him to apply the law in the way he did. Paragraph 175 contains the *ratio*, which has been quoted above in part in the preface. These two paragraphs are crucial to understanding this judgment, and they are quoted in full in the appendix below.

Paragraph 175 contains Sweeney J's balancing of, on the one hand: the public interest in prosecuting those accused of serious crime; and, on the other, the overlapping public interests in: first, 'executive misconduct ... not undermin[ing] public confidence in the criminal justice system and bring[ing] it into disrepute'; and second 'holding officials of the state to promises they have made in full understanding of what is involved in the bargain'. These two reasons are the one idea: 'executive misconduct' must be the John Downey mistake, and promises by officials of the state is the comfort letter. The judge made clear that the former was 'very significantly outweighed' by the latter, words carefully chosen when the balance could have been expressed in many different ways. This was, he concluded, an abuse of process case: 'this is one of those rare cases in which, in the particular circumstances, it [in the words of Lord Lowry] offend's the court's sense of justice and propriety to be asked to try the defendant.' But what were the particular circumstances?

Paragraph 173 contains these. It is difficult to summarize or categorize the 32 findings. However, a number of points may be made. First, John Downey knew he was wanted for the Hyde Park bombing (and, though Mr Justice Sweeney did not go so far, he must have known whether he was guilty or not). Second, the judge rejected firmly the prosecution view of a limited undertaking, to which John Downey must have known he was not entitled (because of the mistake). Third, the judge had twenty/twenty vision of the administrative scheme (revealed in his court over five days). Four, Mr Justice Sweeney accepted the prosecution view that there had been a 'catastrophic failure' regarding John Downey's letter, but he did not – as the government would do – blame the PSNI: 'As yet, there has been no sensible explanation for the various Operation Rapid failures.' A sensible explanation was to take time to emerge. Five, John Downey relied upon his letter, by entering the UK, and he suffered detriment, when he was arrested at Gatwick airport.

It was the prosecution that attributed the Downey mistake to the PSNI. The closing written submissions of the prosecution, by Brian Altman QC and Stuart Baker, included: 'The assurance letter was transmitted to the defendant via Sinn Fein in error in the sense that there was a fundamental failure of those within the PSNI conducting the review in 2007 … to make checks of the PNC or of the material in their own files.'[335] Both of the latter propositions are clearly wrong, as we now know. But, the PSNI being blamed in court by the prosecution, would set a precedent for others. Ministers, following the judgment, were ready to run with the ball.

No doubt, Mr Justice Sweeney toyed with the idea of whether he should permit John Downey to be prosecuted. He had the law – offending justice and propriety – as his master, but that created a very wide discretion. As a criminal lawyer, he did not pursue equitable ideas, such as it was unconscionable of John Downey to rely upon his letter (since he was not entitled to it). Nor was he interested in public-law concepts, about legality – which could have led him to query a great deal of the official conduct which had been revealed. One can only conclude that the judge was mesmerized, by the apparently consensual talk of peace process.[336] This had been a Tony Blair project from the first, not something attributable to a few hidden officials. The judge quoted uncritically Gerry Kelly, Jonathan Powell and Peter Hain in his findings of fact. In doing so, he invited – no doubt unconsciously – a proper constitutional examination, stimulated by his judgment, of the conduct of NI policy in 2000-14.

If John Downey had pleaded guilty in January 2014, he would

---

[335] 2 February 2014 (Downey case papers, tab 1).

[336] He used the phrases: 'an international peace process' (para 173(11)); 'a supporter of the peace process' (para 173(22)); and 'in furtherance of the peace process' (para 173(30)). This was the language of the defence, not of constitutional analysis.

have faced only a maximum of two years in prison, probably on transfer to the Republic of Ireland (if he had requested it). Abuse of process applications rarely succeed. His legal advisers were ready for a relatively risk-free five days. The prosecution appeared disabled, having had to disclose the administrative scheme, by the idea of a PSNI mistake. The defence did not have to pry into Sinn Féin's secrets, given it had UK perfidity to allege. It was John Downey's good luck, and many others misfortune, that Mr Justice Sweeney was listed to referee this criminal justice match to judicial decision.

Given Mr Justice Sweeney's decision was not one that every judge would have made, could it not have been appealed. That question needs asking.

CHAPTER ELEVEN

Why No Appeal?

An order staying the prosecution was made in the Old Bailey, on 21 February 2014, *in camera*. When the prosecution stated in the high court, on 25 February 2014, that it was not appealing, the stay then took effect. The reporting restrictions of the previous Friday were also lifted. Had the prosecution considered appealing the order of Mr Justice Sweeney as unlawful? Yes it did, and it did so promptly. What grounds might there have been? Here, one can only speculate about what might have been considered, and what was probably not thought about.[337]

Abuse of Process Appeals

It is necessary to stress that abuse of process appeals are not common. Defendants lost the right to appeal a failed application immediately, in the early 1990s. The prosecution's limited prosecution right is contained in: part 9 of the Criminal Justice Act 2003. Appeal is to the court of appeal (criminal division), with the leave of the judge or the court of appeal.

Section 58 (general right of appeal in respect of rulings) contains the procedure: the section does not expressly include abuse of process appeals. It permits an adjournment, to consider whether to appeal or not. During any adjournment – which is a matter for the judge – the stay is stayed. But the prosecution is required, if it appeals, to agree that the defendant should be acquitted, if the court of appeal refuses leave or the appeal is abandoned. The stay remains stayed, if there is a decision to appeal, and leave is being sought, from the judge or the

---

[337] In theory, there could have been an application – a second option – in the court of appeal subsequently, to set aside the stay, if, for example, new evidence had been forthcoming. That is different from an appeal of the order.

court of appeal, until there is disposal of the appeal.

The powers of the court of appeal are contained in section 61: it may confirm, reverse or vary any ruling of a judge in the crown court.

But section 67 (reversal of rulings) is crucial: before it reverses a ruling, the court of appeal must be satisfied: '(a) that the ruling was wrong in law; (b) that the ruling involved an error of law or principle, or (c) that the ruling was a ruling that it was not reasonable for the judge to have made.' An appeal is not a second try, with a different judge or judges. The first-instance judge has to have made an error of law. An appellate court often ends up deciding that, whether or not it would have so decided, the judge was entitled to come to his decision; judicial discretion, which is what Mr Justice Sweeney exercised, is very difficult to appeal.

What the Prosecution Did?

Immediately after Mr Justice Sweeney's ruling, on Friday, 21 February 2014, the prosecution asked for an adjournment. On Tuesday, 25 February 2014, it told the judge that it was not seeking leave to appeal.

Evidently, there had been a conference, on the Monday: this was hosted by the crown prosecution service; invited was Brian Altman QC, and probably his junior; the attorney general, Dominic Grieve QC, also attended, with Kevin McGinty. 'We discussed this case in great detail', Dominic Grieve told NIAC, 'before we took the decision not to appeal the judge's judgment.'[338]

We do not know what reasons were considered, and proved decisive. They have to be sought in oral evidence given to NIAC.

Dominic Grieve volunteered to NIAC the (innocent) mistake point: 'not only had there been an initial mistake, but that mistake had been compounded by, on at least two occasions, there being the possibility of it being rectified, but for reasons unexplained, that not happening.'[339] Innocent mistake was clearly not thought to be a runner,

---

[338] NIAC, *Report,* Q2157, 2 July 2014.
[339] NIAC, *Report,* Q2157 & Q2180, 2 July 2014.

because nothing was done on the two subsequent occasions.

Kevin McGinty told NIAC, regarding further abuse of process applications: 'If any other letter has gone out that fits the same facts as Downey in that it is not only wrong but it is known to be wrong by the authorities, then I think we will face the same position that we did with Downey and we would not get past an abuse-of-process argument.'[340]

Barra McGrory – who had no involvement in the case – also put forward the same narrow view of the judgment: 'Mr Downey's [letter] was worth something, because he had been misled into thinking there was no evidence ... the only basis upon which the abuse of process application was allowed ... was that he not only got a letter in error in 2007, but there were two opportunities to rectify that – one in 2008 and one in 2009 – that were not taken. So the view of Mr Justice Sweeney was that the degree of culpability of the state in its mistake was so great that it was an abuse of process of the court.'[341]

The facts of the John Downey case were, in contradistinction: there was an executive promise, right or wrong; and John Downey relied upon it (or rather Gerry Kelly's interpretation). We doubt that John Downey was misled about there being no evidence against him. If Mr Justice Sweeney had wanted to decide on 'the degree of culpability' of the state, he would have explained that and not left it to distinguished interpreters of his judgment.

Two things may have haunted the 24 February 2014 conference: first, the prosecution had disclosed the administrative scheme (in all its departmental variation) incrementally, and Mr Justice Sweeney got the picture of considerable executive substance to John Downey's letter; and second, the judge had not been persuaded by the prosecution to analyze the text of the letter – the so-called statement of fact – leading to the possibility of diminishing its effect to irrelevance (that, after all, had been the premise of the decision to prosecute: Brian Altman QC had advised initially that the letter was not an insuperable obstacle to

---

[340]   NIAC, *Report*, Q576, 30 April 2014.
[341]   NIAC, *Report*, Q1379, 10 June 2014.

prosecution[342]). I have made the point already that the letter to Gerry Kelly said one thing, and the letter for John Downey said something different. But that seems not to have been considered.

Ultimately, the appeal conference had to ask (and answer) the question: after the legal argument of five days, and the disclosed official material, would the court of appeal – regardless of the glare of publicity – say that Mr Justice Sweeney had got it wrong, or would it conclude that it was not unreasonable to have ruled that prosecution would amount to an abuse of process.

Criminal litigation is, of course, adversarial. It appears that the prosecutors, having lost in front of Mr Justice Sweeney, concentrated on what they perceived their weakness to be: a letter issued in mistake. They were not looking closely enough at the defence's strong card: the administrative scheme, as it emerged during the abuse of process application. The judgment of Mr Justice Sweeney, looked at more objectively, taking advantage of time and space, turns on Tony Blair and his peace process – the conclusion which flows from paragraph 175 of the judgment.

Grounds?

Though any appeal would have been to the criminal division of the court of appeal, at that level it is possible to have a wider range of judges consider possible prosecution grounds. There are three possible grounds, which, if they were not considered, should have been considered, at the prosecution conference on Monday, 24 February 2014. They are now academic (as lawyers and others use that word). And they raise wider issues than are considered normally in a criminal appeal.

First, the state of the law on abuse of process. Fair trial is tried and tested. A great variety of points is taken.[343] But the court can often, by modifying procedure, avert the need to abandon a prosecution. Unfair to try (or the integrity of the criminal justice system) undoubtedly

---

[342] NIAC, *Report,* Qs2854-5, 22 October 2014.
[343] *Archbold 2014,* paras 4-75 to 4-98.

exists as a legal reason.[344] But it is at risk of becoming amorphous, and frankly covering other issues. Why does executive misconduct inevitably damage confidence in criminal justice? Could practical solutions not be found by the courts? Are abduction and entrapment not effectively criminal defences, whereas they were not before attachment to abuse of process? This part of abuse of process is at risk of becoming what it claims not to be, namely a case of the courts punishing public figures and bodies by denying them prosecutions. Some or all of these issues may figure, in a review of abuse of process by the supreme court, sooner rather than later.

Second, the question of equity. Equity was once an alternative to law, and its concepts remain distinct in statutory and common law today. It turns on the question of conscience or unconscionability. An aspect of equity has intruded into criminal law, and it was argued – mainly by the prosecution, unsuccessfully – in the John Downey case: (no) detrimental reliance. Less attention was paid the idea that John Downey knew he was not entitled to a comfort letter. How would he have been prejudiced by a fair trial, which the judge held he could have? One must assume that Gerry Kelly interpreted the letter, and the administrative scheme, to John Downey. But the latter chose to take the risks, by entering NI and Great Britain. On a strict reading of the letter, John Downey – not knowing what the PSNI might have done from 21 July 2007 – was showing no detrimental reliance.

Third, the idea of public law. This is a product of the twentieth century, and is displayed most frequently in the administrative court (so-called judicial review). It is the law which is used to assess the actions of ministers, officials and others. It is extraordinary that Mr Justice Sweeney never asked relevant constitutional questions. True, he was not writing the first draft of history. But did he not wonder about Tony Blair, when he (the judge) let himself be impressed by peace process talk (against which Brian Altman QC warned correctly[345])?

Lord Goldsmith, who advised on the administrative scheme from

---

[344] *Archbold 2014,* paras 4.99 to 4.106.
[345] Para 165(11).

2001 to 2007, hinted (in evidence to NIAC) at the exceptional nature of Mr Justice Sweeney's judgment: 'There are a number of cases ... where people have been able to avoid prosecution even for serious crimes on the basis of an abuse of process by the prosecution. It is quite a tough regime. This may be quite a tough example of its operation. If the letter had been corrected, then the situation really would not have arisen, but I understand the legal thinking behind it, though I think that other judges might have reached a different conclusion.'[346] One doubts his point about correcting the letter (Downey, or rather Gerry Kelly, had been sent it). And the possibility of a different decision cuts two ways: it provides an opportunity for appeal; and it permits the court of appeal to dismiss even a leave application.

Lord Pannick QC Intervenes

David Pannick is a leading barrister, who has done government work, and is a crossbench member of the house of lords. He writes a fortnightly legal column for *The Times*. He practises public, and human rights, law. He writes frequently on criminal matters.

On 20 March 2014, he devoted his column to John Downey: 'Should executive misconduct prevent justice in serious crimes'. He began: 'It is very regrettable that the Attorney-General decided not to take the case to the Court of Appeal so the matter could be considered by the Lord Chief Justice [Lord Thomas of Cwmgriedd] and other senior judges.'

David Pannick summarized the OTR issue, for a generally unin-formed audience, and quoted Mr Justice Sweeney's paragraph 175. He went on to criticize the judge: 'It is far from obvious that Mr Justice Sweeney's conclusion was correct in principle. Mr Downey is accused of a crime of the utmost gravity. Mr Justice Sweeney did not find that any public official had deliberately sought to mislead Mr Downey. Indeed, the defence accepted that "the likelihood was that the letter was the product of error". The case-law establishes that the court's discretion to

---

[346] NIAC, *Report,* Q2086, 2 July 2014.

stay proceedings should not be exercised in order to express disapproval of official conduct. Moreover, it is not enough for Mr Downey to show that but for the assurance he would not have entered the jurisdiction.'

Concluding with the attorney general's written parliamentary statement, to the effect that there was no prospect of a successful appeal, David Pannick wrote: 'But how to balance the public interest in trying a man accused of such a heinous crime against an assurance wrongly given because of gross incompetence is a novel issue of principle appropriate for the Lord Chief Justice and the Court of Appeal to determine. Previous cases have involved deliberate and flagrant disregard of legal requirements by the State. It would not have been difficult to draft arguable grounds of appeal that the trial judge erred in principle. An appeal would undoubtedly have been difficult, but would have had at least some prospects of success.'

David Pannick was writing without any knowledge of the thought that had been given to a mistake (mainly by Kevin McGinty). He was also writing before the NIO decided what to do about the existing comfort letters. To conclude: maybe the legal thinking on the John Downey mistake was contaminated – not for the first time – by the politics of NI.

End of the Road?

The attorney general expressed the view to NIAC that John Downey could not be prosecuted in the future. That process had been stayed by Mr Justice Sweeney, in England and Wales. It is the position that John Downey is most unlikely to return to the Old Bailey, regarding the Hyde Park bombing. But there are two other options. The first is that, with the PSNI review of the OTR files (Operation Redfield), something in templates 1 to 5 will emerge. John Downey could be prosecuted in NI, for an offence committed there. But this would require his extradition from the Republic of Ireland, under a European arrest warrant. That assumes he has stopped travelling to NI and to Great Britain.

The second option is admittedly more tenuous. The stay of Mr

Justice Sweeney applies only in England and Wales. It does not bind the NI judiciary. When Neal Graham was completing template 6, regarding Hyde Park, on 2 May 2007, he believed John Downey faced a conspiracy to murder charge.[347] As noted, John Downey had been entered on the police national computer as wanted for conspiracy to murder, on or before 20 July 1982. Most likely, the Hyde Park and Regent's Park bombings were planned in the Republic of Ireland; but there is a possibility that there was a conspiracy in NI. If, and it is only a slight possibility, there was evidence of a NI conspiracy, then, in theory, John Downey could be tried in NI, for his alleged part in a conspiracy which led to bombings in England and Wales.

Given the sorry saga of the Downey trial collapse, how was the administrative scheme assessed in the immediately following months, by the various inquiries established?

---

[347] This manuscript template was disclosed by district inspector Eamonn Corrigan, on 24 January 2014.

CHAPTER TWELVE

Reports

The three official reports into OTRs, mentioned in the preface, are:

- *first*, Dame Heather Hallett CBE, *An Independent Review into the On the Runs Administrative Scheme*, HC 380, 17 July 2014 ('Hallett, *Report*');
- *second*, Police Ombudsman for Northern Ireland ('PONI'), *Public Statement on PSNI Operation Rapid, Matters Arising from the Ruling in R v John Downey*, 20 October 2014 ('PONI, *Report*); and
- *third*, House of Commons, Northern Ireland Affairs Committee ('NIAC'), *The Administrative Scheme for "On-the-Runs": second report of session 2014-15*, HC 177, 24 March 2015 ('NIAC, *Report*').

Here, I look at the setting up of the three inquiries, and then consider each report in turn. The terms Hallett, PONI and NIAC are used to refer mainly to the reports. What do the three reports tell us about the OTR scandal?

In the Wake of Downey

On 26 February 2014 (immediately after Downey and at the request of the PSNI), the Police Ombudsman for Northern Ireland, Dr Michael Maguire, announced that he would investigate the conduct of police officers regarding the Downey letter.

On 11 March 2014, the secretary of state for Northern Ireland, Theresa Villiers, announced that an English court of appeal judge, Dame Heather Hallett DBE, was to provide an independent review of the administrative scheme. This was not a judicial inquiry. Nor was it under the Inquiries Act 2005. And it was time limited to the end of

May (then June) 2014. The NIO offered the judge's clerk civil service support. Dame Heather was offered accommodation in the ministry of justice building in Westminster.

The prime minister, David Cameron, had been involved in the background,[348] not least because NI's first minister, Peter Robinson, was threatening to resign unless there was a speedy judicial inquiry.[349] This explains the imprecisions in the establishment of the Hallett review, with number 10 dealing with the first minister and the NIO communicating with the lord chief justice, Lord Thomas of Cwmgiedd. The terms of reference of the Hallett review (agreed with the first minister) were threefold: one, 'to produce a full public account of the operation and extent of the administrative scheme for OTRs'; two, 'to determine whether any letters sent through the scheme contained errors'; and three, 'to make recommendation as necessary on this or related matters that are drawn to the attention of the inquiry'.[350] The second term of reference had already been amended in negotiations: on 10 March 2014, Julian King, the director general of the NIO, told the lord chief justice, that the reviewer would not have to determine how many other letters were issued erroneously.[351]

Also on 11 March 2014, the Northern Ireland Affairs Committee, in the house of commons, chaired by Laurence Robertson, a conservative MP, decided to launch a parliamentary inquiry simultaneously. Its members included NI MPs, as well as labour and conservative representatives. The terms of reference were more extensive than Hallett, listing sixteen separate issues including 'any other related matters'. NIAC had considerable powers as a departmental select committee, under the standing orders of the house, 'to send for persons, papers and records'.[352] It was determined to use them.

---

[348] Press release, 27 February 2014.

[349] BBC, 26 February 2014.

[350] HC, *Hansard,* vol. 577, col. 22WS, 11 March 2014.

[351] Letter, made available on: *www.judiciary.gov.uk.*

[352] Standing order no. 152(4) (of 19 December 2013).

(1) The Hallett Report

The Hallett report – which appeared first – runs to 147 pages, with eleven appendices. Since publication, it has been embraced by former and existing ministers, but especially by officials, as the definitive work. Dame Heather's conclusion – that the administrative scheme was lawful – is constitutionally inadequate. She made clear that she did not write as a judge: 'I am not sitting in a judicial capacity.'[353] That is why this book does not refer to her as lady justice. She referred to the continuing NIAC inquiry, and described the judicial and parliamentary approaches as complimentary.[354]

Logistics

Dame Heather's initial deadline had been the end of May 2014. She made her 'preliminary findings' on 30 June 2014 (the revised deadline), and, after 'security checks' and 'further representations', she signed off on 11 July 2014.[355] Four months may have been too rushed for the topic.

Dame Heather appears to have avoided the civil-service embrace, to some extent. She appointed Maura McGowan QC, recently chair of the bar council[356] (and now a high court judge), as her leading counsel. Tom Little, the barrister who had been responsible for disclosure in the John Downey case, was junior counsel to the review. Simon Ramsden, a commercial litigator at Norton Rose Fulbright, became solicitor to the review. Aside from her judicial assistant, another solicitor, and a pupil barrister, the other five members of her team were junior officials (including from the ministry of justice).

Dame Heather managed to talk to over forty individuals, some of whom declined to give evidence to NIAC. But her private conversations did not make for necessary distance in examining executive (mis)conduct.

---

[353] Para 1.11.

[354] Para 1.15.

[355] Foreward.

[356] Dame Heather had been chair of the bar council in 1998.

Dame Heather seems not to have appreciated that the Downey case papers (which had been declassified), were in the public domain, ready to be quoted. Her team may well have examined all the documents between its members, but one feels it was overwhelmed.[357] Did Dame Heather read the 'core master bundle containing every significant document in chronological order'?[358] She does not claim to have done so. The team had access to the 228 OTR files, which remain with the PSNI. Dame Heather states she was bound by confidentiality as regards the list of names, though she also draws an unclear distinction between open and closed material.[359] Ultimately, there was a problem with the nature of the review. Dame Heather writes: 'I embarked upon a fact-finding mission rather than a political debate.'[360] Unfortunately, there is inadequate fact finding of a constitutional kind, because she evidently sought to avoid any criticism of Tony Blair, senior ministers and supportive civil servants.

Using the Report

The Hallett report contains much useful material, especially: appendix 5, the OTR tables; and appendix 9, material in the public domain.

Appendix 5

Appendix 5 is the five redacted tables of the 228 OTR applicants. While the PSNI first used this total figure in public,[361] we know from chapter 7 that 23 of these remained 'wanted', with up to an additional 18 cases undecided (meaning that between 187 and 205 got off, one way or another[362]).

It is clear that Hallett obtained considerable disclosure, especially

---

[357] Foreward.
[358] Para 1.28.
[359] Para 1.28.
[360] Para 1.19.
[361] NIAC, *Report,* Q678 (7 May 2014).
[362] Table 7.2.

of the OTR case review files from principally the PSNI.[363] Appendix 5 may also have been prefigured in the so-called OTR spreadsheet, kept seemingly by the NIO.

Appendix 9

Appendix 9 is a compilation of OTR 'material in the public domain'. This is discussed in chapter 8 of the report: public knowledge of the administrative scheme. However, the Hallett interpretation – showing her judging – is neither clear nor convincing.

The data – starting with appendix 9 – refers to over eighty pieces of information, from official statements to Sinn Féin-sourced press stories. The date range, however, is 30 August 1998 to 7 May 2013 – nearly 15 years. Whether one should have known depends upon the consistency of the information revealed over a relatively long period of time, when a great deal else was also happening in NI.

A number of points may be made. First, the government never set out to disclose the administrative scheme, in however a skeletal form. Second, when it appeared to be under pressure, the government deliberately (it would appear) sought to divert attention. (This applies to the much-cited, but rare, parliamentary answers of John Reid (to Quentin Davies), on 1 July 2002, and of Peter Hain [to Lady Hermon], on 7 February and 1 March 2007.[364]) And third, whatever the media was picking up from Sinn Féin, and from various court proceedings latterly, was, in the absence of legal expertise – but especially the responses of government – difficult to assess. NI's finest journalistic sleuths were kept guessing.

There was no straight answer to a straight question, because no MP or peer – seeking to scrutinize government policy – actually knew about the administrative scheme. Time after time, parliamentarians made a stab at the problem: each time, the government was able to deflect attention.

---

[363] Para 1.28.

[364] A parliamentary answer of Tony Blair to Nigel Waterson, on 10 April 2002, may be taken as the precedent for misleading ministerial statements.

There was one occasion on which notice should have been taken, namely the publication of the Eames/Bradley consultative group on the past report, on 23 January 2009. A short summary of the administrative scheme – that term was not used – is given in five paragraphs on pages 120–1. However, the failed NIOB (four paragraphs) had the effect of obscuring the reference to the administrative scheme (one paragraph).[365] Moreover, since Eames/Bradley was subject to immediate controversy, the report having recommended payments to all the dead (including terrorists), there is some defence for not fully studying a report which was politically stillborn on publication.

Owen Paterson, who was one of the most experienced NI shadow secretaries of state, knew nothing of the administrative scheme, before he assumed office in May 2010 (and little of it afterwards, it would appear).

Hallett contains a discussion of appendix 9 in chapter 8. Two conclusions are drawn. First, while the administrative scheme was kept 'below the radar', it was not secret.[366] The following reason for denying secrecy does not make sense: 'Government statements on how OTRs were being dealt with after the Belfast Agreement range from those which might be characterised as accurate and helpful to those which are less than informative.' The government was consistent in its evasiveness: if it had made fully accurate statements on some occasions, the administrative scheme would have been in the public domain; ministers obscured the (private) administrative scheme by referring to the (public) issue of OTRs.

The second conclusion does not logically follow: 'in my view, there was sufficient information in the public domain to alert the close observer of political affairs in Northern Ireland to the fact that some kind of process existed by which OTRs could submit their names for consideration by the police and prosecuting authorities.'[367] There were

---

[365] The source of this information appears to have been the NIO: Shaun Woodward, NIAC, *Report*, Q384, 9 April 2014.

[366] Para 8.55.

[367] Para 8.54.

numbers of close observer of political affairs. But a suspicion about some kind of process was not the same as knowledge. That was kept confined, from 2000 to 2014, to small groups of individuals. If some of the latter gossiped, that did not take matters much further. There was no whistle blower, though Norman Baxter – undoubtedly without intention – is credited as the destroyer of the administration scheme. However, when he blurted out to NIAC in 2009 about OTRs, he was quickly returned to the topic of that inquiry.

In seeking to lance the charge of secrecy (to some extent a straw person), Dame Heather revealed an unwillingness to adequately discuss transparency and accountability in chapter 8. She sits on the fence when she should have been making findings of fact: 'Mr Hain has argued that [his] answers were strictly accurate given the context of the question (the withdrawal of a Bill which would have provided a legislative amnesty for OTRs). Others disagree.'[368] There is no finding here.

Dame Heather may have read the evidence of David (Lord) Trimble to NIAC, on 13 May 2014, when he was asked by Ian Paisley whether he felt betrayed over OTRs: 'I must confess I was quite hurt [at the time of the Downey judgment]. We had had so many meetings with Secretaries of State and with the Prime Minister, and we approached those meetings in a candid manner. There were no hints dropped and no indications. Although some of the questions that we asked came close to containing a broad hint as to what had happened, at the same time, language was used in those questions that would have led us to believe that nothing was being done on the OTR front.'[369]

Legality

In chapter 9 on 'legal issues', there is an attempt to answer the question: was the administrative scheme lawful? I have referred to the need to ask proper public law questions. Having failed to ask the correct questions, it is not surprising that Dame Heather has little by way of answer.

---

[368] Para 8.45.
[369] NIAC, *Report,* Q812.

There are 24 references to Tony Blair, but only eight in the body of the report. All are simply narrative. The Blair letter of 28 December 2006 is quoted in full.[370] However, there is no discussion of the three earlier written promises. The fourth written promise is not analyzed. And this in spite of the prime minister's unqualified promise to 'resolve all the remaining cases' before he resigned.

Lord Williams of Mostyn merits one reference, and Lord Goldsmith two. There is no discussion of the consistent legal advice coming from Tony Blair's law officers.

Nor is there any discussion of how Tony Blair, through Jonathan Powell (and Bill Jeffrey), and some secretaries of state, commanded the executive branch of government. That is the big question of his premiership. To date, his handling of NI affairs has escaped censure. But what if the administrative scheme shows patterning with his conduct of state policy more widely, including on Iraq and Afghanistan?

In contrast to the eight Blair references, there are 127 references to Norman Baxter. Granted, the latter was in charge of Operation Rapid in 2007–8. And granted, the Downey mistake occurred on his watch. But Dame Heather was reporting on the administrative scheme, 2000–14, and this is disproportionate in the extreme. Tony Blair was the key individual, whose legacy includes the John Downey case. Norman Baxter is only one candidate for criticism. The other, more credibly, is Mark Sweeney; there are 18 references to this NIO official, but no discussion of his greater putative mistakes.

The one iconoclastic part of the report is Dame Heather's point about the test for police investigators ('reasonable grounds for suspecting') versus that for prosecutors ('sufficient evidence to afford a reasonable prospect of conviction').[371] She seems not to have appreciated that the administrative scheme was about letting terrorists off, if at all possible. Questions tended to be asked the other way round: is this evidence too weak rather than how could it be made stronger? Dame Heather seems to have failed to distinguish properly the regime under

---

[370] Para 5.11.

[371] Para 2.41.

Sir Alasdair Fraser, 2000–6, and Operation Rapid, from 2007. Under the former, there was a full prosecution review. The PSNI worked with the PPSNI, so the issue was, not investigation, but whether prosecution was viable. Things became less clear in 2007. On the one hand, the failed NIO effort of 2002, with simply a wanted or not wanted answer, appears to have returned with Operation Rapid (not that Peter Sheridan and Norman Baxter knew about the earlier proposal). The PSNI took over. On the other hand, the NIO eclipsed the attorney general's office. The key question remains: what did the PSNI do? It is overly theoretical to refer to different legal tests, since Operation Rapid did not comprise judges or lawyers. It now emerges, for good or ill, that Dame Heather was inspired to take the wrong legal test point, by a third party outside her team (discussed below).

Systemic Failings?

Julian King, in his letter of 10 March 2014, to the lord chief justice, had elaborated on the terms of reference: 'The reviewer should also examine and report on how many errors came to be made, including any systemic failings within the operation of the administrative scheme.'[372] Did this put an idea into Dame Heather's head? Her report, unexciting in so many ways, does contain a potentially radical kernel.

The administrative scheme was run by Whitehall. Senior officials deservedly pride themselves in their Rolls Royce performance. A minister with a problem may expect an administrative solution, with any necessary legislative and presentational add-ons. Yet, in her executive summary, Dame Heather launched an Exocet: 'The administrative scheme was not designed; it evolved. As a result, it lacked proper lines of responsibility, accountability and safeguards (such as risk assessments and mechanisms for review).'[373] It is a measure of Whitehall man and woman, that they have so far limited the damage to their reputations by accepting this Hallett criticism without demur. Not designed but evolved, of course, exonerates each and every individual, regardless of particular contribution.

---

[372] Letter, made available on: *www.judiciary.gov.uk.*
[373] Para 2.26.

Such a catchy phrase should not obscure what the report does not do. There is no empathy for Sir Alasdair Fraser, and his very reluctant willingness to play ball in 2000–6. There is also no assessment of that phase of the administrative scheme, and how it had to be structured. There is no understanding of Peter Sheridan and Norman Baxter, in 2007–8, being driven by unusual political success (Sinn Féin support for the PSNI). And there is certainly no fair assessment of the Downey mistake. Dame Heather develops the police scapegoat theory, and does not look to those who took responsibility for this second, and very different, phase of the administrative scheme in the NIO. Ultimately, her moment of radicalism does not stand up to critical examination. The administrative scheme was so against the grain, it had to operate in a cloak and dagger way. This was not a topic for another inter-departmental committee of officials, proceeding in an ideal way. One imagines that Sir Alasdair Fraser would not have had much time for modern bureaucratic language about 'risk assessments': that was integral to his work. Norman Baxter, working in a quasi-military police culture, under the weight of perceived political interference, would possibly have considered 'mechanisms for review' to be slightly Utopian waffling.

The Sweeney Judgment

Hallett nails its Downey colours to the mast, unconvincingly.[374] The assertion is made (following others) that Downey was decided on unique facts. No other court has to follow Downey, unless it is a 'mistake' case. A reading of the judgment, and in particular the crucial paragraphs 173 and 175, sees the *ratio decidendi* being Downey's detrimental reliance upon his letter of comfort (regardless of his entitlement). That would apply more widely, including to those entitled to a letter.

Devolution of Policing and Justice

Finally, on the devolution of policing and justice in April 2010, Hallett again sits on the fence: prosecution was devolved to NI; but

---

[374] Paras 9.44 to 9.49.

there may have been a national security aspect.[375] Again, there is no decision on the law.

Conclusion on Hallett

The Hallett report addressed its terms of reference, inconsistently and unevenly. The first – a full public account of the administrative scheme – was achieved, but only in part. The report lacks historical analysis, and reads at time like one damned fact after another. Dame Heather pours reasonableness over her cast of characters, Gerry Adams being especially nicely treated.[376]

The second term of reference – other mistakes (in addition to Downey) – was waived by the director general of the NIO. Dame Heather, however, did some original research (inspired by Paul McGowan of Operation Rapid). It is unclear what this goes to: the PSNI had a NI-only focus; it was not ignorant of John Downey and the Hyde Park bombing.

The third term of reference is dealt with in chapter 11: recommendations. Dame Heather addressed five recommendations to the NIO, including seeking legal advice on essentially the existing comfort letters. Four recommendations were addressed to the PSNI, including well-understood terms of reference for Operation Redfield (see below) and proper oversight.

One feels that Dame Heather was trying to extricate the executive from the Downey judgment mess, without adopting a proper lessons-to-be-learned approach. That would explain both those who champion the report as the last word, and those who, if they have heard of it, have not been moved.

(2) The Police Ombudsman's Report

The PONI report, which followed Hallett, failed to rise to the OTR occasion. This is because of the way the office of police ombudsman has been permitted fundamentally to develop.

---

[375] Paras 9.55 to 9.63.
[376] Paras 2.14, 2.62, 4.77, 5.57, 8.40 and 10.57.

The Police Ombudsman

The office of police ombudsman was established by the Police (Northern Ireland) Act 1998, section 62 providing seemingly innocuously: 'The Ombudsman may, in relation to any exercise of his functions..., publish a statement as to his actions, his decisions and determinations and the reasons for his decisions and determinations.' The idea of a section 62 statement quickly became the basis of rapid mission creep by the ombudsman (which the NIO failed to stop), from civilian oversight of serving police officers in the PSNI towards historical inquiries into retired police officers who had served during the years of the troubles in the RUC.

The first police ombudsman was Nuala O'Loan (2000–7), who saw the RUC rebranded as the PSNI. After only a year in office, she published a 14-page statement about the 1998 Omagh bombing, NI's worst atrocity, which blamed the chief constable, Sir Ronnie Flanagan, for an unsuccessful investigation; his reputation was damaged irreparably, but the relatives of those killed were the principal sufferers. They were left with the feeling of being let down badly. The second police ombudsman was Al Hutchinson, a Canadian former police officer (2007–12), who was driven from office by non-governmental organizations. In 2010 (after devolution), he established a historical investigations directorate, tracking the work of the PSNI's historical enquiries team. In September 2011, the chief inspector of criminal justice, Dr Michael Maguire, criticized him fatally.[377] The third police ombudsman (2012–) was, and remains: Dr Michael Maguire. He has continued with historical investigations, and has pursued retired police officers while doing the ombudsman's job of investigating public complaints about current police conduct.

The Downey Judgment

Dr Maguire learned of the Downey judgment, on 25 February

---

[377] *An Inspection into the Independence of the Office of Police Ombudsman for Northern Ireland*, 5 September 2011.

2014, through the media. The following day, the chief constable, Matt Baggott, referred his own service to the PONI, under section 55(4) of the Police (Northern Ireland) Act 1998. But this required possible criminal, or disciplinary, proceedings, neither of which was in play. And the latter could not apply to retired police officers, such as Peter Sheridan and Norman Baxter.

The referral was not a necessary response to Mr Justice Sweeney, who, after all, in paragraph 173 of his judgment, had written carefully (as quoted in chapter 10): 'As yet, there has been no sensible explanation for the various Operation Rapid failures.' The referral was the doing of the NIO, the secretary of state's written statement of 25 February 2014 including (as noted): 'The judge concluded that the error had been made by officers of the PSNI'.[378] Overnight, on 25/26 February 2014, Matt Baggott accepted the NIO line: in doing so, he prejudged his own former officers, all but two of the Operation Rapid team being then retired.[379]

Strangely, the former chief constable, Sir Hugh Orde, then the head of the association of chief police officers in London, issued a press release on 26 February 2014. He referred to 'a very serious error' having been made: 'It is a matter of great personal regret that a crucial oversight was made by a senior officer which resulted in erroneous information being sent to Mr Downey by the Northern Ireland Office and thus prejudicing the current indictment.'[380]

Even without the chief constable, the PONI would have acted (and did so as regards 2008 and 2009 failures to act).[381] Section 55(6) of the Police (Northern Ireland) Act 1998 imposes a similar duty on him. But again, there has to be a suspicion of criminal conduct. And Peter Sheridan and Norman Baxter were beyond disciplinary proceedings.

---

[378] HC *Hansard*, vol. 576, cols. 16WS–17WS.

[379] Norman Baxter told NIAC that the chief constable received the judgment on 21 February 2014, presumably from the NIO. (NIAC, *Report*, Q95, 2 April 2014)

[380] ACPO press release, 26 February 2014.

[381] Para 2.8.

The Ombudsman's Investigation

The PONI investigation began, on 26 February 2014. Dr Maguire was not involved, other than in a directing capacity. Adrian McAllister, the chief executive, and a former acting deputy chief constable from Lancashire, made a substantive contribution, unusually (see below). But Paula Cunningham, a deputy senior investigations officer, took charge; though not a former police officer, she stated she was a civilian trained to investigate such work. It is not known how many people were involved in the investigation. The team interviewed all the Operation Rapid personnel in 2007 (including Peter Sheridan), plus 'other retired and serving police officers, identified as relevant to [the] investigation'.[382] This did not include Sir Hugh Orde. These others remain unidentified. At least one retired officer (not Norman Baxter) refused to cooperate. The report does not state that the PONI examined the Downey case papers (including the prime minister's written promises and the legal opinions of the attorneys general). It is suggested it secured its own documentation in NI, from principally the PSNI and the PPSNI.[383] Active work on the investigation appears to have concluded by late September 2014.

Looking at the circumstances of the swift launch of the investigation, including public responses to the Sweeney judgment,[384] it is difficult to avoid the conclusion that the PONI appears to have pre-judged the case. The investigators started with an assumption that Norman Baxter, and Peter Sheridan, had made a mistake, and they ended with this as their principal conclusion, dressed up in the language of management speak.[385]

---

[382] Para 3.4

[383] Para 3.3.

[384] Para 2.6.

[385] Peter Sheridan told NIAC: 'I believe the Police Ombudsman's report lacked fairness, balance and thoroughness. As someone who has read hundreds of investigations, I got the distinct impression that this was a report where the conclusions had been arrived at and then the evidence would be gathered up. It was followed from one end to the other with hindsight bias, where somebody had viewed the

There are three questions the PONI could have asked himself, overnight on 25/26 February 2014, while absorbing the fallout from the Downey judgment.

First, was the administrative scheme lawful, in whole or only in part? This was not outside his jurisdiction.[386] He seemed to assume the administrative scheme was lawful, and therefore police officers might be guilty of criminality for not running it properly. But what if aspects of it were unlawful? Might Norman Baxter not be an honest man tasked with a job about which he had genuine legal reservations? This was not to be explored in the report.

The second and third questions are most certainly part of the PONI's remit. The second question is: did Sir Hugh Orde act properly in 2006–7, when he established Operation Rapid, but denied its senior officers access to the PSNI's institutional memory?[387] The third (lesser) question is: did Matt Baggott act properly, when he made the referral of 26 February 2014. He can only have done it – wrapped up as a prompt apology spun for the media – to limit damage to his police service generally.

But Dr Maguire was interested only in using his growing powers on lesser targets. An investigation of two chief constables would have been ambitious; but the PONI seemed to want two lesser fry, albeit a detective chief superintendent (Baxter) and an assistant chief constable (Sheridan).

---

events as being more predictable than they really were'. (NIAC, *Report*, Q3149, 11 November 2014)

[386] The PONI should have considered this question, if only following the drafting of paras 6.5 to 6.7. He sees nothing wrong with the administrative scheme. But he then queries the Operation Rapid reviews of earlier reviews. This is illogical.

[387] The PONI should have considered this question, if only following the drafting of para 6.4: 'The Assistant Chief Constable should have been aware of the pervious [sic] work given the information available to him. As a consequence of this lack of knowledge, the Senior Officers who were responsible for [Operation Rapid] were not equipped appropriately to fulfil their role effectively.' The PONI blames Norman Baxter and Peter Sheridan for being in the dark.

It is correct that the Hyde Park families, following the judgment of Sweeney J, made complaints to the PONI.[388] However, these were not decisive in the initiation of the review, much less its structuring.

The Report

The report defines the remit of the investigation narrowly: the Operation Rapid terms of reference; Operation Rapid decision making in May 2007; the letter of 6 June 2007; dealings with the NIO in June/July 2007; the PSNI in 2008 and 2009.[389] All these topics are covered above. They are obvious. But the PONI, by restricting the investigation (when were these defined as the topics?), effectively ensured that the assumption became the conclusion.

The investigation's remit begins, interestingly, with theory: 'The suitability, application and compliance of the Terms of Reference set for the PSNI Operation Rapid.' This idea originated with the PONI's chief executive (not an investigator). As a former senior English police officer (without comparable terrorist experience), he would not be the first to criticize NI colleagues. The terms of reference have been criticized already (chapter 10), but the question should be: what was it that the Operation Rapid officers did? The PONI states: 'My investigation has also examined the intelligence available to the [Operation Rapid] Team in their review of John Downey.'[390] But the report does not answer the key question: how did Operation Rapid assess whether a suspect was wanted or not wanted? Operation Rapid operated pretty much as earlier police officers had done, in 2000–6. Part of the terms of reference (suggesting prosecution rather than arrest) does not contradict that.

Adrian McAllister wears an additional laurel, to his theoretical contribution to the conclusion. It appears that the PONI was in contact with the Hallett review. It is believed – and is not contradicted – that this idea of the wrong legal test was adopted by Dame Heather from this source. One sees group think, following the secretary of state's

---

[388] Para 2.9.
[389] Para 3.2.
[390] Para 3.3.

written statement of 25 February 2014, in play between the Hallett review and the PONI investigation.

The body of the report – chapters 4 and 5 (pp. 10 to 58) – trawls through the documents, these having been put to the witnesses. But there is no attempt to use the latter to bring life to the former. The overriding impression is that the investigators were seeking to attribute a mistake to the PSNI, and in particular Norman Baxter and Peter Sheridan. This they did. There is but one useful finding in all 65 pages: the investigation has tracked the email of Norman Baxter to Peter Sheridan, of 10 May 2007; the PONI report records that the former did not (as he recalled) forward additional papers to Peter Sheridan (the position the latter maintained).[391] That point has been cleared up. However, it goes nowhere, most likely: Peter Sheridan generally rubber stamped Norman Baxter's work.

The PONI made five findings: one, there was 'a lack of clarity, structure and senior leadership'; two, there was 'poor communication'; three, the Operation Rapid terms of reference were 'not suitable'; four, the Downey decision making was 'flawed'; and five, the PSNI failed to advise the PPSNI of the 2008 and 2009 discoveries.

These findings are trite to any administrative structure, and suggest that the PONI was out to get retired police officers. The first finding is credible. But it is not premised on how something like the administrative scheme could have been run. Nor is there any awareness of the unique role played by Sir Alasdair Fraser, hitherto. If it is a criticism of the PSNI, why was Sir Hugh Orde not interviewed? It is most certainly not a criticism of the NIO. The second finding (poor communication) is also trite. The Operation Rapid team did communicate effectively, albeit with new information technology. Their problem was structure: they were working in the dark. The third finding – Adrian McAllister's insight – has not been proved. There is no evidence of a wrong legal threshold in practice. But there is evidence of the PSNI having to reward Sinn Féin for unexpected support.[392] The fourth finding (flaws) is true

---

[391]   Paras 5.23-5.25.

[392]   Even Dame Heather draws this political conclusion: para 5.19: 'While no

but trite. The mistake was bigger than the PSNI. And the fifth finding (the 2008 and 2009 mistakes) assumes institutions do not cover up. The PONI does not ask, much less answer, how, if at all, John Downey's letter, once issued, could have been revoked.

(3) The Northern Ireland Affairs Committee Report

One turns to the NIAC report, of 109 pages (including an annex and two appendices), of 24 March 2015, in search of more. There is much more, not least when one accesses the report in electronic form with its numerous hyperlinks: *http://www.publications.parliament.uk/ pa/cm201415/cmselect/cmniaf/177/177.pdf*

While Hallett took four months, and PONI not much more, NIAC worked on OTRs for over a year. The MPs had other duties, including in their constituencies, but they seemed to have met most weeks when parliament was sitting at Westminster. They worked in public, in the main, and published just about everything.

The report contains, at pages 106–7 (in electronic format), selected documents from the Downey case papers, which may be accessed directly as PDF files.

At pages 107–8, one may access (through hyperlinks in the electronic version) the correspondence between the committee chair and witnesses, including Tony Blair, and those who refused to give evidence in public, seemingly only Gerry Kelly.[393]

Page 105 contains (with hyperlinks in the electronic version) the written evidence of 17 witnesses.

Pages 101–4 list the 60 witnesses (including some repeats) from whom oral evidence was taken. The electronic version carries hyperlinks to each session. Altogether, 3,990 questions were asked by the MPs. This may be a parliamentary record for a select committee inquiry.

---

document I have seen or evidence I have heard reveals that this [namely the PSNI meeting with Sinn Féin on 24 January 2007, followed, four days later, by Sinn Féin's vote to support the PSNI] was the direct reason for Operation Rapid commencing a few days later, it does not appear to be a coincidence.'

[393] Further correspondence is available on NIAC's part of the parliament website.

Virtually all the evidence sessions were open to the public. They were also recorded on video by parliament, and remain available – after broadcasting by BBC Parliament (including numerous repeats) – on the parliament website.

NIAC has assembled, in electronic form, the only available database on the OTR issue. It is unique, and it is invaluable. That is why this book has been written from that archive. Since the Downey case papers speak for themselves, there is no need to discuss the NIAC report which narrates much of the same material.

The government responded formally to the NIAC report, after the general election, on 21 July 2015.[394] Theresa Villiers had responded to Hallett with the 9 September 2014 ministerial statement. Her response to NIAC was characteristically consensual: 'The Government's notes that the Committee's report reinforces the findings of the Hallett report that the implementation of the scheme was unsatisfactory and suffered from a series of systemic failures. The scheme developed piecemeal and without appropriate direction. [] The Committee's report also acknowledges, as did the Hallett report, that errors of fact were made. The Government[s] fully accepts this conclusion. They should not have occurred and the Government has apologized for this on behalf of its predecessors.'[395]

NIAC was told that Downey might not be the end of the OTR story. There is thought to be at least another six 'mistake' cases.[396] There were, of course, at least 187 comfort letters (or equivalent). The chances of another abuse of process application, from a republican defendant, in an English, or, more likely, NI, court, is high. NIAC may, therefore, return to the issue. The current political outcome, the NIO's disavowing of the letters of 9 September 2014, may therefore

---

[394] NIAC, *Second Special Report of Session 1015–16*, 8 pp, HC345.

[395] P. 2.

[396] Private information; Hallett, *Report,* para 7.39 referred to only two (before NIAC reported, one of those – concerning Gareth O'Connor, who disappeared in May 2003 – arose in an inquest: HC, *Hansard,* vol. 591, cols. 729–37, 27 January 2015).

not be the last word on the sorry saga.

It is now time to conclude this account of the administrative scheme, and to pose a major question about the future of the past in NI.

CHAPTER THIRTEEN

Conclusion

The lesson of history, regarding the OTR story, is: Tony Blair and Jonathan Powell should never have embarked upon the project in 1999/2000. That lesson was learned, regardless of the various accounts to be put forward by Hallett, PONI and NIAC in 2014-15, in the Downey trial collapse.

The immediate losers are the 228 OTRs, who were led up to the top of the hill by Gerry Kelly (he presumably still has the letters), only to be led down as a consequence of Adams/McGuinness over-negotiation. (The OTRs might have had their statutory amnesty in 2006, but for Sinn Féin pulling the plug over the inclusion of the security forces.) The principal culprit is the UK government: it violated the principle of the rule of law, by permitting political interference in criminal justice. History will not absolve Tony Blair, and those who did his bidding, with enthusiasm or because they had to: there was no good (and lawful) reason for Operation Rapid, in advance of the political retirement forced by Gordon Brown, other than the prime minister's need to secure his personal legacy with a NI deal.

Operation Redfield

On 7 May 2014 (before Hallett), Matt Baggott told NIAC that the PSNI had decided to review the 228 OTR cases, including John Downey's. The review was to be called Operation Redfield, and it replaced Sir Hugh Orde's less appropriately named one. Criminal justice was back apparently in the hands of the police and prosecutors. Drew Harris, an assistant chief constable also giving evidence, revealed, for the first time, that 95 holders of comfort letters were linked, through intelligence (not evidence), to 295 murders.[397] He expected Operation

---

[397] NIAC, *Report*, Q696, 7 May 2014. Drew Harris actually said 200 murders.

Redfield to take two to three years: he was taking 19 officers off serious crime, and wanted to increase that to 30 officers.[398] Unfortunately, when, as deputy chief constable, he returned to NIAC, to give further evidence on 4 November 2014, he informed MPs that police budgeting meant he could only deploy 17 officers, and it would now take seven to eight years.[399] In March 2015, following legal advice from the secretary of state, the PSNI revised the terms of reference for Operation Redfield; ironically, given the Downey case, it would not be reviewing offences committed in England and Wales (or Scotland?).

Dealing with the Past

Drew Harris also told NIAC on the latter occasion, that the PSNI was establishing 'a legacy investigation branch' to replace the historical enquiries team.[400] Clearly, something was in the wind regarding the past, albeit – it would seem – further legacy litigation. The Eames/Bradley report of 2009 had been still born.[401] If the recommendations – based upon a legacy commission – had been accepted then, it would have been implemented over five years. The Haass/O'Sullivan talks in late 2013 had not even achieved agreement.[402] But they left a list of new adopted institutions, with an alphabet soup of initials. On 23 December 2014, after eleven weeks of talks brokered by the NIO, the Stormont House agreement emerged in Belfast.[403]

The Stormont House Agreement

The Stormont House agreement was between principally the DUP and Sinn Féin: the alliance party supported it; but the Ulster unionist

---

He corrected the figure later: clerk's annotation to earlier transcript.

[398] NIAC, *Report,* Qs 749 & 751, 7 May 2014.

[399] NIAC, *Report,* Qs 3049 & 3054, 4 November 2014.

[400] NIAC, *Report,* Q3054, 4 November 2014.

[401] Report of the Consultative Group on the Past, 23 January 2009.

[402] Proposed Agreement 31 December 2013, *An Agreement among the Parties of the Northern Ireland Executive on Parades, Select Commemorations, and Related Protests; Flags and Emblems; and Contending with the Past.*

[403] There is in fact: a principal agreement of 14 pages; and a 5-page financial annex.

party and SDLP had reservations. It had the – mainly financial – support of the UK government, which makes a difference.

This agreement, under 'the past', provided for: one, an oral history archive; two, a historical investigations unit; three, a UK/Irish independent commission on information retrieval; and, four, an implementation and reconciliation group.[404] The past, and legacy litigation, has become a major topic. Here, I note only the planned historical investigations unit, one of the four proposals on the past. Strangely, OTRs was nowhere mentioned in the Stormont House agreement, after Hallett but before NIAC.

A Fresh Start Agreement

Implementation of the Stormont House agreement was interrupted by two related IRA murders.[405] The UK government was forced to admit that the IRA still existed, but that it was committed to Sinn Féin's political objectives.[406] There followed ten weeks of talks in NI. On 17 November 2015, the NIO published: *A Fresh Start: the Stormont agreement and implementation plan* (67 pp). This document, agreed again principally by the DUP and Sinn Féin, dealt with some issues, such as finance, reform of Stormont and ending paramilitarism. However, it failed to deal at all with the past:[407] 'Despite some significant progress', the NIO stated, 'a final agreement on the establishment of new bodies to deal with the past was not reached. The Government continues to support these provisions of the Stormont House Agreement and to provide better outcomes for victims and survivors. We will now reflect with the other participants on how we can move forward and achieve broad consensus for legislation.'[408]

---

[404] Paras 21 to 55.

[405] Gerard 'Jock' Davison, 5 May 2015; Kevin McGuigan, 12 August 2015.

[406] Lord Carlile QC, Rosalie Flanagan & Stephen Shaw QC, *Paramilitary Groups in Northern Ireland*, 19 October 2015 (7 pp); HC, *Hansard,* vol. 600, cols. 829–42, 20 October 2015.

[407] Pp. 34–5.

[408] Press release, 17 November 2015; *Irish News*, 17 November 2015 (article by

Historical Investigations Unit

The historical investigations unit – if it ever goes ahead – requires legislation.[409] It is to run for five years. And it will come under the NI policing board. Essentially, it is to be a merger of the PSNI's historical enquiries team (now the legacy investigation branch) and the historical investigations directorate of PONI. But the former has full police powers, while the latter has more limited ombudsman powers. The historical enquiries team's work was addressed to victims. The PONI work concerns retired political officers. OTRs are fugitive suspects. It may be assumed that Operation Redfield is to go to the historical investigations unit. The unit is to have a relationship – as part of the policing family – with the PPSNI.

The Downey Myths

The ten so-called Downey myths, which had been reproduced by officials and politicians, on and after 25 February 2014, were listed in the preface. They are repeated below in italics. They are followed by brief comments at the end of this book, based upon the narrative presented above:

- *one, the administrative scheme was lawful;* I disagree. Tony Blair's four written promises crossed the line. This does not apply to the PSNI and PPSNI's involvement in 2000–6, though those who are alive probably regret their involvement. This book is particularly critical of the NIO in 2006, after the collapse of the NIOB in parliament. A legal cloud hangs over Operation Rapid: there is less criticism of individual officers; the focus has shifted to Sir Hugh Orde, and to the NIO under Peter Hain;
- *two, the administrative scheme had not been secret;* I disagree.

Theresa Villiers on historical investigations unit and national security).

[409] The queen's speech, on 27 May 2015, referred to Westminster legislation. In September 2015, the NIO published a paper, *Northern Ireland (Stormont House Agreement) Bill 2015* (33 pp).

The book refers to the paradox, whereby the public face of the OTR issue obscured the private face;

- *three, ministers were not involved in the administrative scheme;* I disagree. The policy was driven heavily from number 10. Peter Hain in the NIO is responsible for Operation Rapid, and for the Downey mistake;

- *four, the comfort letters were only statements of facts;* I disagree. Some may have sought to give a very conditional guarantee to the OTRs. Mr Justice Sweeney declined the prosecution's invitation to go down that road in his analysis of the administrative scheme. His judgment simply refers to executive promises, including the one articulated by Gerry Kelly and communicated to John Downey;

- *five, OTRs were not granted immunity;* I disagree in part. There was no grant of executive immunity. But, through the abuse of process ruling by Mr Justice Sweeney, John Downey secured immunity effectively;

- *six, there was no amnesty for IRA crimes (up to 10 April 1998);* I agree. Effective immunity, if secured by enough people, could become an effective amnesty. There is an important counter-factual question to be answered: how many of the 228 OTRs might have been prosecuted, after extradition where necessary (if it had been possible), between 2000 and 2014? We may obtain an answer in part from Operation Redfield in future years. It will take time;

- *seven, the administrative scheme was necessary to implement the Belfast, and St Andrews, agreement;* I disagree. Tony Blair was very keen to implement UK promises. He went further, and made additional personal promises in a less than transparent peace process. The task for a UK head of government should have been to bring the republicans into democratic politics, without violating the rule of law. Adams and McGuinness succeeded in pushing the UK state further than it needed to go;

- *eight, the judgment of Mr Justice Sweeney was particular to a unique set of facts;* I disagree. The existence of three Downey mistakes is being argued legally. It does not, however, exist in the judgment. Looking at the five-day application thoroughly, it is the position that Mr Justice Sweeney was impressed by the revelation for the first time of the existence of the administrative scheme;

• *nine, the PSNI – in particular the Operation Rapid team – was responsible for Downey escaping prosecution;* I disagree. Norman Baxter and Peter Sheridan deserve exoneration and apology. The PSNI did get things wrong. Much of that is down to Sir Hugh Orde. But it is mainly the responsibility of the NIO. The role of Mark Sweeney, the director of the rights and international relations division, deserves to be highlighted;

• *ten, no ministers nor officials did anything wrong;* I disagree. The administrative scheme deserves to have had a whistle blower (it was not Norman Baxter). This opinion now expressed is a measure of the abuse of power which took place.

The Future: Prosecution or Amnesty?

What is the future for NI, as the PSNI continues with Operation Redfield (while political leaders dither over the historical investigations unit): either the prosecution of republican terrorists and others for past crimes or an amnesty for all troubles offences, committed between 1968 and 1998?

It might be thought – given the critical view of Tony Blair expressed here – that the successful prosecution of all OTRs would be the only way of proceeding. On the contrary, I have come to the opposite conclusion, during the writing of this book, that a statutory amnesty is the only way forward.

However, I am only interested in the idea, if it applies equally to everyone. The lessons of the NIOB of 2005–6 need to be learned.

This view is based upon a complex of reasons for and against, to do with each of the alternatives: prosecution or amnesty. It is not an easy debate to initiate, but it must be done by way of conclusion to this account of government policy gone badly wrong. The question begs to be asked, if not answered conclusively.

Prosecution

The following are important arguments, for or against prosecution:

- *one,* the victims: 3,720 persons died violently, between 1966 and 2006 (and more since),[410] and very many more were injured, creating a huge (and growing) sector of victims and survivors.[411] Each victim deserves justice without question, and varying groups of relatives and supporters have demanded variously, and increasingly, inquiries, inquests, investigations and prosecutions;

- *two,* the perpetrators: the figures for who killed whom are clear; republicans are responsible for nearly 60 per cent of deaths; loyalists for nearly 30 per cent; and the security forces – there were 361 state killings – for less than ten per cent.[412] All of the republican and loyalist killings were unlawful; most (but not all) of the security force deaths were lawful. If all unlawful killings were to be pursued equally, the investigations etc. would be overwhelmingly against republican and loyalist paramilitaries, including those who have now abandoned violence for politics;

- *three,* legacy litigation: this unfortunately goes with the grain of propaganda. The republicans divert attention from themselves as the principal culprits by focussing on state killings and construing loyalist murders simplistically as collusion. The state has archives, and the government seeks to discharge its

---

[410] David McKittrick & Others, eds., *Lost Lives,* Edinburgh & London, 2007, p. 1553.

[411] Victims and Survivors (Northern Ireland) Order 2006, SI 2006/2953; Commission for Victims and Survivors Act (Northern Ireland) 2008. According to the victims and survivors service, an average of ten new victims comes forward each day: *Belfast Telegraph,* 30 October 2014.

[412] Ditto, p. 1553.

legal obligations by limiting disclosure.[413] There are no such requirements imposed on republican and loyalist organization, which are permitted to keep their secrets. The impression is reinforced, by increasing calls for inquests, inquiries and investigations, that the troubles were really about a succession of direct and indirect state abuses which the IRA heroically resisted until it was able to turn to the political struggle for a united Ireland;

- *four*, humanitarian concerns for victims and survivors: grieving is a necessary emotional response to death and injury, and there is a growing need for private and public provision of services, therapeutic, medical and social. Few appear to have asked the macro question in this context: would more people begin to feel better more quickly, with a continuation of sectarian polarization (as has happened) or with genuine reconciliation promoted by the state (as has been attempted in other societies)?;
- *five*, the concept of criminal justice: is it necessary to have open-ended historic investigations (and reparations) or, as most constitutional states do, have a statute of limitation for criminal liability, with different periods for different crimes?;
- *six*, the passage of time: given the standard of proof (beyond a reasonable doubt), it becomes increasingly difficult to convict years after a crime. Witnesses move, disappear and eventually die. Their evidence often deteriorates. They can be more successfully cross-examined. Forensic evidence (which may be enhanced by new techniques) is more likely to be lost or destroyed with years of storage;
- and *seven*, resources: the lord chief justice of NI (Sir Declan

---

[413] Article 2(2) of the 2015 ICIR international agreement lists three: one, prejudice national security; two, risk to life or safety of any person; and three, prejudicial effect on legal proceedings. These, of course, apply to Dublin as well as London.

Morgan),[414] the local attorney general (John Larkin QC)[415] and the chief constable (George Hamilton)[416] have variously indicated that concentrating upon the past means, the criminal justice system cannot deal properly with the present. It follows that NI may have a bleak future: a bad past has distorted a great deal; without a post-troubles present, it may not be possible to overcome such disadvantages.

There has been little spontaneous reconciliation since 1998, even though violence has given way to politics. It is very striking that, for many, time has not healed. This is not helped by the perception that 'bad guys' – including the OTRs – do well in NI. But the instinctive response, to investigate and prosecute all perpetrators (even with only two years in prison), is extremely problematic. We only have Operation Redfield at present. And the number of successful prosecution, after further abuse of process applications, and various defences, is not likely to satisfy many people.

Amnesty

The following are important arguments, for or against amnesty:

- *one*, precedent: the new Irish state legislated three times in 1923–4, to protect from civil and criminal liability: first, UK forces; second, republicans in the war of independence; and third, free state forces in the civil war. Early in the NI troubles, the Stormont government announced an executive amnesty, for the period 5 October 1968 to 6 May 1969;[417]
- *two*, immunities: there has long been special treatment of republicans: between 1997 and 2010, regarding the

---

[414] *Belfast Telegraph*, 17 November 2014; BBC, 18 January 2016 (referring to the 56 pending inquests).

[415] Various media interviews & press reports, 19–20 November 2013.

[416] Speech to British-Irish association, 6 September 2014.

[417] Lord Trimble suggested there was early release of prisoners after the 1956–62 IRA campaign: NIAC, *Report*, Q807, 13 May 2014.

decommissioning of terrorist weapons; between 1998 and 2013, regarding evidence to the Saville inquiry, and the four lesser ones (Robert Hamill, Rosemary Nelson, Billy Wright, and Breen and Buchanan); and from 1999 and continuing, regarding the recovery of the disappeared;[418]

- *three*, the 1998 Belfast agreement: the NIO did not prepare in advance of the talks for the release of terrorist prisoners. Sinn Féin handled the issue badly, failing to look after a complex republican constituency.[419] It did not even demand an amnesty. The text of the agreement was inadequate, and caused problems subsequently. By not signing up to the Belfast agreement, the republicans had no hope of political support for prisoner releases (OTRs did not even register with most people). They certainly gave nothing positive in return for what the UK, and Irish, government gave them in 1998-2000;

- *four*, statutory amnesty: it was Lord Williams of Mostyn, followed by Lord Goldsmith, who put the idea on the agenda after the Belfast agreement, albeit negatively in advice to Tony Blair;

- *five*, officialdom: the NIO, and in particular Sir Quentin Thomas, came up with the idea of excluding the security forces from an amnesty, this idea prevailing between 2001 and 2005;

- and *six*, legislation: the government's NIOB was opposed by all parties in 2005–6, but Sinn Féin pulled the plug when it could no longer deny that the security forces were to be included.

---

[418] President Clinton may have had a hand in this: see his telephone calls to Tony Blair, on 8 and 23 May 1998, following a meeting with WAVE representatives (Clinton presidential library and museum, collection no. 2012-0600-M).

[419] It comprised the following prisoners: (i) those sentenced in NI before 1973; (ii) those sentenced in NI since 1973; (iii) transferees to NI; (iv) transferees to the Republic of Ireland; and (v) escaped prisoners from mainly NI. Sinn Féin went on to elide the following OTRs subsequently: (vi) those subject to extradition requests to the Republic of Ireland and other countries; (vii) volunteers who had not been arrested, and may or may not have been on the run; and (viii) political militants, not members of the IRA, who had helped criminally.

CONCLUSION

The story of the OTRs reveals missed opportunities. The UK (and Irish) government failed to include an amnesty (really two) in the Belfast agreement. Sinn Féin, of course, wanted special treatment, without signing up to the Belfast agreement or having to decommission. Such is its national liberation self-deception. The failure of UK public policy was the subsequent appeasing of the republicans in a less than transparent peace process. The idea of excluding the security forces had been Sir Quentin Thomas's contribution; ironically, this is the card Sinn Féin played to destroy the NIOB.

Prosecution versus Amnesty

Any discussion of prosecution versus amnesty (as a result of this book) will have to take account of the factors listed above, and no doubt others. The prediction regarding prosecution is most likely: whatever of the efforts of the legacy litigators (who are keen on state killings), there will be no general refighting of the troubles through the courts in coming years. The prospects of any amnesty are, of course, slight, given a continuation of the present political standoff. It would be going further than the Belfast agreement. When it was tried in 2005–6, only the labour government and Sinn Féin supported it.

We now know that Tony Blair's secret diplomacy led only to the Downey fiasco. The 228 OTRs are being reviewed, with a view to successful prosecution. Maybe circumstances will emerge, where the idea of properly drawing a line under the past, appeals to different groups, albeit for different reasons. Sinn Féin, out to get the security forces (not that there are likely to be many cases), would be opposed to the principle of equal treatment of all criminal suspects. But do the 228 OTRs want to continue running personal risks, on the slight chance that a member of the security forces – who acted unlawfully – will be prosecuted successfully?

This advocacy of an amnesty is not designed to lock relatives and survivors into their private worlds of grief, while the rest of NI gets on with its life. Yes, inquests, investigations and prosecutions would stop. But, and this is crucial to the idea I am advocating, there would then be an opening of the archives, subject to human rights concerns. The outstanding precedent is the 2012 *Report of the Hillsborough Independent Panel*,[420] into the 1989 Sheffield football tragedy which saw 96 Liverpool fans killed. (This, of course, was followed, by an inquest in Warrington, between March 2014 and April 2016, conducted by Sir John Goldring, a former appeal court judge, in which the jury found that the fans had been killed unlawfully.) Relatives and survivors in NI would learn much more, through the opening of archives, than might emerge in a criminal court or through an inquest. The perpetrators might have to confront their past deeds, with such disclosure. And society generally could begin to see more clearly who killed whom in the NI troubles.

The Stormont House agreement envisages three other institutions, as well as the historical investigations unit. Perhaps the UK and NI governments could try and advance those ideas separately. In advance of her appointment as first minister in January 2016, Arlene Foster (herself a troubles victim) showed the importance of information being disclosed.[421] And, despite the exclusion of the past, the NIO has unilaterally published the international agreement – with more special treatment of republicans – on the independent commission on information retrieval, no doubt to encourage progress.[422]

---

[420] HC 581, 12 September 2012, 389 pp plus *http://hillsborough.independent.gov.uk*
[421] *Belfast Telegraph,* 18 December 2015.
[422] HC, *Hansard,* vol. 604, cols. 43WS–44WS, 21 January 2016. This was signed on 15 October 2015. Article 9 is: inadmissibility of information received by the commission.

APPENDIX

The Judgment of Mr Justice Sweeney

(Extract)

...

PARAGRAPH 173

Applying the burden and standard of proof that I have indicated, and whether as a result of direct evidence or reasonable inference, I find the following core facts:

(1) At all material times the defendant was a citizen of the Republic of Ireland, and was domiciled there.

(2) At all material times from 29 May 1983, save for a short period in 1994, it was recorded on the PNC that the defendant was wanted by the Metropolitan Police for conspiracy to murder on 20 July 1982.

(3) From at least October 1984 onwards, the defendant was aware that he was wanted by the Metropolitan Police in relation to the Hyde Park Bombing.

(4) In November 1989 a final decision was taken not to seek to extradite the defendant from the Republic of Ireland.

(5) From at least the spring of 2000 in private, and from March 2001 in public, the Government assured Sinn Fein that it was sympathetic to the argument that the position of the OTRs was an anomaly and that the issue would be addressed.

(6) The beginnings of what became the administrative scheme in relation to OTRs, which was the product of suggestions made by the Government, can be seen in events, in particular, in April/May 2000.

(7) The beginnings of what became the broadly standard letter sent to those who were not wanted can be found in letters from the Attorney General to the SSNI and the NIO in November 2000 and mid-March 2001.

(8) The standard letter did not amount to an amnesty as such. However, its terms (and in particular the references to the SSNI and the Attorney General) were intended to and did make clear that it was issued in the name of the Government and that the assurances within it could be relied upon with confidence as meaning what they said, namely an unequivocal statement that the recipient was not wanted -with the obvious implication from the remainder that thus the recipient would not be arrested or prosecuted unless new evidence came to light or there was a new application for extradition.

(9) As Mr Powell says in his witness statement: "What each letter was intended to reflect, was that on the basis of information then available to the authorities and carefully considered in each case individually, an assurance was being given that the individual would not be subject to arrest and subsequent prosecution if he or she returned to the United Kingdom ... The intention behind the British Government giving written assurances to individual OTRs was to try to resolve the issue given the failure to find a workable general approach and to provide individual letters that Sinn Fein could use to reassure the individuals concerned that they could return to the UK without fear of arrest".

(10) As Mr Hain says in his witness statement: "It was intended that the assurance be just that, reliable assurances as to the position of the applicants and implicit in that, that the process by which the assurances had come to be given, had been competent and robust."

(11) The assurances given in the letter were not only given in the name of the Government in the course of an international peace process, but were intimately connected with the criminal justice system in respect of very serious offences.

(12) Accordingly, at least until 2007, it was clearly appreciated by those involved in the conduct of the administrative scheme that it was vitally important that the relevant checks were exhaustively and accurately done, and that the results were correctly notified to each recipient. Hence the amount of time and care that was taken in the conduct of the scheme up to 2007.

(13) As Mr Kelly says in his witness statement: "There had been throughout the administrative process a reliance that those responsible for preparing and presenting an assurance (or a refusal) were in a position to provide an unequivocal statement. It was on that basis that Sinn Fein felt able to advise those who had sought its help in asking for such assurances, that they meant what they said and on this basis, that the recipients thereafter believed they were able to organise their lives accordingly."

(14) It was equally appreciated by the Government that an error in telling someone that they were not wanted, when in fact they were, would be an extremely serious matter ("the worst outcome") both politically and legally – with the likelihood of an abuse of process application based upon a breach of the relevant assurance in the letter.

(15) It was such concerns that led, amongst other things, to:
   (a) Correcting the error in relation to the individual referred to in the Attorney General's letter of 29 January 2001.
   (b) The rejection by the DPP(NI) and the PSNI in March/April 2002 of the more rough and ready (and therefore more high risk) approach then being mooted.

(16) In March 2006 the defendant was told that he was wanted – albeit that the relevant letter was not clear as to whether that was in relation to offences in Northern Ireland, to the Hyde Park bombing, or to both.

(17) Operation Rapid commenced in around February 2007.

(18) Checking the PNC was a straightforward process.

(19) At the time of Operation Rapid's review of the defendant's case, it was aware that the defendant was wanted by the Metropolitan

Police in relation to the Hyde Park bombing, but failed to pass that on to the DPP(NI).

(20) That was, as the prosecution conceded, a catastrophic failure.

(21) It was compounded by the fact that:

(a) Operation Rapid was aware of the need to check whether an individual was wanted by another UK police force.

(b) When specifically asked by the NIO (before the issue of the letter to the defendant) whether such a PNC check had been done in relation to the defendant (and others) Operation Rapid informed the NIO that such checks had been done, but failed to mention that the check in relation to the defendant had shown that he was wanted by the Metropolitan Police in relation to the Hyde Park bombing.

(22) When the defendant received his letter he was entitled to and did believe that it was the product of careful and competent further work, and that there had been a genuine and correct change of mind about him – particularly given that he was a supporter of the peace process. He also believed, as a result of assurances (whether direct or indirect) from individuals in Sinn Fein who had been involved in the negotiations with the Government that he could rely upon the assurances given in the letter.

(23) Hence he relied upon the assurance given by the Government that; "The Police Service of Northern Ireland are not aware of any interest in you from any police force in the United Kingdom" – which he rightly believed to be an assurance that if he went to the UK mainland he would not be at risk of arrest or prosecution unless (as the letter went on to say) "... any other outstanding offence came to light, or if any request for extradition were to be received" – neither of which apply in his case.

(24) However that assurance was wholly wrong – he was wanted by the Metropolitan Police in relation to the Hyde Park bombing, which involved the causing of an explosion and four murders. Thus, as the prosecution conceded, the defendant was wholly misled

(25) The defendant was not aware that in 2007 the Attorney General

was no longer as closely involved in the administrative scheme as he had been the case in the past.

(26) The catastrophic failures of Operation Rapid in 2007 were further compounded in 2008, when it was appreciated by Operation Rapid that the DPP(NI) had not been informed in 2007 that the defendant was wanted for the Hyde Park bombing, but no step was taken to put matters right.

(27) The Operation Rapid failures were further compounded in 2009, when it was again appreciated that the defendant was wanted for the Hyde Park bombing, but nothing was done to put matters right.

(28) As Mr Hain said in his witness statement: "No mistake of such importance could or should have been permitted to have gone uncorrected".

(29) As yet, there has been no sensible explanation for the various Operation Rapid failures.

(30) Relying on the letter, the defendant travelled to Canada, and on a number of occasions to Northern Ireland (including visits in furtherance of the peace process) and to the UK mainland.

(31) The defendant was again acting in reliance on the letter when he sought to transit Gatwick Airport on route to Greece on 19 May 2013.

(32) As the prosecution conceded in argument the defendant suffered detriment as a result – by way of arrest, the loss of his freedom for a time, the imposition of strict bail conditions, and being put at risk of conviction for very serious offences (albeit that the latter is tempered, to some extent, by the fact that even if convicted of all the offences he would, in consequence of the 1998 Act, serve no more than two years in prison).

...

PARAGRAPH 175

Given the core facts as I have found them to be, and the wider undisputed facts, I have conducted the necessary evaluation of what has occurred in the light of the competing public interests involved. Clearly, and notwithstanding a degree of tempering in this case by the operation of the 1998 Act, the public interest in ensuring that those who are accused of serious crime should be tried is a very strong one (with the plight of the victims and their families firmly in mind). However, in the very particular circumstances of this case it seems to me that it is very significantly outweighed in the balancing exercise by the overlapping public interests in ensuring that executive misconduct does not undermine public confidence in the criminal justice system and bring it into disrepute, and the public interest in holding officials of the state to promises they have made in full understanding of what is involved in the bargain. Hence I have concluded that this is one of those rare cases in which, in the particular circumstances, it offends the court's sense of justice and propriety to be asked to try the defendant.

INDEX

(All titles are dispensed with except where a judge makes a judicial decision)

G

H

O

P

Printed in Great Britain
by Amazon